VITTORIO DE SICA

Contemporary Perspectives

Edited by Howard Curle and Stephen Snyder

Recognized as a master of Italian cinema, Vittorio De Sica (1902–74) is perhaps best known and most respected for his critically acclaimed neorealist films of the period 1946–55. As this anthology reveals, however, his production was remarkably multifaceted. The essays included here – some newly commissioned, some reprinted, and others in translation – look at De Sica's varied career from many perspectives.

Structured chronologically, the volume begins by introducing readers to De Sica's early popularity as an actor and singer during the years of Italian Fascism, and to his initial directorial efforts before the end of World War II. It was not until the postwar era, however, that De Sica made his mark in film history. Special attention is given to this critical phase of his career, which encompasses the neorealist films that made him famous: *Shoeshine, Bicycle Thieves, Miracle in Milan,* and *Umberto D.*

When the neorealist movement waned after 1955, De Sica returned to his roots in Neapolitan comedy for a series of commercially successful films starring Sophia Loren and Marcello Mastroianni, such as *Marriage Italian Style* and *Yesterday, Today, and Tomorrow,* which won De Sica an Academy Award in 1965. However, in *Two Women,* a film adaptation of Moravia's novel *La ciociara,* which was released in 1960, and in *The Garden of the Finzi-Continis,* one of De Sica's last films, he returned to the subject of World War II and to the human tragedy that is at the heart of his best neorealist productions.

This fine anthology offers a comprehensive critical survey that covers the entire scope of De Sica's career, and is an excellent resource for students, critics, and film enthusiasts.

(Toronto Italian Studies)

HOWARD CURLE is a lecturer in the Film Studies Programme at the University of Manitoba.

STEPHEN SNYDER is Associate Professor in the Film Studies Programme at the University of Manitoba.

VITTORIO DE SICA
Contemporary Perspectives

Edited by
Howard Curle and Stephen Snyder

UNIVERSITY OF TORONTO PRESS
Toronto Buffalo London

© University of Toronto Press Incorporated 2000
Toronto Buffalo London
Printed in Canada

ISBN 0-8020-0654-x (cloth)
ISBN 0-8020-8381-1 (paper)

Printed on acid-free paper

Toronto Italian Studies

Canadian Cataloguing in Publication Data

Main entry under title:

Vittorio De Sica : contemporary perspectives

(Toronto Italian studies)
Includes filmography.
ISBN 0-8020-0654-x (bound)   ISBN 0-8020-8381-1 (pbk.)

1. De Sica, Vittorio, 1901–1974 – Criticism and interpretation.
I. Curle, Howard.   II. Snyder, Stephen.   III. Series.

PN1998.3.D473V57 2000   791.43'0233'092   C00-930166-6

University of Toronto Press acknowledges the financial assistance to its
publishing program of the Canada Council for the Arts and the Ontario
Arts Council.

University of Toronto Press acknowledges the financial support for its publishing activities of the Government of Canada through the Book Publishing
Industry Development Program (BPIDP).

Contents

Acknowledgments

It is with gratitude and pleasure that we thank the following people who have helped make this book possible. First, our contributors, who share our admiration and affection for Vittorio De Sica and his films. Thanks too to our translators, Eugene Walz and Michelle Walz, Hubert Balcaen, and Jean-Pierre Allard. An essential thank you to John Daretta whose De Sica bibliography showed the way.

At the University of Toronto Press we would particularly like to thank Bill Harnum for encouraging our participation in the Toronto Italian Studies series, and our editor Ron Schoeffel for his constant support and enthusiasm. Thanks as well to our readers Bart Testa and Patrick Rumble for their scrutiny of the manuscript and for helpful suggestions, to our typist Carol E. Adams, and to Joan Bulger for her scrupulous eye in preparing the manuscript for publication.

We are grateful to the staff of the Elizabeth Dafoe Library at the University of Manitoba, to Marilyn Loat of the Film Studies Department, University of Manitoba, to Mary Corliss and her staff in the Stills Department of the Museum of Modern Art, New York, and to Lee Amazonas and the staff of the Pacific Film Archive, Berkeley. A warm salute to Pauline Kael for the pleasure her writing has given and for waiving the reprint fee for her *Shoeshine* review.

Finally, personal thanks are owed to colleagues present and past, friends, and loved ones who have sustained and prodded us and been patient along the journey: George Toles, Eugene Walz, Mark West, Frank Burke, Norm Larsen, Bill Simon, Bev Phillips, Donna Lewis, and our students.

This book is for our parents.

HOWARD CURLE
STEPHEN SNYDER

A Note on Film Documentation and Photographs

Vittorio De Sica: Contemporary Perspectives gathers together previously published writings as well as new essays written expressly for this volume. For the new essays we have tried to maintain consistency in regard to film titles and release dates. However, for previously published material, some of it translated from Italian and French, titles and release dates may vary. Our procedure is that the first time a film title appears in the body of an essay, it is given in its original language followed when applicable by the generally used English-language title, then by the release date in the film's country of origin. If this plan produces needless repetition, the procedure is waived. A standardized De Sica filmography concludes the book.

A selection of excellent production stills will be found following page 22. While we recognize that production stills fail to reproduce the exact shot compositions afforded by frame enlargements, we feel that they have the advantage of clarity. With the exception of the photo of De Sica directing *Bicycle Thieves*, which is from Stephen Snyder's personal collection, all photos are from the Stills Archive of the Museum of Modern Art, New York. We are grateful to the Stills Archive for giving us permission to reproduce the stills.

VITTORIO DE SICA

Contemporary Perspectives

Introduction

HOWARD CURLE and STEPHEN SNYDER

In contrast to the major figures of post-World War II Italian cinema –
Rossellini, Fellini, Antonioni, Visconti – Vittorio De Sica has been relatively neglected in English-language film criticism. The commentaries
on his work that do exist have tended to reduce his career to one or
two significant films. At the present time the only full-length study of
De Sica's work in English is John Daretta's *Vittorio De Sica: A Guide to
References and Resources* (1982), which presents primarily a summary of
his career and a critical bibliography. De Sica's directorial work, which
once formed the cutting edge of theory-influenced cinema, has receded
on the film-theory horizon, year by year, to a state of near invisibility.
This gradual displacement of De Sica's neorealist films from centrality
to obscurity is not easily explained. We suspect the neglect may in
some way be related to changes in the temperament of audiences
regarding social issues or, perhaps, to the overt emotional claims that
De Sica's 1940s work imposes on its audience. In a period of film criticism characterized by the exposure of the methods of viewer manipu-
lation used by the film industry a certain distrust of *emotion* in films
has surfaced in some of the more interesting film studies. Mary Ann
Doane's *The Desire to Desire*, a remarkable and well-received book on
women's films, virtually assumes without question that all spectator
emotion generated by a film is to be distrusted. Beyond this trend of
distrust it is also possible that the tense emotional situations represented in De Sica's best work have come to seem somehow remote to
critics and general viewers of the late twentieth century. Some consider De Sica's work sentimental.[1]

De Sica's 1940s films always aimed at the emotional heart of their
audience; but it is our thesis that De Sica's impulse towards producing

emotional reactions has to be understood as part of the postwar world, especially as De Sica saw it. First, for example, within the context of postwar Italy De Sica saw himself not as a purveyor of sentimentality but as a physician supplying a stringent antidote to a prevailing sentimentality: a champion challenging an idealized vision of people which he understood to be a misrepresentation of human life and human living conditions. De Sica has always claimed to hate the heroic lie, which, in preaching false notions of nobility and individual heroism, clouds our perception of ourselves, blurs our connections with others, and substitutes the sentimental lie for the truth. For example, the films of Raffaele Matarazzo, *Catene/Chains* (1949), *Tormento/Torment* (1950), *Figli di nessuno/Nobody's Children* (1951), offer sentimentalized visions of the same themes being treated by De Sica and Zavattini. Matarazzo's films, offering a placatory sit-com vision of life, were box-office hits while De Sica's were often miserable failures. Sentimentality, then, should be better understood within its historical Italian context and should not be readily conflated with any form of emotional prodding.

Beyond the issues of fraud and sentimentality, De Sica in his interviews in the postwar period suggests that he sees in Italians a collective trauma, arising, perhaps, from their having seen and experienced more in the war years than they were capable of digesting. The symptoms of this trauma are made manifest in a collective cauterization of emotion. Such cauterization, in De Sica's view, crystallizes into generalized feelings of isolation among individual people and a self-destructive narrowing of human vision. Because we have neither the will nor the imagination to attempt to communicate with each other, we become insular. In a real sense the emotional impoverishment resulting from the cauterization of feelings fosters a progressive failing of community and communion: it metamorphoses itself into an unwillingness to know or see and a consequent inability on the part of human beings to understand either the lives of other people or the complexities of their own lives (this is, for example, the premise of *La ciociara/Two Women*, 1960). People react to each other only in terms of social programming. De Sica directs his cinema towards this perceived psychic contraction, this hibernation of the impulse to understand, in an effort to generate, not feeling for feeling's sake, but empathy for the sake of restoring a cohesive community in which human beings are able to relate to each other without violence or indifference.

Still, some viewers (some of our students, for example) have argued that De Sica's best films seems to work only negatively. That is to say, he can imagine scenarios of human failure but none of success. What does it mean to pinpoint types of emotional failure if you do not believe in the possibility of change and the realization of some form of success? *Miracolo a Milano/Miracle in Milan* (1950), for example, imagines a social revolution only as a fairy tale; thus, its real message is that change is impossible. *La ciociara* and *Il giardino dei Finzi-Contini/The Garden of the Finzi-Continis* (1970) are equally unable to imagine characters who can imagine change. De Sica has supplied an answer to this sort of charge in the interview with Samuels included in this volume (30–49 below): the job of the artist is to reveal situations, not supply solutions. Still, one may find in some of De Sica's lesser-known films models of change that are persuasively prescriptive. One of the best examples, perhaps, is *Il tetto/The Roof* (1956). In this film the protagonists succeed in creating a viable life for themselves because they can see possibilities of life that exceed accepted norms, and that exist in locations whose possibilities remain invisible to others. Humility, collective action, and the mutual admission of shared helplessness are the keys to reconstructing a habitable world and a human community.

De Sica was the subject of much critical discussion in France in the 1950s: André Bazin's famous essays in *Qu'est-ce que le cinéma?/What Is Cinema?* and Henri Agel's 1955 study. In the 1960s Pierre Leprohon published a book on De Sica, while Agel put together a De Sica issue of *L'Avant-scène du cinéma*, but these works are relatively unacademic, written for a general audience. A great deal of English criticism of the same period, from that of Lindsay Anderson to Eric Rhode, amounts to a postmortem on neorealism. Rhode's 'Why Neorealism Failed' is typical of the essays on De Sica in *Sight and Sound* and even in such French journals as *Positif*. And, as far as we can tell, the only major, academic, book-length Italian criticism on De Sica was a 1972 issue of *Bianco e nero* (which is represented in this collection by an essay by Phillip Cannistraro, 86–93 below).

Among English-language studies of neorealism Roy Armes's *Patterns of Realism* (1971) is still the most extensive, although David Overby's anthology *Springtime in Italy* (1978) widens the perspective. John Daretta's bibliography has been updated by Bert Cardullo's *What Is Neorealism?* (1991). Research on Fascist-era Italian cinema continues to yield fresh perspectives on the antecedents and early years of neorealism, as in the essays of Sam Rohdie and Ted Perry. Recently, De Sica's work has begun to receive appreciative examination from a number of different perspectives. Robert Kolker in *The Altering Eye* (1983) updates De Sica's views on realism; Millicent Marcus in *Italian Film in the Light of Neorealism* (1986) writes on two De Sica films, emphasizing historical contexts other than neorealist theory; P. Adams Sitney in his recent book *Vital Crises in Italian Cinema* (1995) explores the problem of individuality and collectivity in De Sica's work in political terms; and an essay by Marcia Landy (included in this volume, 94–100 below) situates De Sica's work in terms of its historically embedded discourses. Meanwhile, neorealism has become such a problematized concept that almost no one feels comfortable in using the term uncritically. The major texts of neorealism (Bazin and Zavattini) have been harrowed for errors by French critics (beginning with Godard) and eventually given an intriguing revision by Gilles Deleuze in his two-volume work *Cinema 1* and *Cinema 2* (1988 and 1989). De Sica's neorealism has also been repositioned as a comic strategy by Christopher Wagstaff and made the subject of neoformalist analysis by Kristin Thompson.

Bicycle Thieves as a Film Icon

However problematic De Sica's status within film culture, neorealism itself has remained significant for subsequent generations of filmmakers. In particular, De Sica's *Ladri di biciclette / Bicycle Thieves* (1948) seems to possess a mythic hold on filmmakers, serving as inspiration and icon of the realist project. In Italian cinema this use of *Bicycle Thieves* emerges especially in the second wave of neorealism during the early 1960s. Pier Paolo Pasolini concludes his first feature film, *Accattone* (1961), with the eponymous hero stealing a motorbike, an event which leads to his death. Pasolini's next film, *Mama Roma* (1962), has Lamberto Maggiorani, De Sica's non-professional lead from *Bicycle Thieves*, cast as a hospital patient robbed by the slum-dweller protagonist. In 1975 Ettore Scola put De Sica himself and *Bicycle Thieves* at the centre of *C'eravamo tanto amati / We All Loved Each Other So Much* (1974), his critical epic of Italian life (and cinema) since World War II. In this film a screening of *Bicycle Thieves* in a community hall erupts into a quarrel which rehearses the debate between Giulio Andreotti, then Undersecretary of Culture in the Christian Democratic government, and neorealism's defenders. But the key episode in *We All Loved Each Other So Much* is a television game show in which the contestant, Nicola, an irritable left-wing film critic, misconstrues a question about why Bruno weeps at the end of *Bicycle Thieves*. Nicola assumes that the correct answer should acknowledge that De Sica humiliated the young actor (Enzo Staiola) by accusing him of pilfering cigarette butts, which De Sica himself had planted in the boy's pocket tin, as a method of getting him to cry on cue. The exposure of the 'constructed' nature of De Sica's method is not what the show's master of ceremonies wants as a correct answer. Like the majority of the film's viewers, the game show host insists on maintaining the fictional source of Bruno's tears, that is, the humiliation suffered by his father. Thus, while Scola pays homage to De Sica, he also deconstructs his movie and the unsullied 'humanism' of the man: De Sica was not above using cruelty.

Allusions to De Sica's work in other films have often been harmlessly funny, sometimes more serious but perhaps condescending. The essentially benign world of *Pee-Wee's Big Adventure* (Tim Burton, 1985) presents a parody of Ricci's search for his bicycle but one largely invisible to an audience that no longer has any historical contact with *Bicycle Thieves*. The parody is negated by its very gentleness and by the childlike view of the working class presented in the film. Maurizio Nichetti's *Ladri di saponetti/The Icicle Thief* (1989), however, ostensibly uses De Sica's original film to explore the slippery nature of reality itself but ultimately strikes a condescending attitude, as if to say, 'How simple those neorealist times were.' Equally cynical but more sophisticated is Robert Altman's *The Player* (1992). Here *Bicycle Thieves* is playing at a Los Angeles revival house where a disgruntled screenwriter has retreated from failed attempts at pitching story ideas. He is trailed to the cinema by the young movie executive who has been receiving the screenwriter's postcard death threats. After unctuously implying that he is considering a remake of *Bicycle Thieves* that will be true to the film's ending, the executive accidentally kills the writer. In the illusionary world of Los Angeles, where De Sica himself helplessly waited to pitch story ideas to executives in the 1950s, *Bicycle Thieves* is reduced to a mere simulacrum of the real, and, even less, to a sign of artistic integrity to be forgotten with the raising of the lights in the cinema.

Undoubtedly more complimentary to De Sica is Gianni Amelio's *Il ladro di bambini/Stolen Children* (1990), which uses the situation of *Bicycle Thieves* without condescension. Amelio takes a policeman (more exactly, a *carabiniere*) named Antonio and makes him the source of a dawning moral awareness. The odyssey this time is one in which the quest to deliver two children, a sister and brother, to a Sicilian orphanage gradually loses its urgency through the *carabiniere*'s perceived need to restore a sense of childhood to the children. Only when Antonio spontaneously assumes his original duties by apprehending a thief is the spell that the threesome have made for each other broken. The kinship of *Stolen Children* to *Bicycle Thieves* culminates in a remarkable two-shot of the sister and brother sitting on a curb. The dawn light (as opposed to late-afternoon light in *Bicycle Thieves*), the whizzing cars (as opposed to bicycles), the pair facing forward, their backs to the camera (as opposed to facing the camera), all recall the memorable scene of father and son from late in De Sica's film. But, strikingly, Amelio has the sister, through word and gesture, express a Maria-like concern for her brother, suggesting a sympathetic but radical reimagining of De Sica's movie.

Amelio is not alone, of course, in emulating De Sica's method and empathy for children. The case of Satyajit Ray is well known; in 1950 he went from Bombay to London to pursue a career in advertising, saw *Bicycle Thieves*, and, 'gored' by the experience, determined to film *Pather Panchali* (Robinson, 71). In fact the whole tradition of postwar films about children, from René Clément's *Jeux interdits / Forbidden Games* (1952), to Kobei Oguri's *Doro no Kawa / Muddy River* (1981), Hector Babenco's *Pixote* (1981), and Mira Nair's *Salaam Bombay!* (1988), testifies to De Sica's influence. One could even argue that François Truffaut's *Les quatre cents coups / The 400 Blows* owes as much to De Sica as it does to Jean Vigo. Most recently, Iranian cinema has confirmed neorealism and De Sica's legacy. Kianush Ayari's *Abadani-ha / The Abadanis* (1993) is virtually a reworking of *Bicycle Thieves* in contemporary Tehran, and Abbas Kiarostami's *Khaireh-ye Doust Kojast? / Where Is the Friend's House?* (1987) and his script for Jafar Panahi's *Badkonake Sefid / The White Balloon* (1995) attest to De Sica's humanist vision.

Career Overview

Vittorio De Sica was born on 7 July 1902 in the small town of Sora, south of Rome, but when he was barely three, his family moved to Naples, a city whose exuberance had a lasting effect on his own character and his subsequent films. Biographical commentators like Daretta have noted that De Sica himself overplayed the poverty of his family; in fact, his father, Umberto De Sica, was a journalist and later a clerk for the Banca d'Italia. De Sica claimed that there was a bordello near the family house and that he spent his childhood talking with the ladies. The family, however, moved to Florence in 1907 and then a year later to Rome. De Sica's interest in the movies was spurred by the fact that on occasion his father used to fill in for the pianists who accompanied the silent films.

Although trained in accounting and military service, the young De Sica parlayed an excellent singing voice and a strikingly handsome countenance into theatre work. During World War 1 he performed with a musical group that entertained soldiers in the military hospitals in Naples. Fortunately the war ended for Italy before De Sica was draftable, and when he did enter the service, his regiment encouraged him to perform in benefits and regimental theatrics.

Eventually De Sica was encouraged in his move from business to entertainment by his father, who in his profession as journalist had many contacts with show-business people. Vittorio had a small role in Tatiana Pavlova's theatre company in 1923, graduating to lead parts in musical comedies via Luigi Almiranto's troupe, where his breakthrough success came with the musical revue *Za Bum*. By 1930 he was a matinee idol who attracted the interest of Mario Camerini. De Sica starred in Camerini's 1932 film *Gli uomini, che mascalzone! / Men Are Such Rascals,* and his subsequent work with Camerini made both of them national celebrities, De Sica becoming known as the Italian Maurice Chevalier. The script for Camerini's *Daro un millione / I'll Give a Million* (1935) was by Cesare Zavattini, who would later create with De Sica masterpieces of neorealism. Thus, the two men began working together before neorealism was much of a concept in anyone's mind, and, significantly, the work of both men in this early period was more in the realm of comedy than realism. De Sica's early film work, then, even his directorial thinking, was primarily comedic, supplying little hint of the serious neorealist artist to come. It is well to keep in mind De Sica's roots in comedy when evaluating his middle-period Sophia Loren films, which represent, in fact, not so much a departure from form as a return to comedic roots.

Between 1931 and 1940 De Sica acted in twenty-three films as well as starring in and directing stage productions and radio shows. In 1937 he married the actress Giuditta Rissone. Perhaps he might never have turned to directing films but for his dissatisfaction with his lead role in *Manon Lescaut* (1939) and especially with Carmine Gallone's direction of the film. For his directorial debut De Sica chose a relatively safe project: a romantic comedy in the Camerini mode entitled *Rose scarlatte / Two Dozen Red Roses* (1940), an adaptation by Aldo De Benedetti of his own play which De Sica had starred in and directed in 1936. De Sica was satisfied with the result, and two other light comedies followed: *Maddelena zero in condotta / Madeline, Zero for Conduct* (1941) and *Teresa Venerdì / Mademoiselle Friday* (1941) [more provocatively titled *Doctor*

Beware for its North American release in 1951 to exploit Anna Magnani's postwar popularity]. In both these films De Sica is also the male lead, presenting himself as a sensitive, thoughtful, and compassionate physician, arguably the role that De Sica would assume artistically in his great films following the war. *Un garibaldino al convento / A Garibaldian in the Convent* (1942), a romantic drama set during the Risorgimento, was less successful. However, De Sica's next film was a breakthrough. *I bambini ci guardano / The Children Are Watching Us* (1943) confirmed De Sica's skill with actors, especially children (already evident in *Teresa Venerdì*). Together with Luchino Visconti's *Ossessione / Obsession*, made the previous year, *The Children Are Watching Us* presages the critical but compassionate eye of neorealism.

Now estranged from his wife but unable to obtain a divorce, De Sica began living with the actress Maria Mercader in 1942. (In order to divorce Rissone and marry Mercader, in 1968 De Sica became a French citizen. The couple had two children, Manuel, a composer, who has written scores for some of his father's later films, and Christian, who has had a career as a pop singer and film director.) By 1942 Mussolini's Italy was in the midst of a losing war. In 1944 De Sica was invited by Hitler's propaganda minister, Goebbels, to make a film in Prague, but an invitation by the Catholic Cinema Centre in Rome provided a welcome excuse to turn down Goebbels's offer. Instead De Sica made *La porta del cielo / The Gates of Heaven* (1945), the story of a religious pilgrimage, but the Vatican considered the film unsatisfactory.

The struggle against fascism and the rebuilding of Italy's war-torn social fabric formed the neorealist focus in Italian cinema over the next eight years. De Sica was both honoured and criticized for the moral indignation he shared with his fellow neorealists, Roberto Rossellini, Luchino Visconti, Giuseppe De Santis, and others.[2] De Sica's first postwar film, *Sciuscià / Shoeshine* (1946), upset the Italian Ministry of Justice and the Department of Correction, but won a special award at the 1947 Academy Awards, the beginning of a tendency for neorealist films to be more sympathetically received in foreign countries than in Italy. *Shoeshine* was a failure with Italian movie-goers who, although enthusiastic about Rossellini's patriotic *Roma, città aperta / Open City* (1945) and De Santis's provocative *Riso amaro / Bitter Rice* (1948), flocked mostly to comedies starring the popular Neapolitan actor Totò, to spectacles like Alessandro Blasetti's *Fabiola* (1947), and to the previously mentioned domestic melodramas of Matarazzo. Mostly Italians seemed to prefer American movies, now flooding the Italian cinemas after the lifting of the war-time ban. In order to promote Italian films the Christian Democrats, victors in the general election of 1948, passed the Andreotti Law (named for the under-secretary in charge of culture, Giulio Andreotti) which established quotas (*programmazione obbligatoria*) on imported films and provided loans to indigenous producers. Having alienated the authorities with *Shoeshine*, De Sica could not expect a subsidy and consequently he found financing difficult. In a much documented incident Hollywood producer David O. Selznick agreed to back *Ladri di biciclette/Bicycle Thieves* (1948) if De Sica would accept Cary Grant as the unemployed worker (see Samuels interview below, 34). De Sica declined, ventured to Paris and London where *Shoeshine* had been so warmly received, but was again disappointed, and finally financed the film himself with a consortium of Italian businessmen. De Sica would resume his connection with Selznick in the next decade with *Stazione termini/Indiscretion of an American Wife* (1953), an unfortunate attempt to graft neorealism to the Hollywood performance style of Jennifer Jones and Montgomery Clift, and *A Farewell to Arms* (1957) in which he acted a supporting role.

Bicycle Thieves was well received: a Silver Ribbon at the Italian Film Awards, a Hollywood Oscar, and numerous other accolades, including Lotte Eisner's praise as the best Italian film since the war. In Italy the film was reasonably successful at the box office, and it has come to be the film most associated with De Sica's name.

For his next film De Sica went to a novel by Zavattini, *Totò il buono/Toto the Good* (published 1943), and in homage to his collaborator he created a neorealist fairy tale, *Miracolo a Milano/Miracle in Milan* (1950). A blend of fantasy and realism, the film reveals the influence of Charlie Chaplin and René Clair. Left-wing critics began deserting De Sica with *Miracle in Milan*; to earlier accusations of sentimentality they now added that of whimsy. But De Sica's principal critical nemesis was to be the Italian government. De Sica's next film, *Umberto D.* (1952), was his most uncompromising application of the Zavattini aesthetic. Upon its release Giulio Andreotti sent De Sica an open letter which in part stated: 'We ask the man of culture to feel his social responsibility, which should not be limited to description of the abuses and miseries of a system and a generation ... If it is true that evil can be fought by harshly spot-lighting its most miserable aspects, it is also true that De Sica has rendered bad service to his country if people throughout the world start thinking that Italy in the middle of the twentieth century is the same as in *Umberto D.*' (quoted in Furhammar and Isaksson, 90).

Umberto D. was not a success at the time although it is now regarded by many, including De Sica, as his finest film. De Sica now found it increasingly difficult to raise money for neorealist projects, and moreover, tastes were changing in the culture as a whole. For economic survival the director turned to the commercial cinema for his livelihood.

Although De Sica had been performing in films throughout the neorealist period, he turned to acting in earnest after the financial failure of *Umberto D.* Especially successful were his performances in the roles of Baron Donati in Max Ophuls's *Madame de ... / The Earrings of Madame D.* (1953) and the *carabiniere* in Luigi Comencini's *Pane, amore e fantasia / Bread, Love and Dreams* (1954). The latter film is a good example of *neorealismo rosa*, or pink neorealism, a prettified version of the Zavattini ideal. *Neorealismo rosa* films were star-making vehicles for Gina Lollobrigida and Sophia Loren. De Sica himself contributed a film (his first in colour) to this cycle, *L'oro di Napoli / The Gold of Naples* (1954), which he directed and in one episode of which he acted the role of an aging gambler. De Sica himself was notorious for his compulsive gambling; it is reported that during the making of *The Monte Carlo Story* (1956) De Sica lost up to $10,000 a night at the tables (Sargeant, 46). During this period De Sica also spent some time in Hollywood, negotiating with David O. Selznick over a project that eventually became *Miracle in the Rain* (1956) directed by Rudolph Mate, and vainly waiting for telephone calls to be returned by Howard Hughes. As far as anyone knows, De Sica never saw Hughes, but he did meet Chaplin, who impressed him greatly. De Sica even found time to join the cast of the television series *The Four Just Men* (1959).

De Sica made one last effort at rigorous (black-and-white) neorealism in *Il tetto / The Roof* (1956), but the film was dismissed as journalistic by critics and ignored by audiences. Yet the film features some memorable sequences of familial tension and an alert eye to Rome's changing cityscape.

Four years separate *The Roof* from De Sica's next film, *La ciociara / Two Women* (1960). In this period De Sica portrayed a swindler who is persuaded to impersonate a resistance figure in Rossellini's *Il Generale della Rovere / General Della Rovere* (1959). Not only does De Sica's performance rank with his Baron Donati in *Madame D.* as his finest, but it presages the pursuit of invisibility that De Sica's own directorial career would take in the next decade. De Sica's early 1960s films partake of some of the reformist spirit of his neorealist projects while departing from those films in style. *Two Women*, which earned Sophia Loren an Academy Award for best actress in 1960, along with the less successful *The Condemned of Altona* (1962), can be understood as De Sica's contribution to the Italian cinema's revisionist interpretation of World War II.[3] *Il giudizio universale/The Last Judgment* (1961), a satire with an international cast, concerns reactions to the postponement of the Last Judgment, an oblique metaphor of our evaluation of social responsibility.

The commercial thrust of De Sica's work in the 1960s eventually concentrates on satire (*Il boom*, with Alberto Sordi, 1963), burlesque (*After the Fox*, with Peter Sellers, 1966), and light sex comedy (*Ieri, oggi, domani/Yesterday, Today and Tomorrow*, 1963, and *Matrimonio all'italiana/Marriage Italian Style*, 1964), the latter genre enormously successful vehicles for Sophia Loren and Marcello Mastroianni. While these films lack the poetic quality of the earlier work, their thematic structures are in fact no less complex. One could argue that the turn from neorealism to comedy embodies not an abandonment of the concerns of neorealism so much as a turning on De Sica's part to themes that we might identify as postmodernist. That is, De Sica's earlier work seems readily at home in a modernist tradition whose fundamental interests include a Marxist-influenced goal of progress and human liberation. By contrast, the later comedies subtly or overtly explore issues such as the construction of cultural identity, the function of language in culture, the role of image in language, the nature of the cinema medium, and the historicity of history. Furthermore, these movies of the mid-1960s, even the most mediocre like *Woman Times Seven* (1967) or *A Place for Lovers* (1968), continue De Sica's meditations on the issues of gender conditioning that are evident in the early films.

Finally, in the 1970s De Sica made two films, *Il giardino dei Finzi-Contini/The Garden of the Finzi-Continis* (1970) and *Una breve vacanza/A Brief Vacation* (1973), that prompted critics to suggest that the aging master had returned to form. *The Garden of the Finzi-Continis* won an Academy Award as best foreign film and prompted Pauline Kael to write an essay in the *New Yorker* on the fall and rise of De Sica's career. These final films reclaimed for De Sica his stature as film auteur and major artist.

Vittorio De Sica died in Paris on 13 November 1974.

De Sica the Actor

It is possible to argue that De Sica played just one character in the course of his acting career, a version of the *bravo ragazzo* role he filled in the 1930s (discussed by Francesco Bolzoni in *Quando De Sica era Mister*

Brown [When De Sica Was Mr. Brown] (2–33): a pleasant, compassionate, and rather passive figure who seems to be a healer or physician in disguise. In *Teresa Venerdì* (1941), of course, De Sica is a physician. This persona is more mature than that of the *bravo ragazzo* (good-hearted youth), weighed down with responsibilities and with an óften unspoken knowledge of the human heart. Progressively in these performances the camera focuses on De Sica's eyes, his gaze. He peers out at his audience with the look of a depressed angel, his eyes sweeping the landscape in an indictment of failed compassion.

The issue of identity is central to the roles De Sica played in his matinee-idol period in the 1930s. For example, in the Camerini film *Men Are Such Rascals*, which gave De Sica his stardom, he plays a chauffeur/mechanic named Bruno, who attempts to win a cosmetician, Marianne, the daughter of a taxi driver, by assuming a role. In order to impress Marianne Bruno borrows his boss's car, assuming another identity which he maintains in front of Marianne until the boss's wife turns up and demands Bruno's services (remarkably close to Chaplin's *City Lights*, released the previous year). From the outset the film establishes the notion that the two lovers are made for each other, but throws a number of synthetic plot complications in their way to keep this truth obscured from them.

Signor Max (Camerini, 1937) reworks this pattern of identity slippage. De Sica plays Gianni, a modest news-stand clerk who becomes impressed by the stories and advertising in American magazines. On an excursion he drops some of the magazines in front of a group of tourists who assume that he, Gianni, is American. Attracted to one of the tourists, he goes along with the mistake, assuming the identity Signor Max. In his book *Popular Film Culture in Fascist Italy* James Hay describes De Sica's character in these films as being 'decent' but fundamentally 'conformist' – a good boy.[4] It can be argued that this persona constitutes an essential aspect of De Sica's directorial personality as well, or at least one that contributes to an understanding of the filmmaker who would make the sort of films he made in the 1960s. For the reader interested in the relationship of De Sica's pre-neorealist career – as both actor and director – to his major films, Philip Cannistraro's essay (86–93 below) provides an interesting and different view. For Cannistraro there is no break in continuity between the phases of De Sica's career. From his role as the archetypical 'little man' in his early films De Sica as director merely graduated from playing small people to celebrating *directorially* small people and their lives.

Another not incompatible point of view in examining De Sica the actor is possible. In Rossellini's *General Della Rovere* (1959) De Sica plays the role of a petty gambler (a man of layered fraudulent identities) impersonating the general, an important resistance figure. As the story progresses, his character has a moral transformation and assumes the role of general seriously – becoming a good general to the point of sacrificing his life for the partisan cause and liberation from Nazi tyranny. The moral reprobate and role player becomes, in the course of time, not only a 'good' person but a healer or physician. His change is galvanized by his assumption of a theatrical role. The film, of course, is Rossellini's, with due credit to Sergio Amidei's screenplay, yet the role is quintessentially De Sica's. Rossellini has cast De Sica as himself, in the sense that he has cast him in the role that De Sica, a real-life gambler, previously constructed for himself: a role as director/healer which he became. In a recent essay on Rossellini Peter Brunette notes of De Sica's role here: 'the *abime* of representation and the self opens up at our feet as the continuity and certainty of self-identity seem to be threatened' (Brunette, 214). Stephen Snyder's essay in this collection (226–41 below) continues the exploration of De Sica's role playing (acting) into the 1960s, emphasizing the relationship between self and visibility.

De Sica and Realist Style

Much debate over the constructed nature of realism has occurred since the early days of Bazin's realist theories and his celebration of De Sica's style. At present almost no one considers De Sica's films to be pure unstructured realism. Indeed, some essays in this collection go to considerable lengths to disclose the various ways in which De Sica's realist images are highly structured. Nevertheless, even if we discard Bazin's concept of pure realism, there remains the question of what De Sica's style is all about. John Berger provides one answer to the question of what De Sica is up to in a comment on *Umberto D.*: 'Umberto D. comes to abide in us because the film reminds us of all the reality that we potentially share with him, and because it discards the reality which distinguishes him from us, which has made him separate and alone. The film shows what happened to the old man in life and, in the showing, opposes it. This is why film – when it achieves art – becomes like a human prayer. Simultaneously a plea and an attempt to redeem' (Berger, 21). Berger's notion is, we think, probably fairly close to De

Sica's own physician-directed view of his work. Neorealism becomes a prayer for human solidarity rather than a reflection of a vague consensus reality.

In a *New Yorker* article, 'The Fall and Rise of Vittorio De Sica,' Pauline Kael comments on De Sica's style: 'De Sica achieved images that one feels to be essences of human experience – suffering or joy turned into poetry ... Because of De Sica's selflessness and the way he has disappeared into the subject, those great films stay almost incredibly distinct in the memory' (48). Yet De Sica's disappearance into his characters has not always been an act of selflessness so much as an act of escape. Still, there is something to Kael's remark, and she supplies the perfect example at the end of the same article, which is a review of *The Garden of the Finzi-Continis*: 'The anxious face of the dignified old lady, who a moment later crumples in tears on her granddaughter's shoulder, is one of those faces lit from within by the director's love' (Kael, 53). In fact, throughout her reviews of De Sica's films Kael has pointed her readers towards the intricate emotional trajectory of De Sica's art. This insistence amounts to a claim that the essence of neo-realism lies not so much in the reclamation of a real, given world but rather in the reclamation of the viewer's *emotional* reserves. De Sica's realism, as Berger puts it, is a way of making us inhabit lives we would rather not experience. Such a view of film at the present time is as much evidence of directorial failure as it is of success, a form of ideological subterfuge. The jury, however, is still out on the interpellative function of cinema and the whole issue of viewer response.

Nevertheless, the insistence upon the humanist and sometimes sentimental side of De Sica's work has fostered an exaggerated and inaccurate conception of both the man and his work. For example, Edward Bell, tired of the rhetoric of De Sica's proclamations of love for everything, notes in the *Village Voice* in October 1991, on the occasion of a De Sica retrospective in New York: 'De Sica received four Academy Awards, but he never got the one that would have suited him and Zavattini best, the Oscar for most relentless anthropocentrism ... Ricci procures a bike with some desperation, and it is anthropomorphized into a savior. When the thing is stolen Ricci and his young son Bruno scour a street market in fear the bike has been dismembered and sold for parts. The camera cranes in on piles of frames and wheels and it is difficult to escape the impression that these are not metal bits but a human body that has been torn limb from limb' (Bell, 23).

De Sica himself has fostered this kind of complaint with his stream of somewhat deceptive comments which often sound as though he were quoting Bazin (in his most seraphic mood) on himself. For example, a remark of De Sica's that Bell sees as typical: 'The humanity of cinema! Any form of spectacle, any manifestation of art cannot estrange itself from this basic tenet: Humanity!' (Bell, 23); and in 'De Sica on De Sica' (30–49 below) there is more of the same. But these remarks disguise a great deal of what actually goes on in a De Sica film, in which the viewer may find it difficult to detect this rhetorically inflated pro-humanity view of life that De Sica seems never to tire of proclaiming. De Sica the director and De Sica the self-publicist were seldom the same figure. For example, in his 1966 book on De Sica Leprohon has gone some way to challenge the popular view of De Sica as an anti-intellectual film-maker (as compared to Rossellini). Leprohon includes a very interesting statement from one of De Sica's assistant directors, Yves Boisset:

> If directing is a matter of choice, De Sica's is instinctive, certainly, but also of an implacable logic. In a few seconds he saw and understood what characterized to the maximum a location or an atmosphere ... From a very pointed observation of reality De Sica rebuilds a purely abstract world that draws only its superficial power lines from reality. De Sica's universe is a mean universe. Filled with faults, egoism, unjustness, and haughtiness, De Sica is far from being the legendary handsome serene Italian ... The real De Sica is this aging man who in sixty years has refused to accept injustice and stupidity. Vittorio De Sica's power does not reside in his apparent generosity, which is only a mask, but in the hatred he avows towards false values. The real De Sica is forever the author of *Umberto D.*, the film that ruined him. (Leprohon, 98–9)

Compare these remarks from the 1960s with those of Nicola Chiaromonte in 1949 on watching De Sica work on *Bicycle Thieves*:

> Nine-tenths of De Sica's talent consists in knowing exactly what he can do and doing it with great diligence and patience. He directs a movie much the same way as Stanislavski directed a play. A scenario is to him a series of notes indicating places and atmospheres that he wants to use. Then come weeks and weeks of careful work on the spot, which involves getting really to know every milieu that is going to be represented, even in details that will never appear on the screen. Since the war, fortune tellers have become a very important part of Italian life. The scenario of *Bicycle Thieves* required

two scenes in a fortune teller's room. De Sica's collaborators had discovered
a woman seer whom they thought was inimitable and tried to bribe her into
acting her own part, in her own apartment. The woman was incorruptible.
The only solution left was to go to her place day after day, posing as her clients, and noting down every detail, from the awed whispers of people waiting in the corridor to be received by the 'holy woman' to the hundreds of
sacred images and fetishes hanging on the walls of the sibyl's temple. In due
time the mental photographing was completed. The whole thing had to be
reconstructed and the right actors found. It took a lot of time and trouble,
since De Sica didn't want any professional actors. But De Sica is ready to
wait as long as necessary to get the right touch. He knows Rome, loves the
Roman way of life, enjoys catching it on film and, as people say of him, he
could lure even a sack of potatoes into acting.   (Chiaromonte, 623)

The conventional view of De Sica as a sentimentalist was something
of a mask that De Sica created for himself. It is not that De Sica was
cynical about life and people, but rather that he was able, even during
his rhetorical effusions, to remember that all people are capable of
destructive behaviour. His treatment of the Finzi-Contini family, for
example, in his last masterwork is indeed loving, but at the same time
ruthlessly critical of the cultural 'incest' that conditions their life and
death. De Sica was not a sentimentalist when it came to defending
views on culture in which he believed (just as he could be stubbornly
obstinate in negotiations with producers); and these views did not necessarily have as their tenet the fundamental goodness of mankind.
People are more often 'made' good in a De Sica film by being submerged in trial, suffering, and forced reflection. Ricci, for example, is
not especially good at the beginning of *Bicycle Thieves*; if anything, he
seems rather 'dotty,' especially in his behaviour towards Bruno. In fact
the loss of his bicycle can be attributed to his carelessness and preoccupation with his own woes. Ricci (as Mark West argues below, 137–59)
is not by any means a good man for whom we uncritically agonize, but
a self-absorbed, unaware man for whom we feel some degree of scorn
at the film's beginning; he is guilty of refusing to see, but in that quality he resembles most of De Sica's major characters from beginning to
end: Umberto, for example, who in his petit-bourgeois crustiness
refuses to see his kinship with the maid Maria and at one point bluntly
interrupts her tearful confrontation with her soldier boyfriend; or even
Totò in *Miracle*, who has a great deal to learn about people and what
they really want. We come to care about Ricci as he becomes aware of
the world himself, as his simple ignorance is shown to be of no value in

the world – at the moments when his dimness cracks and his concern for Bruno becomes apparent, at the moments of his defeat (in the church, or at the thief's house). He achieves his humanity fully for us only when Bruno, recognizing his father's victimization, takes his hand at film's end.

As a director De Sica was as much a reconstructor of reality as a discoverer of it. Thus, it is important to understand that De Sica films aim not only at a love for everything, which Bazin praised, but as well at an x-ray of everything, a representation of reality that reveals the power lines, the abstract infrastructures, and the psychological motives in the humanity he celebrated verbally. As he became older, he began to enjoy experimenting more and more and regretted the times when he had lacked capable technical collaborators to follow through on experiments (see 'De Sica on De Sica,' 48 below). De Sica belongs as much to the tradition of constructed reality (the tradition of Georges Méliès) as he does to that of Louis Lumière.

Notes

1 For an indication of the capacity of *Bicycles Thieves* to elicit tears see Sue Harper and Vincent Porter, 'Moved to Tears: Weeping in the Cinema in Postwar Britain,' *Screen* 37:2 (Summer 1996), 152–73.
2 For Rossellini see Tad Gallagher, *The Adventures of Roberto Rossellini* (New York: Da Capo, 1998); for Visconti see Henry Bacon, *Visconti: Explorations of Beauty and Decay* (Cambridge: Cambridge University Press, 1998); for De Santis see Antonio Vitti, *Giuseppe De Santis and Postwar Italian Cinema* (Toronto: University of Toronto Press, 1996).
3 See, for instance, Mario Monicelli's *La grande guerra / The Great War* (1959), where the ostensible focus is World War I; and Nanni Loy's *Le quattro giornate di Napoli / The Four Days of Naples* (1962).
4 Hay also analyses two other films in which De Sica starred: *Ai vostri ordini signora / At Your Service Madame!* (Mario Mattoli, 1939) and *Grandi magazzini / Department Store* (Mario Camerini, 1939).

References

Agel, Henri. *Vittorio De Sica*. Paris: Editions Universitaires, 1955.
Agel, Henri, editor/author. *Vittorio De Sica*, an entire issue of *L'Avant-scène du cinéma* (15 October 1978).

Armes, Roy. *Patterns of Realism: A Study of Italian Neo-Realist Cinema*. New York: Barnes, 1971.

Anderson, Lindsay. 'Paramount at Cannes.' *Sight and Sound* 26:1 (Summer 1956), 16–21.

Bazin, André. *What Is Cinema?* 2 volumes. Selected and translated by Hugh Gray. Berkeley: University of California Press, 1971.

Bell, Edward. '"Human, Molto Human."' *Village Voice* 29 November 1991.

Berger, John. *Keeping a Rendezvous*. New York: Vintage, 1991.

Bolzoni, Francesco. *Quando De Sica era Mister Brown*. Torino: RAI/Edizioni Italiani, 1984.

Brunette, Peter. *Roberto Rossellini*. New York: Oxford University Press, 1987.

Cardullo, Bert. *What is Neorealism? A Critical English Language Bibliography of Italian Cinematic Realism*. Lanham, Md.: University Press of America, 1991.

Chiaromonte, Nicola. 'Rome Letter: Italian Movies.' *Partisan Review*, 16:6 (June 1949), 621–30.

Daretta, John. *Vittorio De Sica: A Guide to References and Resources*. Boston: G.K. Hall, 1982.

Doane, Mary Ann. *The Desire to Desire: The Woman's Film of the 1940s*. Bloomington: Indiana University Press, 1987.

Deleuze, Gilles. *Cinema 1: The Movement Image; Cinema 2: The Time-Image*. Translated by Hugh Tomlinson and Barbara Habberjam. Minneapolis: University of Minnesota Press, 1988; 1989.

Furhammar, Lief, and Folke Issaksson. *Politics and Film*. Translated by Kersti French. New York: Praeger, 1971.

Hay, James. *Popular Film Culture in Fascist Italy: The Passing of the Rex*. Bloomington: Indiana University Press, 1987.

Kael, Pauline. 'The Fall and Rise of Vittorio De Sica.' *New Yorker* 47 (18 December 1971), 48–53. Reprinted in Pauline Kael, *For Keeps* (New York: Dutton, 1994), 16-17.

Kolker, Robert Philip. *The Altering Eye: Contemporary International Cinema*. Oxford: Oxford University Press, 1983.

Leprohon, Pierre. *Vittorio De Sica*. Paris: Seghers, 1966. All quotations from this work have been translated by Eugene and Michelle Walz.

Marcus, Millicent. *Italian Film in the Light of Neorealism*. Princeton: Princeton University Press, 1986.

Overby, David, editor. *Springtime in Italy: A Reader in Neorealism*. London: Talisman, 1978.

Perry, Ted. 'The Road to Neorealism.' *Film Comment* 14:6 (November–December 1978). 7–13.

Rhode, Eric. 'Why Neorealism Failed.' *Sight and Sound* 30:1 (Winter 1960), 27–32.

Robinson, Andrew. *Satyajit Ray: The Inner Eye.* Berkeley: University of California Press, 1989.

Rohdie, Sam. 'Italian Neorealism 1941–1943.' *Australian Journal of Screen Theory* 15/16 (1983), 133–62.

Samuels, Charles Thomas, editor. *Encountering Directors.* New York: Putnam's, 1972.

Sargeant, Winthrop. 'Profiles: Bread, Love, and Neo-realismo – 1.' *New Yorker* 33:19 (29 June 1957), 35–58.

Sitney, P. Adams. *Vital Crises in Italian Cinema.* Austin: University of Texas Press, 1995.

Thompson, Kristin. *Breaking the Glass Armor.* Princeton: Princeton University Press, 1988.

Wagstaff, Christopher. 'Comic Positions.' *Sight and Sound* 2:7 (November 1992), 25–7.

De Sica on De Sica

A Portrait of De Sica and His Philosophy

An exceedingly handsome man, standing about six feet tall, with dark eyes and a thick, wavy, immaculately groomed head of hair, [De Sica] has a carefully pre-served figure that even today betrays only a little of the fullness of middle age. There is about him the air of unabashed patrician elegance that often character-izes the well-turned-out Italian male, and even when he is off the set, he closely resembles, except for the absence of a moustache, the courtly marshall of cara-binieri that he impersonated so tellingly in Bread, Love and Dreams. *Car-rying himself erect at all times, with the veteran actor's regard for effect, he walks in a manner that conveys an almost kingly impression of tranquillity and equilibrium. His voice is quiet and well modulated, and he expresses himself with just a trace of Mediterranean floweriness. When he sits, he drapes himself – unconsciously, it appears, and probably from long years of theatrical habit – in a graceful pose, perhaps with his knees crossed, his left hand in the pocket of his jacket, and a cigarette in the fingers of his right hand as he rests his right elbow on a convenient end table in an attitude of careless ease. The effect sug-gests the leading man in an extremely urbane, if slightly old-fashioned bedroom comedy, and it is heightened by De Sica's way of dressing, which is fastidious almost to a fault and nearly always more formal than the occasion calls for. It is by no means easy to determine what is going on inside his head, for his face, though an expressive one, is, like his body, a carefully controlled instrument, trained to meet the requirements of the stage and the camera. From time to time, it may become clouded by some slight annoyance, but he never loses his poise, and both his quick smile and his momentary lapses into seriousness conform to the general pattern of the personality he chooses to reveal – that of a cultivated, self-assured, and infinitely courteous Italian man of the world.*

De Sica in his *bravo ragazzo* persona as Bruno in Mario Camerini's *Gli uomini che mascalzoni / Men Are Such Rascals* (1932)

De Sica (centre) in Mario Camerini's *Daro un milione / I'd Give a Million* (1935)

De Sica in his healer persona as the paediatrician in his own *Teresa Venerdì* (1941)

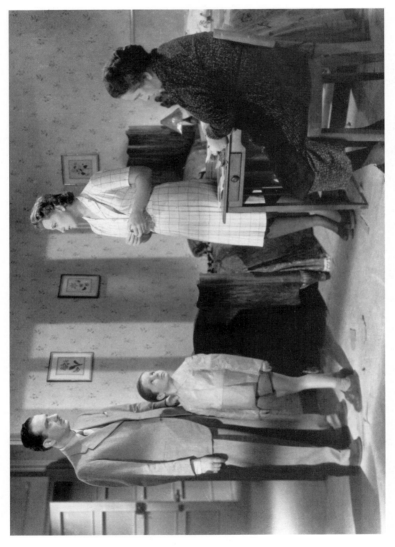

The child (Luciano De Ambrosis) torn between his father (Adriano Rimoldi) and his mother (Isa Pola) in *I bambini ci guardano / The Children Are Watching Us* (1943)

Antonio (Lamberto Maggiorani) and his son Bruno (Enzo Staiola) surrounded by hostile fellow-Romans in *Ladri di biciclette / Bicycle Thieves* (1948)

Vittorio De Sica on the set of *Ladri di biciclette / Bicycle Thieves* (1948)

Francesco Colisano as Totò (holding the dove, lower right) in De Sica's neorealist fantasy, *Miracolo a Milano / Miracle in Milan* (1950)

The pensioner Umberto (Carlo Battisti) gazing dejectedly upon his dishevelled accommodations in *Umberto D.* (1952)

The *carabiniere* (De Sica) and the midwife (Marisa Merlini) in Luigi Comencini's *neorealismo rosa* hit *Pane, amore e fantasia / Bread, Love and Dreams* (1953)

De Sica as the count, with his valet (Mario Passante), in the gambler episode of De Sica's omnibus film *L'oro di Napoli* / *The Gold of Naples* (1954)

Giorgio Listuzzi and Gabriella Pallotta as the young newlyweds, home at last in their hastily built shelter in De Sica's final neorealist drama, *Il tetto* / *The Roof* (1956)

Cesira (Sophia Loren) and her daughter, Rosetta (Eleonora Brown), in
La ciociara / Two Women (1960)

Neapolitan exuberance and plenitude: Adelina (Sophia Loren), her husband, Carmine (Marcello Mastroianni), and the children in the 'Adelina' episode of *Ieri, oggi e domani* / *Yesterday, Today and Tomorrow* (1963)

Starlet (Britt Ekland), aging star (Victor Mature), and director (Peter Sellers) in De Sica's parodic, self-mocking farce, *After the Fox* (1966)

Micòl Finzi-Contini (Dominique Sanda) and Giorgio (Lino Capolicchio) bicycling through the family estate in De Sica's elegiac *Il giardino dei Finzi-Contini* / *The Garden of the Finzi-Continis* (1970)

Vittorio De Sica (1964)

Only by directing can I express what is within me. The Lord and the Lumière brothers have provided me with this wonderful method of writing. I find philosophy very difficult to understand, but nevertheless I have a favorite philosopher – Seneca, the Roman Stoic. I like to think over his moral observations. Besides, I feel particularly well acquainted with him because I once impersonated him in a film. I am basically an unhappy man. Life gives me always the impression of cruelty. I read the newspaper – crimes, murders, divorces, and so on. I do not find evidence of sincerity or solidarity there. I love humanity, I trust humanity, but humanity has a way of disillusioning me. The pictures I direct are nearly always melancholy. This comes from the contrast between my love and my disillusion. I am an optimist. I love life. I seek perfection. If my art seems pessimistic, it is a consequence of my continuing optimism and its disillusion. At least I have enthusiasm. It is necessary to all professions to have enthusiasm in order to have success.

This 'portrait' of De Sica on page 22 and De Sica's own description of his philosophy are from Winthrop Sargeant, 'Profiles: Bread, Love, and Neo-realismo – 1,' *New Yorker* 33:19 (29 June 1957), 40–1, 45–6.

Getting into Cinema

During the First World War, I toured the hospitals in Naples with an amateur troupe, singing Neapolitan *canzonette*. According to my father, I was very good and had very dramatic expressions. The war was finished and the family moved to Rome. I gained my diploma in accountancy and enrolled at the University in the Faculty of Political and Commercial Science. That tragic and aristocratic poverty was still prevalent in the family. One day what was bound to happen came to pass. I met a friend in the street.

'What are you doing,' he asked.

'I'm an accountant,' I said rather haughtily, but I added: 'I'm looking for a job so I can help my father.'

He told me he was working as a walk-on at the theatre, that they were looking for someone else. So I went to see Tatiana Pavlova and made my debut in *Sogno d'amore* – as a waiter.

From Vittorio De Sica, 'The Most Wonderful Years of My Life,' in *Films and Filming* 2:3 (December 1955), 5. Translated by John Francis Lane

On *I bambini ci guardano* / *The Children Are Watching Us* (1942)

The Children Are Watching Us was a compromise between the old formula and the new: but for Zavattini and me it was a decisive experience ... In those difficult times, my thoughts turned more to the children than to the adults who had lost all sense of proportion. This was truly the moment when the children were watching us. They gave me the true picture of how our country was morally destroyed.

From *Films and Filming*, 2:3 (December 1955), 5

On *Sciuscià* / *Shoeshine* (1946)

I knew two of them, Scimmietta (little monkey) and Capellone (big cap). Scimmietta slept in a lift in via Lombardia, and he was lucky to have a grandfather who loved him. This family warmth saved him. Capellone was nobody's child, completely alone in the world, with his big head deformed by rickets ... As soon as they earned three or four hundred lire from cleaning shoes, they ran to the nearby Villa Borghese park and hired a horse. Later in writing the script, Zavattini made of the horse an exquisitely poetic touch ... There are some characters which demand professional actors, while there are others which can come to life only through a certain face ... Capellone and Scimmietta would not do: they were too ugly, almost deformed.

From *Films and Filming*, 2:3 (December 1955), 5

On *Stazione Termini* / *Indiscretion of an American Wife* (1953)

I must say that I like the film: it is full of faults but it convinces me. I would not make it again as I would all my other films. Work on it was very complicated. For some extraordinary reason, many people think that all the scenes shot of the station life were authentic, 'stolen from reality.'

From Vittorio De Sica, 'Hollywood Shocked Me,' in *Films and Filming* 2:5 (February 1956), 13 Translated by John Francis Lane

On *Umberto D.* (1951)

One of the first evenings I was in Hollywood, Merle Oberon invited
me to her home ... She organized a dinner in my honour, inviting the
whole film aristocracy from Chaplin to Sam Goldwyn. Knowing that I
had brought with me a copy of *Umberto D.* she persuaded me to let her
run it ... When the projection finished ... I looked at Chaplin: everyone
else had risen and they were all gesticulating. He still sat there immo-
bile, with his eyes closed. Two minutes went by. I began to feel sick in
the stomach and a sort of panic seized me. Then he spread out his arms
and opened his eyes.

I saw he was crying like a baby.

He said: 'De Sica, it's great, a great film ... but it won't please the
Americans, or very few of them.' Later he spoke again and described it
as an 'academic' work, that he preferred *Bicycle Thieves* and *Shoeshine*
because they are closer to the public, more accessible to them, and
could move anyone be he an intellectual or an illiterate.

From *Films and Filming*, 2:5 (February 1956), 12

On Casting *Ladri di biciclette* / *Bicycle Thieves* (1948)

Among the queue of parents bringing their children for me to see, I
noticed this man holding his little son by the hand. I beckoned him to
come forward. He lifted up the child and held it out to me ... 'No,' I
said, 'I'm interested in you, not your child.' I did a film test of him
immediately; the way he moved, the way he sat down, his gestures
with those hands hardened from work, the hands of a working man,
not an actor ... I made him promise that after the film he would forget
the cinema and would go back to his job ...[1]

Finding a child for *Bicycle Thieves* was not so easy. In desperation,
I decided to start shooting anyway ... During a pause, while I was
talking to Maggiorani, and becoming irritated with the people who
were pushing around me, I noticed amongst them an odd-looking
child with a round face and a weird nose and large expressive eyes.
It was Enzo Staiola – I felt that our Neapolitan Saint Jannarius had
sent him to me. Indeed, it was proof that everything was alright ... that

first day's shooting of *Bicycle Thieves* was one of the most satisfying of my life.

From Vittorio De Sica, 'Money, the Public and *Umberto D.*,' in *Films and Filming* 2:4 (January 1956), 28. Translated by John Francis Lane

On *Miracolo a Milano / Miracle in Milan* (1950)

In spite of the fact that in reality things are quite different, often in fiction we read about the power and heartlessness of the rich and the humble resignation of the poor. The struggle is unequal; but the poor man, by dint of prodigious courage and presence of mind, emerges victorious in the end, just when it seems that he is fated to succumb. Very often, love is his guiding force, inciting him to victory. Thus, once again, virtue triumphs and evil is punished.

Miracle in Milan, despite certain realistic overtones capable of varied, even antithetical, interpretations on the social level, is simply a fairy story and only intended as such ...

Once again, ... I have remained faithful to the world of my imagination. But, from the stylistic point of view, *Miracle in Milan* opened up new paths for me. Its content is humanist, but its inspiration, the climate in which the characters evolve, their way of thinking and behaving, and their very fate itself, is more closely related to the legends of the North, to [Hans Christian] Andersen, for example, than to the reality of our present-day Latin world. There is no hymn in praise of poverty – as I read somewhere to my horror – nor any condemnation of riches ... This is a fable, slightly wistful, perhaps, but quietly optimistic within its poetic framework ... Men and angels are to be found here living on good terms together. Totò works miracles for all comers and works them, obviously, for the benefit of those who need them – that is to say, the poor. But these people, with their dreamy, ingenuous looks, do not ask only for things that will satisfy their material needs and alleviate their distress. They ask also for superfluous, even ridiculous things, to appease some secret longing for them.

In this style I had two masters, Clair and Chaplin, towering above me with all the force of their genius; their example drew me on and yet, at the same time acted as a restraint and a warning to me: it was a dangerous attraction.

From Vittorio De Sica, "How I Direct My Films," preface to the English edition of the screenplay, *Miracle in Milan* (New York: Orion Press, 1968), 1–9

'Letter to Zavattini' (1953)

My dear Zavattini,
I hope you will be kind enough to explain to our friends from the Roman Circle of Cinema my absence from their theoretical debates. I am grateful for your affectionate and insistent invitations. My absence occurs through no lack of goodwill on my part, as you know, but primarily because I am not a theoretician and, consequently, fear theoretical discussions even though I recognize their basic importance – and, secondly, there is a lack of time because our beautiful profession leaves us no leisure time. I follow, as well as I can, the cultural activities of the Circle through the news that colleagues give me or your bulletins, and I believe that such activity itself is one of the best signs of the concrete life of our cinema, of that Italian cinema that certain people consider dead at the very moment that it manifests its existence in a vital way, through its attempts and its errors as well as its successes.

In brief, as you see, I am anything but pessimistic, and I would like to insist that, despite the fact that the capitalistic nature of our production restricts the inspiration of our artists, we manage, on average, to produce about ten films a year which are made with above-average ambitions and contain positive values; such films could be defined as having 'indicative' values (and I should spare these details to one such as yourself who is continually blazing new trails). Of course, it is necessary that these ten good films, as soon as possible, become twenty, then thirty, then forty, and, in order to facilitate the development of our cinema, that the competent authorities assure the first and all-important condition of that development which is, we all agree, freedom.

On this score, also, the press can continue to play a useful role, provided it avoid personal and seditious facts ... the press is in a position to enlighten the public concerning our works, to prepare it for that revolution which is taking place since the cinema has grown aware that its limitations go beyond that of mere entertainment – or, to put this another way, that entertainment has assumed an increasingly precise role in the fashioning of public attitudes. I was reflecting on this exact matter yesterday as I was reviewing the articles published on *Stazione Termini* [*Indiscretion of an American Wife*], and I was noticing that a small proportion (fortunately insignificant) found in the film a pretext to pretend that you and I should split up and bring to an end a partnership that has lasted more than ten years. Well, our case, as modest in importance as it may be, is significant in relation to the general problem to which I was referring above, and to the political or private passions which sometimes hurt the workings of criticism. You and I have asked the press to judge us severely; we have read its judgments with care and we have drawn some lessons from it; but we have always been astonished and saddened by judgments which, instead of being based upon ethical or aesthetic analysis of film, are motivated by feelings of friendship or enmity – if not worse.

Thus, what is the basis for trying so hard to separate us? Has our collaboration, so natural and close, affected the Italian cinema in an adverse way? I have the feeling that such an insistence was done with so much bitterness and nastiness because all possible means were used to pit one against the other: they came very close to succeeding. It all started with *Miracle in Milan* and all the forces were released with *Indiscretion of an American Wife*. It is certain that none of these critics were encouraging us ten years ago at the time of *The Children Are Watching Us* or *The Gates of Heaven*, when the very identity of our inspiration was already obvious, when we were already giving evidence of a complete mutual understanding. We didn't get any encouragement from anyone, may I insist, and we were very much on our own, you and I, each having confidence in the other, and that is how *Bicycle Thieves* was made. I know that the script for *Bicycle Thieves* is due to your unrelenting talent, and we both know how unpopular an event it was; but I felt that it really expressed my view of the world and that I would know how to express it as if I had always felt that way. Do you recall that someone even remarked to us upon reading the script: 'That is not cinema'? None of those critics liked your white horse of *Shoeshine*; they did not want such a tragic ending nor did they want to see that the theft of a poor bicycle would provoke such misery and that the other characters such as the kind Totò or old Umberto D. would upset the quiet life of a group that had already forgotten the war. But I have never doubted, and I do not believe that the two brothers, during the war and postwar periods, could have been more united than we were in aspiring towards the same goals. We knew what we wanted. When the long labour of production came for me and we had to stay apart for several months, I would find you upon my return always ready to pursue our thoughts and always overflowing with this human fantasy, with this enlightened enthusiasm, of that ethical consistency that never failed you. And why have we separated? Today, as I go over the newspaper accounts, it seems that I fully realize for the first time in a startling way the grave injustice that was done to you and, consequently, to me in showing your scripts in opposition to my production, or even by denying the very authorship of these scripts in order to sow discord where there has always been agreement.

I realize that a letter that should have been of a few lines only has become very long, a kind of outpouring on this Sunday afternoon. I do not complain about it because it has thus given me one more opportunity to affirm publicly the indestructible links of esteem and affection that bind us together and that, on the very eve of a new joint effort, I hope with all my heart this effort will not be our last.

From *Cinema nuovo* 2:16 (1 August 1953), 70. Translated by Hubert Balcaen

On Character

When I make a picture I love all the characters, their vices and defects. My work is human work. There is always an excuse, even for the criminal. Humanity is a very deep mystery ... I have a concept of the art of interpretation ... Always in my mind I have a concept of the character. Often actors suggest something too exaggerated or too sentimental.

Robert Flaherty was the first in my life. And King Vidor's *The Crowd*, in 1928, was the first of the neorealist pictures.

From "Viva De Sica," *Newsweek* 79 (10 January 1972), 58

Perhaps it's presumptuous, but it would be hard to renounce this conviction that I have: to believe myself capable of understanding men, their feelings, their troubles, their dramas. This conviction is based on long, hard experience. I too have suffered long and hard. From my youth, I've known deception, bitterness, renunciation. It's an unforgettable experience that follows us our entire lives, and that perpetrated itself in the peremptory and mysterious need to look around oneself with comprehensive and generous eyes to bring forward, from behind their appearances and inventions, the secret drama of each man. We remind ourselves of the great principles of the French Revolution: Liberty, Equality, Brotherhood. We believe; we need to believe, even when the new atrocities committed in the world should make us doubt mankind's humanity. But suffering contains both the poison and its antidote. In their ordeals humans return to the forgotten bases of our culture, of our faith, of our very nature itself. They return to the words and teachings of Christ. And with them, to Art, whose language is essentially humane. And consequently, to cinematographic art as well.

From Pierre Leprohon, *Vittorio De Sica* (Paris: Seghers, 1966), 109. Translated by Eugene Walz and Michelle Walz

An Interview with Charles Thomas Samuels

Samuels: Signor De Sica, how did you meet Zavattini and what made you decide to collaborate with him?

De Sica: I met him when I had decided to film a novel by Cesare Giulio Viola, called *Prico*. A short time before that, I had met Zavattini in Milan and had thought, 'Here is a writer I would like to work with.' I admired his style, which had just then been revealed in his novel *They're Talking So Much about Me*. The film we made together, *The Children Are Watching Us*, had a great success because of the poetry and melancholy of a marriage failing before the witness of a child, who learns that adults make mistakes, who is forced to suffer his mother's adultery and his father's suicide. But when it came out, we were in the middle of our Fascist period, that absurd little Italian republic of ours, and I was asked to go to Venice to lead the Fascist film school. I refused, so my unfortunate little film came out without the name of its author.

S: Your collaboration with Zavattini seems to me the most fruitful partnership between director and writer in film history. Has it been completely untroubled?

DS: Sometimes producers, after discussing a project with Zavattini and me, have turned to other writers, thus disturbing our rapport. But in these so-called betrayals, I was never at fault. Unfortunately, our producers often make films with American backing, so sometimes they say they want an Anglo-Saxon flavor and hire an English-speaking writer. But I stoutly maintain that a good film must reflect the country of its origin. A French film must be truly French; a Yugoslav film, truly Slavic; etc. When one starts making these Italo-English, Italo-American films, he is bound to fail.

S: Would you go so far as to disown those films you made outside of Italy, such as *A Young World*?

DS: Not *A Young World*, because that film deals with an international problem which is still being talked about. When we decided to make it, a million women a year were dying in France because of abortions. The film was a defense of the birth control pill, and it argued that abortion should be a recognized fact, dealt with efficiently and not hidden. At this very moment, there is a scandal in France because of all those prominent women who declared they had abortions in order to oppose the law against it. Look at all the trouble their sincerity has brought them!

S: Signor De Sica, you are one of the most famous of neorealists. What does neorealism mean to you?

DS: I recently discussed this question with a British journalist. You know, people think that neorealism means exterior shooting, but they are wrong. Most films today are made in a realistic style, but they are actually opposed to neorealism, to that revolution in cinematic language which we started and which they think to follow. Because neorealism is not shooting films in authentic locales; it is not reality. It is reality filtered through poetry, reality transfigured. It is not Zola, not naturalism, verism, things which are ugly.

S: By poetry, don't you mean scenes like the one in *The Bicycle Thief*, where the father takes his son to the *trattoria* in order to cheer the boy up only to be overcome with the weight of his problems?

DS: Ah, that is one of the few light scenes in the film.

S: But sad at the same time.

DS: Yes, that is what I mean by poetry.

S: Was that scene improvised?

DS: It was written in advance, but of course, during the moment of filming, gestures are produced by the actors that reflect their dreams and taste. I knew there must be some shift in the scene to show the change in the father's heart, and I directed toward that end.

S: You say that neorealism is realism filtered through poetry; nonetheless, it is harsh because you forced your compatriots right after the war to confront experiences they had just suffered through. Didn't they resist?

DS: Neorealism was born after a total loss of liberty, not only personal, but artistic and political. It was a means of rebelling against the stifling dictatorship that had humiliated Italy. When we lost the war, we discovered our ruined morality. The first film that placed a very tiny stone in the reconstruction of our former dignity was *Shoeshine*.

S: Usually, audiences resist such reconstruction.

DS: In fact, *Shoeshine* failed. It is easy to see why. After the war, Italians were hungry for foreign films. They flocked first to American, then to Russian movies, but both proved a great disillusionment. Slowly, bit by bit, the public came back to their own. Rossellini, Zavattini, and I came out too early. Many films that were shown then would have a greater success if they were new today.

S: Do you know the films of Olmi?

DS: Of course.

S: What do you think of them?

DS: I like them very much. He is a very delicate director. He doesn't try to *épater le bourgeois*; he says what he thinks in his own way: simple, modest, humble.

S: I'd like to know what you think of his contemporaries. Bellocchio?

DS: I don't like him. He is too propagandistic and presumptuous.

S: Pasolini?

DS: He is good, particularly in his Roman films, like *Accattone*, but I also admire his *Oedipus Rex*.

S: Don't you find his theme banal?

DS: Perhaps Pasolini is a bit too literary, too educated. It's been said that Shakespeare is better played by ignorant than by overly cultivated actors. Pasolini imposes his immense cultivation on his work; he could probably use more freedom, greater simplicity.

S: I find that Godard has badly influenced most of these directors.

DS: Godard is a master, a totally personal artist, but the inventor of the New Wave. He created followers, imitators, and imitation is always deplorable.

S: What about his most important Italian imitator, Bertolucci?

DS: No, Bertolucci is our best young director. I liked him from the first, when he showed *La commare secca* to me. He is a young man with a new vision of cinema.

S: How do you compare his *Conformist* with your *Garden of the Finzi-Continis*?

DS: They are totally different.

S: They have similar subjects and the same leading lady.

DS: Okay, but Sanda is not very good in his film. Still, the picture is very beautiful, except for a certain willful and eccentric estheticism. For example, when the father's madhouse is made to look like the Roman Senate, I find the effect too *recherché*, too painterly. Bertolucci admits that he follows Magritte. Another young director I like is Carmelo Bene;[2] unlike all the others, he has a sense of humor. And he doesn't make propaganda, which for me isn't art.

S: How do you feel the younger critics treat you? For example, the *Cahiers du cinéma* group.

DS: They have never liked my films, and they are welcome to their opinion. I am never affected by critics I don't esteem. I go my own way, mistaken or not. I trust my conscience and my sensibility. On the other hand, I have listened to those critics who said that De Sica made no important films since *Umberto D.*, and who, fortunately, feel there has been a revival with *The Garden of the Finzi-Continis*. They are right, because I made too many films that depended on the will of American financiers. For example, I made a film with Sophia Loren, which earned her an Oscar. I made films that are ... too industrial, not as deeply felt as *Umberto D.* When I offered that film to Rizzoli, he said, 'Why do you want to make *Umberto D.*? Why don't you make *Don Camillo*? I will give you a hundred million lire, half of the grosses.' But I was full of noble intentions then; I didn't make *Don Camillo*, I made *Umberto D.*[3] But soon my money ran out, because I financed *Umberto D.*, *The Bicycle Thief*, and *Shoeshine* myself, and I became dependent on producers, who wanted me to make films I won't say that I didn't believe in but that I would rather not have made.

S: Are you nostalgic for the earlier days?

DS: Very. *Umberto D.* was made absolutely without compromise, without concessions to spectacle, the public, the box office.

S: Even fewer than *Bicycle Thief*?

DS: Look, for me, *Umberto D.* is unique. Even though it has been the greater critical success, *The Bicycle Thief* does contain sentimental concessions.

S: Nevertheless, it is wonderful. How, having made such films, could you produce a thing like *A Place for Lovers*?

DS: That was the result of a misunderstanding. I had read in the papers that a friend of mine, Rondi, had an enormous theatrical success with a play of his called *The Lovers*. I told my manager about it, and without even giving me time to see the play, he purchased the rights. I kept saying, 'Wait. I only read about it in the paper.' But he didn't wait. Still the play was not a bad one; it simply wasn't good material for a movie.

S: Why?

DS: *Love Story* is a great success, but in my film the lovers are adults of forty and thirty-six. A love affair between adults isn't as touching as one between young people.

S: What about *Brief Encounter*? Your rule doesn't hold up.

DS: Yes, *Brief Encounter* is beautiful.

S: Even allowing for the ill-suited subject, why did you smother it in such beautiful scenery and chic costuming? It seems to me a film about Faye Dunaway's wardrobe.

DS: Faye Dunaway brought her personal dressmaker with her. That's the way with all actresses!

S: Such a film gives ammunition to those who use your later works to dismiss your entire career.

DS: It was a mistake. Like all artists, I make mistakes.

S: Why do you use professional actors now, whereas you made your best films without them?

DS: In Italy there are about a hundred actors; fewer, if you are critical. In life there are millions. If I find a person with the particular appearance, virtues, and defects that fit my character, I take him from the streets when I cannot find what I need in a professional. For example, in *The Garden of the Finzi-Continis* Dominique Sanda and Lino Capolicchio are perfect for their parts, but Sanda's father I found in the street. Her mother is a Turinese countess, her grandmother a Russian extra. For *The Bicycle Thief* only one producer would give me money. David O. Selznick was the only one who saw value in the project, but he wondered whom I would cast as the father. I replied that I wanted a real Italian worker because I found no one suitable among the available professionals (Mastroianni would have done, but he was too young then, only eighteen). You know whom Selznick wanted? Cary Grant. Grant is pleasant, cordial, but he is too worldly, bourgeois; his hands have no blisters on them. He carries himself like a gentleman. I needed a man who eats like a worker, is moved like a worker, who can bring himself to cry, who bats his wife around and expresses his love for her by slamming her on the shoulders, the buttocks, the head. Cary Grant isn't used to doing such things, and he can't do them. Therefore, Selznick refused to give me money, and I had to beg to finance the film, as I always have had to beg. For my commercial movies, money was always available. I want to make Flaubert's *A Simple Heart* now, but the producers want me to amplify the love affair in it. You can't betray Flaubert. If they will let me make *A Simple Heart*, I will; if not, not.

S: How do you direct nonprofessionals?

DS: I explain and explain, and I am very convincing. I seem to have a special gift for making myself understood by actors. Either I play the part or I explain it, slowly, patiently, with a smile on my face and never any anger.

S: Do you have many takes?

DS: No.

S: If it isn't right?

DS: If it isn't right, I sometimes repeat, but usually I keep what I have shot. But I rehearse and rehearse and rehearse.

S: Is it difficult for you to act for others, as, for example, in *General Della Rovere*?

DS: That was my best role because the film was made by a director I esteem.

S: You are also very good for yourself, especially in *The Gold of Naples*.

DS: That was painful. I couldn't see myself and kept asking the cameramen and mechanics, 'Do you believe me? How am I doing?' A line of dialogue can be said a thousand ways; you need someone behind the camera to tell you which is the right one.

S: You have the rushes.

DS: Yes, but in Italy there is never enough money. Producers always tell you that once a thing is shot it must remain that way.

S: You've explained why you made your commercial films, but I still can't fathom how you and Zavattini, not only neorealists but leftists, could have made a film like *Woman Times Seven*, a wish fulfillment for the middle class.

DS: *Woman Times Seven* was a compilation of sketches that Zavattini had lying about. We were among the first to make films of sketches, and when Joseph Levine asked us to make another of them, Zavattini pulled some out of his drawer. It was a bit dishonest. The film is too long, but there are some cute things in it.

S: Bresson complained to me that you neorealists were violating reality by dubbing, since the voice is the truest expression of personality.

DS: It's not the voice; it's what one says.

S: Still, why do you dub?

DS: Because I didn't have the money. *The Bicycle Thief* cost a hundred thousand dollars, *Shoeshine* twenty thousand. With such budgets, I couldn't afford sound cameras.

S: You've worked in color and black and white. Which do you prefer?

DS: Black and white, because reality is black and white.

S: That's not true.

DS: Color is distracting. When you see a beautiful landscape in a color film, you forget the story. Americans use color for musicals. All my best films were made in black and white.

S: What do you think of the color experiments of Antonioni?

DS: He is an esthete. He takes red apples and paints them white.

S: Most critics today maintain that the true film artist writes what he directs.

DS: That's not true. Directing is completely different from writing; it is the creation of life. If *Bicycle Thief* had been directed by someone else, it would have been good, but different from the film I made.

S: Does this mean that you think dialogue less important than images?

DS: Images are the only important things. Let me give you another example of what I mean. Five films have been made of *The Brothers Karamazov*, all bad. Only one came close to Dostoyevsky: the version by Fedor Ozep.[4] That's how the director is an author. In all these films the same story was used, but only one of them was any good.

S: You have often said that you greatly value René Clair and Charlie Chaplin. How have they influenced you?

DS: In no way.

S: Not even in *Miracle in Milan*?

DS: No, that is a wholly personal film. I detest imitations. In fact, I sometimes don't go to see a certain film for fear I'll want to imitate it.

S: How does your success affect you?

DS: Success has never made me drunk. I have never told myself one of my films is wonderful; I have always thought I could have done better. I want always to improve. When I have done something badly, I recognize it; when I do something well, I want to do better.

S: Do you see your old films?

DS: Yes, and sometimes I am pleased by them. Recently I saw that unfortunate film *Good Morning Elephant*, which was signed by

Gianni Franciolini but which I directed and in which I and my wife, Maria, played. It is delightful.[5] Another film of mine that had no success, *The Roof,* seems to me one of my best.

S: That film seems unusually polemical, am I right? Under the credits, for example, we see the Italian flag. The film seems your judgment on Italy.

DS: To a certain extent, because, you know, the housing problem is still an issue for us. But I was primarily interested in recording a way of life. You see, it is customary to place a flag of Italy atop a house when it is completed. To me, this film is sincere and interesting, as well as humble. The actors are delightful.

S: But too pretty.

DS: No. I'll tell you a story about that. Sophia Loren wanted to play the feminine lead. In fact, she has always reproached me for not letting her. But, as I told her, if she were in that situation, people wouldn't give her a little shack but a palace. She is too beautiful, whereas Pallotta was a dumpy girl with a fat ass.

S: Could the film have succeeded if the lovers were ugly?

DS: The cinema has certain terrible requirements. One is that love stories be told about beautiful people. I know of only one film where this rule was ignored: *Marty.* Unfortunately, the public is not convinced when lovers are not handsome.

S: Why are there so many sounds of jets in the film?

DS: I'm glad you noticed them; they were an important auditory element to me. That sound evokes faraway worlds, power, the joy of escape.

S: Why are you so drawn to the destruction of young children as a theme for your films?

DS: Because children are the first to suffer in life. Innocents always pay.

S: This is what you show in *The Children Are Watching Us.* But something even more remarkable in that film is the general decency of the characters. Even that nosy neighbor turns out to be all right, in the moment when she brings the maid a glass of water. Does this represent your belief about mankind?

DS: All my films are about the search for human solidarity. In *Bicycle Thief* this solidarity occurs, but how long does it last? Twenty-four hours. One experiences moments, only moments of solidarity. That glass of water is one of them. Two hours later there will be no more union; the people won't be able to bear one another.

S: But it is important that the moment occurred.

DS: One needs something that lasts longer.

S: Is that possible?

DS: No. Human incommunicability is eternal.

S: Incommunicability or egoism?

DS: Let me tell you something. I wanted to call my films from *Shoe-shine* on, not by their present titles, but 'Egoism #1, #2, #3.' *Umberto D.* is 'Egoism #4.'

S: One of the greatest performances on film is given by the man who plays the father in *The Children Are Watching Us*. Who was he?

DS: A dubber named Cigoli.[6]

S: The film is splendid. With so many traps for sentimentality, I marveled at how you avoided them. And the characters are so rich, except the aunt.

DS: Ah, she was a bourgeoisie truly of the second rank, a coquette. But you are talking of a film that I made over thirty years ago and scarcely remember.

S: There is a strange shot in the film: The grandmother's mill seems to be made up of two photos joined at the middle.

DS: I spliced the shot because there was no mill on the set.

S: A particularly fine moment occurs when the father is leaving the resort. As Nina sees him off at the train, we also watch the leave-taking of that vulgar young couple.

DS: A prostitute changing bordellos and her young man. I put that in as an ironic comment on the similarity between this good and well-intentioned husband who will be betrayed by his bourgeoisie wife as if she were a prostitute.

S: Did you believe in your next film, *The Gates of Heaven*?

DS: No. I made it only to save myself from the Germans. As a matter of fact, the Vatican didn't find it orthodox enough and destroyed the negative. We were in the middle of the war then. I was invited by a messenger of Goebbels to go and direct a German film school at Prague, because, you see, I was then at the top of my fame as a director. I told the envoy to give me time to think, but in truth, I was shaking because I knew they could put me on a train any time they wanted to. Then the Italian Fascists began insisting that I go to direct their school in Venice. I was saved by a marvellous man, D'Angelo, who was truly an angel and who asked me to make a film for the Vatican. I said yes immediately, knowing that the Vatican tie would keep me alive. All the time the Fascists kept asking me when I would finish that Vatican film and come to Venice, and I kept telling them, I was at work on it. It took me two years; I completed it the day the Americans entered Rome. It was made to order. There are some good things in it, but the final scene of the miracle is horrible. It was a film made only to save me from the Fascists.[7]

S: *Shoeshine* is more polemical than *The Roof*, isn't it?

DS: Of course. That is the result of the war, whose first victims were those poor youngsters, ruined by Americans, money, the black market in cigarettes. And then we put them in prison!

S: How did you get the details of prison life?

DS: I frequented the jails and spoke to the inmates. But, you know, the idea for this film was born years earlier. As soon as the war was over, three men and I formed a film journal, which was forbidden to publish after four numbers because it reflected Communist ideas. In the journal we ran a series of interviews with directors, including myself. In my interview I said that I wanted to make a film about shoeshine boys, and I even photographed some of these youngsters and published the results. One year later a producer asked me to make this very film, but he gave me a plot line that was terrible. I said that I would make the film but not with that story. Instead, I went to Zavattini, and we came up with this tale about the boys and their love for that horse.

S: One theme in the film is not developed: homoerotic love among the adolescents. Why?

DS: Because it revolted me.

S: It comes out very strongly in the shower scene where one of the boys beats Interlinghi [the hero].

DS: Yes, the element is present. The boys are nude, and the motive for the fight is jealousy. You're right, but it isn't developed.

S: Is it possible that you instinctively felt that development of this theme would harm the polemic?

DS: Yes. The other is a peripheral tragedy, a secondary unhappiness.

S: Don't you find the ending of the film melodramatic?

DS: I had intended to shoot the last sequence outdoors, but the producer didn't have the money to wait for good weather, as one must in exterior shooting. I wanted to photograph several sunrises and sunsets, and this would have required a week. He gave me two days, so the scene had to be shot indoors on a set. The original ending was beautiful, but I didn't have the money to shoot it properly. The film cost only twenty thousand dollars.

S: The ending isn't convincing.

DS: Twenty thousand dollars!

S: Why do you use music in *The Bicycle Thief* so often to provoke an emotional response?

DS: I am against music, except at a moment like the end of *The Garden of the Finzi-Continis* when we hear the Hebrew lament, but the producers always insist on it.

S: You said that this film [*Bicycle Thief*] contains a compromise ...

DS: Not a compromise; a concession. A small, romantic sentimentality in that rapport between father and son.

S: But that is the most moving thing in the film.

DS: Look, I agree that *Bicycle Thief* and *Umberto D.* are my best films, but I stoutly maintain that the latter is superior.

S: So do I, but you've no need to denigrate the earlier film. The son's forgiveness of the father isn't at all sentimental. It is the dawning of his maturity. It is absolutely essential to the meaning of the film.

DS: I am pleased to hear you say that. So many have criticized me for it.

S: Don't listen to them. I've also heard criticism of the end of *Umberto D.* by people who don't realize the dreadful irony that Umberto is saved only because of the dumb brute instinct for self-preservation that makes his dog refuse to be run down by the train.

DS: Yes, that ending is ironic.

S: In *The Bicycle Thief* why do you have Ricci put up a poster of Rita Hayworth as Gilda?

DS: Because she is so far away from his world, and he clumsily ruins this image of that woman.

S: Why did you include the scene of the workers rehearsing a show?

DS: In that Fascist period, it was dangerous to show a Communist cell. I included a polemical discussion of salaries and unemployment, but I made it take place as the workers are trying to divert themselves with a badly made spectacle that also contrasts with the melancholy of the hero in search of his stolen bicycle.

S: Why did you turn to fantasy after these neorealist films?

DS: After the success of *Bicycle Thief* Zavattini and I were afraid that neorealism would become a formula, so we decided to try the style in all genres of film, even fantasy and musical comedy. I liked and bought a book called *Let's Give Everyone a Horse as a Rocking Horse*, but, as a present to Zavattini, I decided instead to make a film out of his old novel *Totò, the Good*. That made him very happy.

S: Why did you present the angels as you do?

DS: I turned to an American makeup man, whom Alexander Korda had recommended to me. This man, who came from Hollywood, was a drunkard. The makeup for the film cost more than everything else, because the man got a thousand dollars a week and took so long. Besides he wasn't any good; that's why the angels look that way.

S: Too balletic.

DS: Exactly. The makeup is the worst thing in the film, and it cost the most. The film cost five hundred thousand dollars, half of that for makeup.

S: Why in *Umberto D.* did you choose a professor for the title role: a man whose life is so different from the character's?

DS: Battisti was a dignified bourgeois. All the neorealist films were made in favor of the proletariat, always forgetting the poor middle class. Furthermore, at that time, one kept reading in the newspapers stories of suicide. When a young man with his whole life ahead of him kills himself, he is crazy. But when an old man hasn't the strength to face his few remaining years, he represents the maximum grade of human despair. That's what I wanted to show.

S: How did such a man learn to act a character like Umberto when he himself was, in real life, famous and powerful?

DS: He was the character physically. Rizzoli, the producer, always complained that Battisti was so unpleasant. 'Why don't you make him up?' he would say. 'Why don't you take Ruggero Ruggeri instead?' I kept saying that I could not imagine changing Umberto D.'s face and that Ruggero Ruggeri was too aristocratic, with a magnificent voice, a great actor, but not Umberto. I looked for Umberto D. everywhere. I went to every old folks' home. I went to see retired people, old workers in pensions. I searched every institution but never found him. One day I saw Battisti on the street and knew immediately that he was the man. I followed him to the university where he was giving lectures, and I stayed put so that he wouldn't disappear. I took him to my office and gave him a test right there.

S: Was he reluctant?

DS: He was totally bewildered. A man like that, a man of letters and high culture, he didn't know me or the cinema ...

S: In the film, he seems crotchety, a bit of a pedant.

DS: He had to be like that. I needed an old man who was totally anti-pathetic because the old are unpleasant. He fights, but he cannot make it any longer. Reality is stronger than him, so he wants to kill himself.

S: Now we come to your awful *Indiscretion of an American Wife*. What kind of trouble did Selznick give you on that film?

DS: Every day he sent me forty- or fifty-page letters, detailing every-thing. They were in English; when I translated them, I arrived at work no earlier than noon. So I stopped reading them and began throwing them away as soon as they arrived. I would agree with everything he said and do things my own way.

S: Do you agree with me that this film is a failure?

DS: It's funny: You don't like it, but many people did.

S: Don't you think that Montgomery Clift and Jennifer Jones are ter-rible?

DS: The film was made for Jones. I found myself in Hollywood, where I was to make a film taken from a television comedy. Thornton Wilder and I prepared a script that was wonderful. Then the imbecile producer cancelled everything. He started say-ing that we couldn't film the picture on the streets of Chicago but must make it in Hollywood with back projection because that cost less. I broke the contract, paid my penalty, and left, thanks to Selznick who had purchased the script for *Stazione Termini* from Zavattini. I accepted this assignment in order to return to Italy.

S: Jones' neurosis is so great that I can't believe the love affair.

DS: She was hypersensitive in real life, too. I had terrible problems with that production. I produced the film myself and spent my own money to rent Terminal Station at night and to fill it with trains and people. At least twice, she arrived distraught, having quarreled with her husband, Selznick, and she threw her hat in the toilet, so that we had to fish it out because we had only one which she used in every scene in the film.

Then she took her shoes off and ran back barefoot to the hotel, leaving me and all the other people in the railroad station. Twice she pulled that trick on me, and it cost me four million lire each time.

S: Another problem with the film is that Clift doesn't seem too masculine and some of the dialogue, by Capote, doesn't give the right impression either.

DS: Yes, they were both pederasts.

S: Why didn't you make any film for the five years between *The Roof* and *Two Women*?

DS: Because I was in America.

S: What did you do there?

DS: Nothing. I lost a year on that script with Thornton Wilder. I lost time working with poor Dudley Nichols. I lost a year being under contract to that madman Howard Hughes.

S: Madman?

DS: He kept me a whole month in Hollywood without showing up. My contract forced me to stay in Los Angeles, and people kept saying, 'Don't you like Los Angeles?' 'Sure,' I answered, 'but I want to work. I'm not used to being kept, like a prostitute.' I was well cared for. They gave me this marvellous hotel, this swimming pool, birds singing outside my window all day. But I wanted to work.[8]

S: Why did you make *Two Women* in cinemascope?

DS: Because it was the fashion in that period.

S: Do you think it a good method?

DS: No.

S: What do you think of the Moravia novel?

DS: I like it. It tells about the countryside where I was born.

S: Don't you find it melodramatic? Can you believe that the young girl, after being raped, would so quickly turn to sexual license?

DS: That's the way it is in the novel. She does it for revenge.

S: It seems opposite to the kind of truth I find in *The Children Are Watching Us* and *Umberto*.

DS: Yes, it is forced drama.

S: Are you satisfied with that moment in the film when they find the girl nursing a dead baby?

DS: No, but that too is in the novel. Perhaps it is too contrived, but, then, women did lose children in the war.

S: Do you like *The Last Judgment*?

DS: Very much. You know, it was never exported.

S: That's regrettable. I think it a first-rate film. I was very surprised to discover it and *Il boom* here. Only the scenes with Mercouri and Manfredi seem wrong to me.

DS: That was a mistake.

S: But I thought, while watching the film, that it must have been made in a mood of great gaiety.

DS: Yes, I was very enthusiastic about it. De Laurentiis lost money on it, however, and it has never been widely shown. That is too bad, because it's one of my best films.

S: I agree. Perhaps it doesn't appeal because of its cynicism, which is exceeded by *Il Boom*. In the latter film, when Sordi goes to the rich woman he thinks will settle his financial problems by taking him as her lover only to find that she merely wants to buy his eye for her husband, why do you end the discovery scene by holding on that wooden angel?

DS: He has false hopes of a profitable adventure with a rich old woman, and she, out of her egoism, entertains equally false hopes. Amid all this asking of favors and false hope I show a false angel.

S: Isn't this type of symbolic detail new to you?

DS: Yes. Robbe-Grillet has made popular this use of objects surrounding the character. It is a new mode.

S: Has this influenced you much?

DS: No, but Robbe-Grillet has been a great influence on Antonioni.

S: Why did you make another American film, *The Condemned of Altona*?

DS: Ponti wanted it; I didn't.

S: It is wholly uncinematic.

DS: You know, Antonioni called it an essay in direction, an anticinematic text that De Sica made with a skill one wouldn't expect him to show.

S: The play is good, but Abby Mann's script diminishes Sartre.

DS: I agree. This film was one of the causes of a breach between me and Zavattini. Zavattini had written a screenplay, but Ponti insisted on having Abby Mann.

S: Why did you use that pompous music of Shostakovich?

DS: Shostakovich wrote me a letter saying that I used this music for a Fascist film, but where is that film Fascist?

S: How do you feel when you direct actors like Robert Wagner and Fredric March?

DS: Melancholy. Someone who made *Umberto D.* cannot be making *The Condemned of Altona*. The producer asked for it.

S: I am deeply disturbed by such films; they give ammunition to those who want to forget your great achievements, and they cause works like *The Last Judgment* and *Il Boom* to be ignored.

DS: I have made many mistakes.

S: For money?

DS: For money. The lack of sufficient money to make the films I want makes me dependent on others. I want to make Flaubert's *A Simple Heart* now, but I must reply on American capitalists who want Flaubert turned into Erich Segal.[9]

S: Did you participate in *Boccaccio '70* also for money?

DS: That sketch was merely a divertissement.

S: In *Yesterday, Today, Tomorrow*, who had the idea of teaming Loren and Mastroianni?

DS: Ponti. But you know, this is the first film with sketches enacted by the same people.

S: I like the first and last parts, but the middle is wholly unconvincing. I don't believe for a minute that Loren as the rich industrialist's wife really wants to change her life; hence the switch is no surprise.

DS: We needed a sketch in the middle to make three.

S: Your next film, on the other hand, is an entertainment that is highly skillful. Part of the excellence is due to a faster cutting tempo.

DS: That was inspired by the French New Wave directors, who gave us a push in that direction.

S: One of the best scenes in *Marriage, Italian Style* is Loren's signing the contract for her apartment. Did she contribute any of the gestures?

DS: I directed it all.

S: Do you believe the ending? Why should this woman, who knew the man so well, be happy at her marriage?

DS: She doesn't love him; she marries to give her sons a name.

S: Why did you use freeze frames in the wedding scene?

DS: To speed up a subject that is so banal.

S: How much of *After the Fox* is due to Neil Simon?

DS: Everything.

S: How did you find working with Peter Sellers?

DS: Sellers is a good friend, for whom I feel great affection. He had made films that I admired, and I wanted to make one with him myself; but I wasn't able to because of Neil Simon.

S: How do you feel about *A Young World*?

DS: It was very difficult for me. I was in a new, completely unknown atmosphere and so had to make myself over. Moreover, I had terrible fights with the French censors. In the original film there is a scene where a man sells himself to an older woman in order to get money for his girlfriend's abortion. The French wanted to send me to jail for it because I was exposing the existence of male prostitution.

S: And then we come to *Sunflower*. How could you have made this film?

DS: When I accepted that film, it was called 'Giovanna,' and Zavattini had written the script. It was a very simple story of a Calabrese woman whose husband had gone to Sweden to become a miner. When he doesn't come back, Giovanna leaves Calabria, makes the difficult trip to Sweden, and learns in Stockholm from some Italians there that the husband has gone to a town in the Arctic. Once there, she meets his wife and child, but she doesn't say who she is. She reports herself as her husband's sister, so the wife takes her in with great affection and tells her whole life story: how she met Giovanna's husband, about their baby, about their desire to go to Italy to meet his mother. Giovanna cries; in order not to show this, she washes her face in the sink. Immediately, her husband comes back from work, his face begrimed. They look at one another; she runs away screaming. The end. Now comes Mr. Ponti, who says, 'Never can Sophia Loren be abandoned by any man. Mastroianni must have lost his memory in the war. He must go after her.' Can you imagine that? What a nice story it was originally, so simple and so true. He comes in, she screams, and that is all.

S: That's the moment I wished *Sunflower* would end.

DS: It doesn't, thanks to Mr. Carlo Ponti.

S: But how could you have agreed to it? Why didn't you abandon the film?

DS: So much time had already been spent preparing it. The shooting had started. It was weak of me not to have left.

S: And of course, you take all the blame.

DS: Yes; me and Zavattini, whereas the fault is wholly Ponti's.

S: And things are worse. In the film, when Loren returns from Moscow, she actually looks younger than before her ordeal.

DS: I didn't notice that. So much depends on the actress. I don't

worry too much about makeup; I am interested in the performance. I didn't notice she had this wig made to make her look
younger. She has her personal makeup man, paid by her.

S: Is the battle scene in the film a stock shot or something you
made?

DS: I think part was stock, but the rest was made.

S: Don't you think the superimposition of the red flag over the carnage is a bit artificial?

DS: That's a stupid effect which Ponti wanted. Anyway, I didn't direct
it. It was shot by the second unit, headed by a Russian director.

S: That's the poignance of being a film director!

DS: My experience with this film was so terrible that I decided to
rebel, and my rebellion is *The Garden of the Finzi-Continis*.

S: Why didn't Zavattini write the script this time?

DS: After *Sunflower*, Zavattini and I have been a bit estranged.
Because even Zavattini sided with Ponti, so I was left alone, with
Ponti, Zavattini, and Tonino Guerra against me. So I separated
from Zavattini and made *The Garden of the Finzi-Continis* as vengeance. After the disaster of *Sunflower* I wanted to make a true De
Sica film, made just as I wanted it. I accepted this subject because
I intimately feel the Jewish problem. I myself feel shame because
we all are guilty of the death of millions of Jews. Why were they
killed? Because a criminal, a lunatic wanted that. But the Italian
Fascists are also guilty. So am I. I wasn't a Fascist, but I belong to
the country that collaborated with Hitler. I wanted, out of conscience, to make this film, and I am glad I made it.

S: I've heard that the author of the novel, Giorgio Bassani,
renounces the film.

DS: Ah, because of the character of the father, which has been mini-
mized in the film. But I think the character is well treated.

S: Why did you use foreign actors?

DS: I needed someone foreign for the heroine, Micòl, because she is a
difficult, ambiguous personality with an unstated incestuous
love of her brother. I couldn't find among my Italians anyone
with the face she needed. But Dominique Sanda is marvellous,
with her hard, cold face.

S: Do you feel that the film shows the connection between Micòl's
private difficulties and the historic tragedy of the war?

DS: Micòl's drama is far from the other. She only suffers the consequences of racial laws.

S: Don't you think the film should have been longer so as to give equal development to both subjects?

DS: Perhaps, but I wanted this effect: The Germans come little by little. They are only the first symptoms. We are only at the door of the tragedy.

S: That's true. But there are problems. For example, when Giorgio goes to the girl who runs the shooting gallery, she tells him that Malnate, who has been killed, used to be her lover, but we never saw that. Something crucial seems to have been left out. I have the impression of a film having to rush to include all the events of a *roman-fleuve*.

DS: Yes, perhaps that was done too quickly. Four years go by too quickly. It's a defect of the screenplay.

S: Do you find the colors a bit in disharmony with the story? The color is so beautiful; the story so bleak.

DS: I should have done what Antonioni did, paint everything white, or what you say Olmi has done: use underexposure.

S: Why didn't you?

DS: Because I made it very quickly, with very little money.

S: The garden is justly marvellous, but so is everything else.

DS: That's right. The second half shouldn't be so beautiful. I should have made it grey or reversed *The Last Judgment* and made the first part color and the second black and white. That's a good idea. I wanted to achieve effects like those in Huston's *Reflections in a Golden Eye*, but my cameraman was incapable.

S: As far as you're concerned, why does Micòl sleep with Malnate?

DS: Because she is jealous of her brother. Her brother loves Malnate, and she wants to take him away from her brother.

S: Doesn't she also do it to abase herself? She, who hates sex, goes to bed with a man whom, as she herself says, she finds too hairy? But don't you find it coincidental that Giorgio arrives just in time to see this?

DS: That was in the novel. Like all true lovers, at a moment of crisis, he has a sixth sense.

S: If you could remake the film, would you want it to be greyer not only in literal color, but figuratively, in tone?

DS: Already it is very sober. It was a very difficult film to make. The novel was so difficult to turn into a motion picture. I had to read four horrible screenplays before I found the one we could use. I am being presumptuous at this moment, but I believe that it is a good film. I am happy that I made it because it brought me back to my old noble intentions. Because, you see, I have been ruined by lack of money. All my good films, which I financed by myself, made nothing. Only my bad films made money. Money has been my ruin.

Editors' Notes

1 Lamberto Maggiorani (1910–83) [Ricci] appeared in other films including De Sica's *Il giudizio universale* (1961) and Pasolini's *Mama Roma* (1962).
2 Carmelo Bene, born 1937, has made a career primarily in the theatre as an actor/director. His films are: *Nostra Signora dei Turchi / Our Lady of the Turks* (1968), *Capricci* (1969), *Don Giovanni* (1971), *Salome* (1972), and *Un Amleto di meno / One Less Hamlet* (1973). For more on Bene see Marc Siegel, 'Contesting Cinema: A Carmelo Bene Project,' in *Cineaction* 47 (September 1998), 30–5.
3 *Le petit monde de Don Camillo / The Little World of Don Camillo* (1951), directed by Julien Duvivier, starring Fernandel.
4 Fedor Ozep's German-made *Dimitri Karamasoff / Karamazov* (1931) starred Fritz Kortner as Dimitri and Anna Sten as Grushenko.
5 *Buongiorno, elefante! / Good Morning Elephant* (1952), from a script by Suso Cecchi d'Amico and Cesare Zavattini.
6 Emilio Cigoli (1909–80) had roles in several other films, including *Shoeshine*.
7 For more on *La porta del cielo / The Gates of Heaven* see Nino Lo Bello, 'The Missing Masterpiece,' *Saturday Review* 12:1 (January/February 1986), 89.
8 For more on De Sica's Hollywood sojourn see his article 'Hollywood Shocked Me,' *Films and Filming* 2:5 (February 1956), 12–13.
9 *Un cuore semplice / A Simple Heart* was eventually filmed in 1978 by Giorgio Ferrara from a script by Zavattini and starring Adrianna Asti.

Some Ideas on the Cinema

CESARE ZAVATTINI

Cesare Zavattini (1902–89) was the central theoretician of neorealism, although he owes a debt, as do almost all intellectuals of the left, to the Marxist philosopher Antonio Gramsci (1891–1937). In turn, Zavattini's writings in realist film theory were extended by André Bazin and Siegfried Kracauer in the 1950s. Zavattini scripted scores of films but his most outstanding are those that he made with De Sica. The two men shared a close personal relationship from about 1940 to De Sica's death in 1974. Most of Zavattini's work has the moral agenda of awakening people to the actualities of the world around them, to the connection of human being to human being, relationships that had been blurred or effaced by twenty years of Fascist rhetoric.

I

No doubt one's first and most superficial reaction to everyday reality is that it is tedious. Until we are able to overcome some moral and intellectual laziness, in fact, this reality will continue to appear uninteresting. One shouldn't be astonished that the cinema has always felt the natural, unavoidable necessity to insert a 'story' in the reality to make it exciting and 'spectacular.' All the same, it is clear that such a method evades a direct approach to everyday reality, and suggests that it cannot be portrayed without the intervention of fantasy or artifice.

The most important characteristic, and the most important innova-

Cesare Zavattini, 'Some Ideas on the Cinema,' *Sight and Sound* 23:2 (October–December 1953), 64–9. Edited from a recorded interview published in *La revista del cinema italiano* 2 (December 1952). Translated by Pier Luigi Lanza

tion, of what is called neorealism, it seems to me, is to have realised
that the necessity of the 'story' was only an unconscious way of dis-
guising a human defeat, and that the kind of imagination it involved
was simply a technique of superimposing dead formulas over living
social facts. Now it has been perceived that reality is hugely rich, that
to be able to look directly at it is enough; and that the artist's task is not
to make people moved or indignant at metaphorical situations, but to
make them reflect (and, if you like, to be moved and indignant too) on
what they and others are doing, on the real things, exactly as they are.

For me this has been a great victory. I would like to have achieved it
many years earlier. But I made the discovery only at the end of the
war. It was a moral discovery, an appeal to order. I saw at last what lay
in front of me, and I understood that to have evaded reality had been
to betray it.

Example: Before this, if one was thinking over the idea of a film on,
say, a strike, one was immediately forced to invent a plot. And the
strike itself became only the background to the film. Today, our attitude would be one of 'revelation': we would describe the strike itself,
try to work out the largest possible number of human, moral, social,
economic, poetic values from the bare documentary fact.

We have passed from an unconsciously rooted mistrust of reality, an
illusory and equivocal evasion, to an unlimited trust in things, facts and
people. Such a position requires us, in effect, to excavate reality, to give
it a power, a communication, a series of reflexes, which until recently we
had never thought it had. It requires, too, a true and real interest in what
is happening, a search for the most deeply hidden human values, which
is why we feel that the cinema must recruit not only intelligent people,
but, above all, 'living' souls, the morally richest people.

II

The cinema's overwhelming desire to see, to analyse, its hunger for
reality, is an act of concrete homage towards other people, towards
what is happening and existing in the world. And, incidentally, it is
what distinguishes 'neorealism' from the American cinema.

In fact, the American position is the antithesis of our own: while we
are interested in the reality around us and want to know it directly,
reality in American films is unnaturally filtered, 'purified,' and comes
out at one or two removes. In America, lack of subjects for films causes
a crisis, but with us such a crisis is impossible. One cannot be short of

themes while there is still plenty of reality. Any hour of the day, any place, any person, is a subject for narrative if the narrator is capable of observing and illuminating all these collective elements by exploring their interior value.

So there is no question of a crisis of subjects, only of their interpretation. This substantial difference was nicely emphasised by a well-known American producer when he told me: 'This is how *we* would imagine a scene with an aeroplane. The 'plane passes by ... a machine-gun fires ... the 'plane crashes ... And this is how *you* would imagine it. The 'plane passes by ... The 'plane passes by again ... the 'plane passes by once more ...'

He was right. But we have still not gone far enough. It is not enough to make the aeroplane pass by three times; we must make it pass by twenty times.

What effects on narrative, then, and on the portrayal of human character, has the neorealist style produced?

To begin with, while the cinema used to make one situation produce another situation, and another, and another, again and again, and each scene was thought out and immediately related to the next (the natural result of a mistrust of reality), today, when we have thought out a scene, we feel the need to 'remain' in it, because the single scene itself can contain so many echoes and reverberations, can even contain all the situations we may need. Today, in fact, we can quietly say: give us whatever 'fact' you like, and we will disembowel it, make it something worth watching.

While the cinema used to portray life in its most visible and external moments – and a film was usually only a series of situations selected and linked together with varying success – today the neorealist affirms that each one of these situations, rather than all the external moments, contains in itself enough material for a film.

Example: In most films, the adventures of two people looking for somewhere to live, for a house, would be shown externally in a few moments of action, but for us it could provide the scenario for a whole film, and we would explore all its echoes, all its implications.

Of course, we are still a long way from a true analysis of human situations, and one can speak of analysis only in comparison with the dull synthesis of most current production. We are, rather, still in an 'attitude' of analysis; but in this attitude there is a strong purpose, a desire for understanding, for belonging, for participating – for living together, in fact.

III

Substantially, then, the question today is, instead of turning imaginary situations into 'reality' and trying to make them look 'true,' to make things as they are, almost by themselves, create their own special significance. Life is not what is invented in 'stories'; life is another matter. To understand it involves a minute, unrelenting, and patient search.

Here I must bring in another point of view. I believe that the world goes on getting worse because we are not truly aware of reality. The most authentic position anyone can take up today is to engage himself in tracing the roots of this problem. The keenest necessity of our time is 'social attention.'

Attention, though, to what is there, *directly*: not through an apologue, however well conceived. A starving man, a humiliated man, must be shown by name and surname; no fable for a starving man, because that is something else, less effective and less moral. The true function of the cinema is not to tell fables, and to a true function we must recall it.

Of course, reality can be analysed by ways of fiction. Fictions can be expressive and natural; but neorealism, if it wants to be worthwhile, must sustain the moral impulse that characterised its beginnings, in an analytical documentary way. No other medium of expression has the cinema's original and innate capacity for showing things that we believe worth showing, as they happen day by day – in what we might call their 'dailiness,' their longest and truest duration. The cinema has everything in front of it, and no other medium has the same possibilities for getting it known quickly to the greatest number of people.

As the cinema's responsibility also comes from its enormous power, it should try to make every frame of film count, by which I mean that it should penetrate more and more into the manifestations and the essence of reality.

The cinema only affirms its moral responsibility when it approaches reality in this way.

The moral, like the artistic, problem lies in being able to observe reality, not to extract fictions from it.

IV

Naturally, some film-makers, although they realise the problem, have still been compelled, for a variety of reasons (some valid, others not), to 'invent' stories in the traditional manner, and to incorporate in these stories some fragments of their real intuition. This, effectively, has served as neorealism for some film-makers in Italy.

For this reason, the first endeavour was often to reduce the story to its most elementary, simple, and, I would rather say, banal form. It was the beginning of a speech that was later interrupted. *Bicycle Thieves* provides a typical example. The child follows his father along the street; at one moment, the child is nearly run over, but the father does not even notice. This episode was 'invented,' but with the intention of communicating an everyday fact about these people's lives, a little fact – so little that the protagonists don't even care about it – but full of life.

In fact *Paisà, Open City, Sciuscià, Bicycle Thieves, La terra trema*, all contain elements of an absolute significance – they reflect the idea that everything can be recounted; but their sense remains metaphorical, because there is still an invented story, not the documentary spirit. In other films, such as *Umberto D.*, reality as an analysed fact is much more evident, but the presentation is still traditional.

We have not yet reached the centre of neorealism. Neorealism today is an army ready to start; and there are the soldiers – behind Rossellini, De Sica, Visconti. The soldiers have to go into the attack and win the battle.

We must recognize that all of us are still only starting, some farther on, others farther behind. But it is still something. The great danger today is to abandon that position, the moral position implicit in the work of many of us during and immediately after the war.

V

A woman is going to buy a pair of shoes. Upon this elementary situation it is possible to build a film. All we have to do is to discover and then show all the elements that go to create this adventure, in all their banal 'dailiness,' and it will become worthy of attention, it will even become 'spectacular.' But it will become spectacular not through its exceptional, but through its *normal* qualities; it will astonish us by showing so many things that happen every day under our eyes, things we have never noticed before.

The result would not be easy to achieve. It would require an intensity of human vision both from the creator of the film and from the audience. The question is: how to give human life its historical importance at every minute.

VI

In life, in reality today, there are no more empty spaces. Between things, facts, people, exists such an interdependence that a blow struck for the cinema in Rome could have repercussions all over the world. If this is true, it must be worthwhile to take any moment of a human life and show how 'striking' that moment is: to excavate and identify it, to send its echo vibrating into other parts of the world.

This is as valid for poverty as for peace. For peace, too, the human moment should not be a great one, but an ordinary daily happening. Peace is usually the sum of small happenings, all having the same moral implications at their roots.

It is not only a question, however, of creating a film that makes its audience understand a social or collective situation. People understand themselves better than the social fabric; and to see themselves on the screen, performing their daily actions – remembering that to see oneself gives one the sense of being unlike oneself – like hearing one's own voice on the radio – can help them to fill up a void, a lack of knowledge of reality.

VII

If this love for reality, for human nature directly observed, must still adapt itself to the necessities of the cinema as it is now organised, must yield, suffer and wait, it means that the cinema's capitalist structure still has a tremendous influence over its true function. One can see this in the growing opposition in many places to the fundamental motives of neorealism, the main results of which are a return to so-called 'original' subjects, as in the past, and the consequent evasion of reality, and a number of bourgeois accusations against neorealist principles.

The main accusation is: *neorealism only describes poverty*. But neorealism can and must face poverty. We have begun with poverty for the simple reason that it is one of the most vital realities of our time, and I challenge anyone to prove the contrary. To believe, or to pretend to believe, that by making half a dozen films on poverty we have finished with the problem would be a great mistake. As well believe that, if you have to plough up a whole country, you can sit down after the first acre.

The theme of poverty, of rich and poor, is something one can dedicate one's whole life to. We have just begun. We must have the courage to explore all the details. If the rich turn up their noses especially at *Miracolo a Milano*, we can only ask them to be a little patient. *Miracolo a Milano* is only a fable. There is still much more to say. I put myself among the rich, not only because I have some money (which is only the most apparent and immediate aspect of wealth), but because I am also in a position to create oppression and injustice. That is the moral (or immoral) position of the so-called rich man.

When anyone (he could be the audience, the director, the critic, the State, or the Church) says, 'STOP the poverty,' i.e. stop the films about poverty, he is committing a moral sin. He is refusing to understand, to learn. And when he refuses to learn, consciously, or not, he is evading reality. The evasion springs from lack of courage, from fear. (One should make a film on this subject, showing at what point we begin to evade reality in the face of disquieting facts, at what point we begin to sweeten it.)

If I were not afraid of being thought irreverent, I should say that Christ, had He a camera in His hand, would not shoot fables, however wonderful, but would show us the good ones and the bad ones of this world – in actuality, giving us close-ups of those who make their neighbours' bread too bitter, and of their victims, if the censor allowed it.

To say that we have had 'enough' films about poverty suggests that one can measure reality with a chronometer. In fact, it is not simply a question of choosing the theme of poverty, but of going on to explore and analyse the poverty. What one needs is more and more knowledge, precise and simple, of human needs and the motives governing them. Neorealism should ignore the chronometer and go forward for as long as is necessary.

Neorealism, it is also said, *does not offer solutions. The end of a neorealist film is particularly inconclusive.* I cannot accept this at all. With regard to my own work, the characters and situations in films for which I have written the scenario, they remain unresolved from a practical point of view simply because 'this is reality.' But every moment of the film is, in itself, a continuous answer to some question. It is not the concern of an artist to propound solutions. It is enough, and quite a lot, I should say, to make an audience feel the need, the urgency, for them.

In any case, what films *do* offer solutions? 'Solutions' in this sense, if they are offered, are sentimental ones, resulting from the superficial way in which problems have been faced. At least, in my work I leave the solution to the audience.

The fundamental emotion of *Miracolo a Milano* is not one of escape (the flight at the end), but of indignation, a desire for solidarity with certain people, a refusal of it with others. The film's structure is intended to suggest that there is a great gathering of the humble ones against the others. But the humble ones have no tanks, or they would have been ready to defend their land and their huts.

VIII

The true neorealistic cinema is, of course, less expensive than the cinema at present. Its subjects can be expressed cheaply, and it can dispense with capitalist resources on the present scale. The cinema has not yet found its morality, its necessity, its quality, precisely because it costs too much; being so conditioned, it is much less an art than it could be.

IX

The cinema should never turn back. It should accept, unconditionally, what is contemporary. *Today, today, today.*

It must tell reality as if it were a story; there must be no gap between life and what is on the screen. To give an example:

A woman goes to a shop to buy a pair of shoes. The shoes cost 7,000 lire. The woman tries to bargain. The scene lasts, perhaps, two minutes. I must make a two-hour film. What do I do?

I analyse the fact in all its constituent elements, in its 'before,' in its 'after,' in its contemporaneity. The fact creates its own fiction, in its own particular sense.

The woman is buying the shoes. What is her son doing at the same moment? What are people doing in India that could have some relation to this fact of the shoes? The shoes cost 7,000 lire. How did the woman happen to have 7,000 lire? How hard did she work for them, what do they represent for her?

And the bargaining shopkeeper, who is he? What relationship has developed between these two human beings? What do they mean, what interests are they defending, as they bargain? The shopkeeper also has two sons, who eat and speak: do you want to know what they are saying? Here they are, in front of you ...

The question is, to be able to fathom the real correspondences between facts and their process of birth, to discover what lies beneath them.

Thus to analyse 'buying a pair of shoes' in such a way opens to us a vast and complex world, rich in importance and values, in its practical, social, economic, psychological motives. Banality disappears because each moment is really charged with responsibility. Every moment is infinitely rich. Banality never really existed.

Excavate, and every little fact is revealed as a mine. If the gold-diggers come at last to dig in the illimitable mine of reality, the cinema will become socially important.

This can also be done, evidently, with invented characters; but if I use living, real characters with which to sound reality, people in whose life I can directly participate, my emotion becomes more effective, morally stronger, more useful. Art must be expressed through a true name and surname, not a false one.

I am bored to death with heroes more or less imaginary. I want to meet the real protagonist of everyday life, I want to see how he is made, if he has a moustache or not, if he is tall or short, I want to see his eyes, and I want to speak to him.

We can look at him on the screen with the same anxiety, the same curiosity as when, in a square, seeing a crowd of people all hurrying up to the same place, we ask, What is happening? What is happening to a real person? Neorealism has perceived that the most irreplaceable experience comes from things happening under our own eyes from natural necessity.

I am against 'exceptional' personages. The time has come to tell the audience that they are the true protagonists of life. The result will be a constant appeal to the responsibility and dignity of every human being. Otherwise the frequent habit of identifying oneself with fictional characters will become very dangerous. We must identify ourselves with what we are. The world is composed of millions of people thinking of myths.

X

The term neorealism – in a very Latin sense – implies, too, elimination of technical-professional apparatus, screen-writer included. Handbooks, formulas, grammars, have no more application. There will be no more technical terms. Everybody has his personal shooting-script. Neorealism breaks all the rules, rejects all those canons which, in fact, exist only to codify limitations. Reality breaks all the rules, as can be discovered if you walk out with a camera to meet it.

The figure of a screen-writer today is, besides, very equivocal. He is usually considered part of the technical apparatus. I am a screen-writer trying to say certain things, and saying them in my own way. It is clear that certain moral and social ideas are at the foundation of my expressive activities, and I can't be satisfied to offer a simple technical contribution. In films which do not touch me directly, also, when I am called in to do a certain amount of work on them, I try to insert as much as possible of my own world, of the moral emergencies within myself.

On the other hand, I don't think the screenplay in itself contains any particular problems; only when subject, screenplay and direction become three distinct phases, as they so often do today, which is abnormal. The screen-writer as such should disappear, and we should arrive at the sole author of a film.

Everything becomes flexible when only one person is making a film, everything continually possible, not only during the shooting, but during the editing, the laying of tracks, the post-synchronisation, to the particular moment when we say, 'Stop.' And it is only then that we put an end to the film.

Of course, it is possible to make films in collaboration, as happens with novels and plays, because there are always numerous bonds of identity between people (for example, millions of men go to war, and are killed for the same reasons), but no work of art exists on which someone has not set the seal of his own interests, of his own poetic world. There is always somebody to make the decisive creative act, there is always one prevailing intelligence, there is always someone who, at a certain moment, 'chooses,' and says, 'This, yes,' and 'This, no,' and then resolves it: reaction shot of the mother crying Help!

Technique and capitalist method, however, have imposed collaboration on the cinema. It is one thing to adapt ourselves to the imposed exigencies of the cinema's present structure, another to imagine that they are indispensable and necessary. It is obvious that when films cost sixpence and everybody can have a camera, the cinema would become a creative medium as flexible and as free as any other.

XI

It is evident that, with neorealism, the actor – as a person fictitiously lending his own flesh to another – has no more right to exist than the 'story.' In neorealism, as I intend it, everyone must be his own actor. To want one person to play another implies the calculated plot, the fable, and not 'things happening.' I attempted such a film with Caterina Rigoglioso; it was called 'the lightning film.' But unfortunately at the last moment everything broke down. Caterina did not seem to 'take' to the cinema. But wasn't she 'Caterina'?

Of course, it will be necessary to choose themes excluding actors. I want, for example, to make a report on children in the world. If I am not allowed to make it, I will limit it to Europe, or to Italy alone. But I will make it. Here is an example of the film not needing actors. I hope the actors' union will not protest.

XII

Neorealism does not reject psychological exploration. Psychology is one of the many premises of reality. I face it as I face any other. If I want to write a scene of two men quarrelling, I will not do so at my desk. I must leave my den and find them. I take these men and make them talk in front of me for one hour or for twenty, depending on necessity. My creative method is first to call on them, then to listen to them, 'choosing' what they say. But I do all this not with the intention of creating heroes, because I think that a hero is not 'certain men' but 'every man.'

Wanting to give everyone a sense of equality is not levelling him down, but exalting his solidarity. Lack of solidarity is always born from presuming to be different, from a *But*: 'Paul is suffering, it's true. I am suffering, too, *but* my suffering has something that ... my nature has something that ...' and so on. The *But* must disappear, and we must be able to say: 'That man is bearing what I myself should bear in the same circumstances.'

XIII

Others have observed that the best dialogue in films is always in dialect. Dialect is nearer to reality. In our literary and spoken language, the synthetic constructions and the words themselves are always a little false. When writing a dialogue, I always think of it in dialect, in that of Rome or my own village. Using dialect, I feel it to be more essential, truer. Then I translate it into Italian, thus maintaining the dialect's syntax. I don't, therefore, write dialogue in dialect, but I am interested in what dialects have in common: immediacy, freshness, verisimilitude.

But I take most of all from nature. I go out into the street, catch words, sentences, discussions. My great aids are memory and the shorthand writer.

Afterwards, I do with the words what I do with the images. I choose, I cut the material I have gathered to give it the right rhythm, to capture the essence, the truth. However great a faith I might have in imagination, in solitude, I have a greater one in reality, in people. I am interested in the drama of things we happen to encounter, not those we plan.

In short, to exercise our own poetic talents on location, we must leave our rooms and go, in body and mind, out to meet other people, to see and understand them. This is a genuine moral necessity for me and, if I lose faith in it, so much the worse for me.

I am quite aware that it is possible to make wonderful films, like Charlie Chaplin's, and they are not neorealistic. I am quite aware that there are Americans, Russians, Frenchmen and others who have made masterpieces that honour humanity, and, of course, they have not wasted film. I wonder, too, how many more great works they will again give us, according to their particular genius, with actors and studios and novels. But Italian film-makers, I think, if they are to sustain and deepen their cause and their style, after having courageously half-opened their doors to reality, must (in the sense I have mentioned) open them wide.

De Sica: *Metteur en Scène*

ANDRÉ BAZIN

This essay by André Bazin, dating from 1952, was originally published in Italian by Edizione Guanda (Parma, 1953), and then published in French in Bazin's two-volume Qu'est-ce que le cinéma? *(Paris, 1962); it is presented here in Hugh Gray's English translation of the Italian version of the work. The essay is, thus,* not *contemporary (notwithstanding the title of this volume), but it demands inclusion in any collection of writings on De Sica because it was one of the first studies of De Sica as a neorealist film-maker, and it has had a formative influence on much of the subsequent criticism of his work. In general, Bazin's discussion takes a moral line, arguing that De Sica's cinema is a vehicle or an agent of increased love and understanding among people.*

In the discussion of Bicycle Thieves *in this essay the names of Ricci and his son Bruno are sometimes confused. For clarity we have inserted Ricci's name in brackets where he has been misidentified as Bruno.*

I must confess to the reader that my pen is paralyzed by scruples because of the many compelling reasons why I should not be the one to introduce De Sica to him.

First, there is the presumption implied in a Frenchman wanting to teach Italians something about their own cinema in general, and, in particular, about the man who is possibly their greatest director. Besides, when I imprudently accepted the honor of introducing De

André Bazin, 'De Sica: *Metteur en scène*,' in *What Is Cinema?* trans. Hugh Gray (Berkeley: University of California Press, 1971), II, 61–76. Copyright © 1967 by The Regents of the University of California

Sica in these pages, I was particularly conscious of my admiration for *Ladri di Biciclette / Bicycle Thieves* (1948) and I had not yet seen *Miracolo a Milano / Miracle in Milan* (1950). We in France have, of course, seen *Bicycle Thieves, Sciuscià / Shoeshine* (1946), and *I bambini ci guardano / The Children Are Watching Us* (1942), but lovely as *Shoeshine* is, and revealing as it is of the talents of De Sica, it bears, side by side with certain sublime discoveries, traces of the apprentice director. The scenario occasionally succumbs to melodramatic indulgence, and the direction has a certain poetic elegance, a lyrical quality, that today it seems to me De Sica is concerned to avoid. In short, we do not have there as yet the personal style of the director. His complete and final mastery is revealed in *Bicycle Thieves* to such an extent that the film seems to include all the efforts that went into the making of its predecessors.

But can one judge a director by a single film? This film is sufficient proof of the genius of De Sica, but not of the future forms that this genius will take. As an actor, De Sica is no newcomer to the cinema, but one must still call him 'young' as a director – a director of the future. In spite of the resemblances we will observe between them, *Miracle in Milan* differs greatly in inspiration and structure from *Bicycle Thieves*. What will his next film be? Will it reveal trends that appear only of minor importance in the previous works? In short, we are undertaking to speak of the style of a director of the first order on the basis of just two films – one of which seems to conflict with the orientation of the other. This is all right if one does not confuse the role of a critic with that of a prophet. I have no trouble explaining why I admire *Thieves* and *Miracle* but that is something very different from pretending to deduce from these two films what are the permanent and definitive characteristics of their maker's talent.

All the same we would willingly have done that for Rossellini after *Roma città aperta / Rome, Open City* (1945) and *Paisà / Paisan* (1946). What we would have been able to say (and what we actually wrote in France) ran the risk of being modified by Rossellini's subsequent films, but not of being given the lie. The style of Rossellini belongs to a different aesthetic family. The rules of its aesthetics are plain to see. It fits a vision of the world directly adapted to a framework of *mise-en-scène*. Rossellini's style is a way of seeing, while de Sica's is primarily a way of feeling. The *mise-en-scène* of the former lays siege to its object from outside. I do not mean without understanding and feeling – but that this exterior approach offers us an essential ethical and metaphysical aspect of our relations with the world. In order to understand this statement one need only compare the treatment of the child in *Germa-nia anno zero / Germany, Year Zero* (1947) and in *Shoeshine* and *Bicycle Thieves*.

Rossellini's love for his characters envelops them in a desperate awareness of man's inability to communicate; De Sica's love, on the contrary, radiates from the people themselves. They are what they are, but lit from within by the tenderness he feels for them. It follows that Rossellini's direction comes between his material and us, not as an artificial obstacle set up between the two, but as an unbridgeable, ontological distance, a congenital weakness of the human being which expresses itself aesthetically in terms of space, in forms, in the structure of his *mise-en-scène*. Because we are aware of it as a lack, a refusal, an escape from things, and hence finally as a kind of pain, it follows that it is easier for us to be aware of it, easier for us to reduce it to a formal method. Rossellini cannot alter this without himself passing through a personal moral revolution.

By contrast, De Sica is one of those directors whose sole purpose seems to be to interpret their scenarios faithfully, whose entire talent derives from the love they have for their subject, from their ultimate understanding òf it. The *mise-en-scène* seems to take shape after the fashion of a natural form in living matter. Despite a different kind of sensibility and a marked concern for form, Jacques Feyder in France also belongs to this family of directors whose one method of work seems to be to treat their subject honestly. This neutrality is illusory but its apparent existence does not make the critic's task any easier. It divides up the output of the film maker into so many special cases that, given one more film, all that has preceded it might be called into question. It is a temptation therefore to see only craftsmanship where one is looking for style, the generous humility of a clever technician meeting the demands of the subject instead of the creative imprint of a true *auteur*.

The *mise-en-scène* of a Rossellini film can be readily deduced from the images he uses, whereas De Sica forces us to arrive at his *mise-en-scène* inductively from a visual narrative which does not seem to admit of it.

Finally and above all, the case of De Sica is up to now inseparable from his collaboration with Zavattini, even more than is that of Marcel Carné in France with Jacques Prévert. There is no more perfect example in the history of the cinema of a symbiosis of screen writer and director. The fact that Zavattini collaborates with others, while Prévert has written few stories or scripts for anyone but Carné, makes no difference. On the contrary, what it allows us to conclude is that De Sica is the ideal director for Zavattini, the one who understands him best and most intimately. We have examples of the work of Zavattini without De Sica, but nothing of De Sica without Zavattini. We are therefore undertaking arbitrarily to distinguish that which truly belongs to De Sica and all the more arbitrarily because we have just referred to his at least apparent humility in the face of the demands of the scenario.

We must likewise refuse to separate, as something against nature, what talent has so closely joined. May De Sica and Zavattini forgive us – and, in advance, the reader, who can have no interest in my scruples and who is waiting for me to get on with my task. I would like it understood, however, for my own peace of mind, that I aim only to attempt a few critical statements which the future will doubtless call into question; they are simply the personal testimony of a French critic writing in 1951 about work full of promise, the qualities of which are particularly resistant to aesthetic analysis. This profession of humility is in no sense just an oratorical precaution or a rhetorical formula. I beg the reader to believe that it is first and foremost the measure of my admiration.

It is by way of its poetry that the realism of De Sica takes on its meaning, for in art, at the source of all realism, there is an aesthetic paradox that must be resolved. The faithful reproduction of reality is not art. We are repeatedly told that it consists in selection and interpretation. That is why up to now the 'realist' trends in cinema, as in other arts, consisted simply in introducing a greater measure of reality into the work: but this additional measure of reality was still only an effective way of serving an abstract purpose, whether dramatic, moral, or ideological. In France, 'naturalism' goes hand in hand with the multiplication of novels and plays *à thèse*. The originality of Italian neorealism, as compared with the chief schools of realism that preceded it and with the Soviet cinema, lies in never making reality the servant of some *a priori* point of view. Even the Dziga-Vertov theory of the 'Kino-eye' only employed the crude reality of everyday events so as to give it a place on the dialectic spectrum of montage. From another point of view, theater (even realist theater) used reality in the service of dramatic and spectacular structure. Whether in the service of the interests of an ideological thesis, of a moral idea, or of a dramatic action, realism subordinates what it borrows from reality to its transcendent needs. Neorealism knows only immanence. It is from appearance only, the simple appearance of beings and of the world, that it knows how to deduce the ideas that it unearths. It is a phenomenology.

In the realm of means of expression, neorealism runs counter to the traditional categories of spectacle – above all, as regards acting. According to the classic understanding of this function, inherited from the theater, the actor expresses something: a feeling, a passion, a desire, an idea. From his attitude and his miming the spectator can read his face like an open book. In this perspective, it is agreed implicitly between spectator and actor that the same psychological causes produce the same physical effect and that one can without any ambiguity pass backwards and forwards from one to the other. This is, strictly speaking, what is called acting.

The structures of the *mise-en-scène* flow from it: decor, lighting, the angle and framing of the shots, will be more or less expressionistic in their relation to the behavior of the actor. They contribute for their part to confirm the meaning of the action. Finally, the breaking up of the scenes into shots and their assemblage is the equivalent of an expressionism in time, a reconstruction of the event according to an artificial and abstract duration: dramatic duration. There is not a single one of these commonly accepted assumptions of the film spectacle that is not challenged by neorealism.

First, the performance: it calls upon the actor to *be* before expressing himself. This requirement does not necessarily imply doing away with the professional actor but it normally tends to substitute the man in the street, chosen uniquely for his general comportment, his ignorance of theatrical technique being less a positively required condition than a guarantee against the expressionism of traditional acting. For De Sica, Bruno was a silhouette, a face, a way of walking.

Second, the setting and the photography: the natural setting is to the artificial set what the amateur actor is to the professional. It has, however, the effect of at least partly limiting the opportunity for plastic compositions available with artificial studio lighting.

But it is perhaps especially the structure of the narrative which is most radically turned upside down. It must now respect the actual duration of the event. The cuts that logic demands can only be, at best, descriptive. The assemblage of the film must never add anything to the existing reality. If it is part of the meaning of the film as with Rossellini, it is because the empty gaps, the white spaces, the parts of the event that we are not given, are themselves of a concrete nature: stones which are missing from the building. It is the same in life: we do not know everything that happens to others. Ellipsis in classic montage is an effect of style. In Rossellini's films it is a lacuna in reality, or rather in the knowledge we have of it, which is by its nature limited.

Thus, neorealism is more an ontological position than an aesthetic one. That is why the employment of its technical attributes like a recipe do not necessarily produce it, as the rapid decline of American neorealism proves.[1] In Italy itself not all films without actors, based on a news item, and filmed in real exteriors, are better than the traditional melodramas and spectacles. On the contrary, a film like *Cronaca di un amore / Story of a Love Affair* (1950) by Michelangelo Antonioni can be described as neorealist (in spite of the professional actors, of the detective-story-like arbitrariness of the plot, of expensive settings, and the baroque dress of the heroine) because the director has not relied on an expressionism outside the characters; he builds all his effects on their way of life, their way of crying, of walking, of laughing. They are caught in the maze of the plot like laboratory rats being sent through a labyrinth.

The diversity of styles among the best Italian directors might be advanced as a counter argument and I know how much they dislike the word neorealist. Zavattini is the only one who shamelessly admits to the title. The majority protest against the existence of a new Italian school of realism that would include them all. But that is a reflex reaction of the creator to the critic. The director as artist is more aware of his differences than his resemblances. The word neorealist was thrown like a fishing net over the postwar Italian cinema and each director on his own is doing his best to break the toils in which, it is claimed, he has been caught. However, in spite of this normal reaction, which has the added advantage of forcing us to review a perhaps too easy critical classification, I think there are good reasons for staying with it, even against the views of those most concerned.

Certainly the succinct definition I have just given of neorealism might appear on the surface to be given the lie by the work of Lattuada with its calculated, subtly architectural vision, or by the baroque exuberance, the romantic eloquence of De Santis, or by the refined theatrical sense of Visconti, who makes compositions of the most down-to-earth reality as if they were scenes from an opera or a classical tragedy. These terms are summary and debatable, but can serve for other possible epithets which consequently would confirm the existence of formal differences, of oppositions in style. These three directors are as different from one another as each is from De Sica, yet their common origin is evident if one takes a more general view and especially if one stops comparing them with one another and instead looks at the American, French, and Soviet cinema.

Neorealism does not necessarily exist in a pure state and one can conceive of it being combined with other aesthetic tendencies. Biologists distinguish, in genetics, characteristics derived from different parents, so-called dominant factors. It is the same with neorealism. The exacerbated theatricality of Malaparte's *Cristo probitio* may owe a lot to German expressionism, but the film is nonetheless neorealist, radically different from the realist expressionism of a Fritz Lang.

But I seem to have strayed a long way from De Sica. This was simply that I might be better able to situate him in contemporary Italian production. The difficulty of taking a critical stand about the director of *Miracle in Milan* might indeed be precisely the real indication of his style. Does not our inability to analyze its formal characteristics derive from the fact that it represents the purest form of neorealism, from the fact that *Bicycle Thieves* is the ideal center around which gravitate, each in his own orbit, the works of the other great directors? It could be this very purity which makes it impossible to define, for it has as its paradoxical intention not to produce a spectacle which appears real, but rather to turn reality into a spectacle: a man is walking along the street and the onlooker is amazed at the beauty of the man walking.

Until further information is available, until the realization of Zavattini's dream of filming eighty minutes in the life of a man without a cut, *Bicycle Thieves* is without a doubt the ultimate expression of neorealism.

Though this *mise-en-scène* aims at negating itself, at being transparent to the reality it reveals, it would be naïve to conclude that it does not exist. Few films have been more carefully put together, more pondered over, more meticulously elaborated, but all this labor by De Sica tends to give the illusion of chance, to result in giving dramatic necessity the character of something contingent. Better still, he has succeeded in making dramatic contingency the very stuff of drama. Nothing happens in *Bicycle Thieves* that might just as well not have happened. The worker could have chanced upon his bicycle in the middle of the film, the lights in the auditorium would have gone up and De Sica would have apologized for having disturbed us, but after all, we would be happy for the worker's sake. The marvellous aesthetic paradox of this film is that it has the relentless quality of tragedy while nothing happens in it except by chance. But it is precisely from the dialectical synthesis of contrary values, namely artistic order and the amorphous disorder of reality, that it derives its originality. There is not one image that is not charged with meaning, that does not drive home into the mind the sharp end of an unforgettable moral truth, and not one that to this end is false to the ontological ambiguity of reality. Not one gesture, not one incident, not a single object in the film is given a prior significance derived from the ideology of the director.

If they are set in order with an undeniable clarity on the spectrum of social tragedy, it is after the manner of the particles of iron filings on the spectrum of a magnet – that is to say, individually; but the result of this art in which nothing is necessary, where nothing has lost the fortuitous character of chance, is in effect to be doubly convincing and conclusive. For, after all, it is not surprising that the novelist, the playwright, or the film maker should make it possible for us to hit on this or that idea, since they put them there beforehand, and have seeded their work with them. Put salt into water, let the water evaporate in the fire of reflection, and you will get back the salt. But if you find salt in water drawn directly from a stream, it is because the water is salty by nature. The workman, Bruno [Ricci], might have found his bike just as he might have won in the lottery – even poor people win lotteries. But this potential capacity only serves to bring out more forcefully the terrible powerlessness of the poor fellow. If he found his bike, then the enormous extent of his good luck would be an even greater condemnation of society, since it would make a priceless miracle, an exorbitant favor, out of the return to a human order, to a natural state of happiness, since it would signify his good fortune at not still being poor.

It is clear to what an extent this neorealism differs from the formal concept which consists of decking out a formal story with touches of reality. As for the technique, properly so called, *Bicycle Thieves*, like a lot of other films, was shot in the street with nonprofessional actors but its true merit lies elsewhere: in not betraying the essence of things, in allowing them first of all to exist for their own sakes, freely; it is in loving them in their singular individuality. 'My little sister reality,' says De Sica, and she circles about him like the birds around Saint Francis. Others put her in a case or teach her to talk, but De Sica talks with her and it is the true language of reality that we hear, the word that cannot be denied, that only love can utter.

To explain De Sica, we must go back to the source of his art, namely to his tenderness, his love. The quality shared in common by *Miracle in Milan* and *Bicycle Thieves*, in spite of differences more apparent than real, is De Sica's inexhaustible affection for his characters. It is significant then, in *Miracle in Milan*, that none of the bad people, even the proud or treacherous ones, are antipathetic. The junkyard Judas who sells his companions' hovels to the vulgar Mobbi does not stir the least anger in the onlookers. Rather would he amuse us in the tawdry costume of the 'villain' of melodrama, which he wears awkwardly and clumsily: he is a good traitor. In the same way the new poor, who in their decline still retain the proud ways of their former fine neighborhoods, are simply a special variety of that human fauna and are not therefore excluded from the vagabond community – even if they charge people a lira a sunset. And a man must love the sunset with all his heart to come up with the idea of making people pay for the sight of it, and to suffer this market of dupes.

Besides, none of the principal characters in *Bicycle Thieves* is unsympathetic. Not even the thief. When Bruno [Ricci] finally manages to get his hands on him, the public would be morally disposed to lynch him, as the crowd could have done earlier [later] to Bruno [Ricci].[2] But the spark of genius in this film is to force us to swallow this hatred the moment it is born and to renounce judgment, just as Bruno [Ricci] will refuse to bring charges.

The only unsympathetic characters in *Miracle in Milan* are Mobbi and his acolytes, but basically they do not exist. They are only conventional symbols. The moment De Sica shows them to us at slightly closer quarters, we almost feel a tender curiosity stirring inside us. 'Poor rich people,' we are tempted to say, 'how deceived they are.' There are many ways of loving, even including the way of the inquisitor. The ethics and politics of love are threatened by the worst heresies. From this point of view, hate is often more tender, but the affection De Sica feels for his creatures is no threat to them, there is nothing threatening or abusive about it. It is courtly and discreet gentleness, a liberal generosity, and it demands nothing in return. There is no admixture of pity in it even for the poorest or the most wretched, because pity does violence to the dignity of the man who is its object. It is a burden on his conscience.

The tenderness of De Sica is of a special kind and for this reason does not easily lend itself to any moral, religious, or political generalization. The ambiguities of *Miracle in Milan* and *Bicycle Thieves* have been used by the Christian Democrats and by the Communists. So much the better: a true parable should have something for everyone. I do not think De Sica and Zavattini were trying to argue anybody out of anything. I would not dream of saying that the kindness of De Sica is of greater value than the third theological virtue[3] or than class consciousness, but I see in the modesty of his position a definite artistic advantage. It is a guarantee of its authenticity while, at the same time, assuring it a universal quality. This penchant for love is less a moral question than one of personal and ethnic temperament. As for its authenticity, this can be explained in terms of a naturally happy disposition developed in a Neapolitan atmosphere. But these psychological roots reach down to deeper layers than the consciousness cultivated by partisan ideologies. Paradoxically and in virtue of their unique quality, of their inimitable flavor, since they have not been classified in the categories of either morals or politics, they escape the latter's censure, and the Neapolitan charm of De Sica becomes, thanks to the cinema, the most sweeping message of love that our times have heard since Chaplin.

To anyone who doubted the importance of this, it is enough to point out how quick[ly] partisan critics were to lay claim to it. What party indeed could afford to leave love to the other? In our day there is no longer a place for unattached love but since each party can with equal plausibility lay claim to being the proprietor of it, it means that much authentic and naïve love scales the walls and penetrates the stronghold of ideologies and social theory.

Let us be thankful to Zavattini and De Sica for the ambiguity of their position – and let us take care not to see it as just intellectual astuteness in the land of Don Camillo, a completely negative concern to give pledges on all sides in return for an all-around censorship clearance. On the contrary it is a positive striving after poetry, the stratagem of a person in love, expressing himself in the metaphors of his time, while at the same time making sure to choose such of them as will open the hearts of everyone. The reason why there have been so many attempts to give a political exegesis to *Miracle in Milan* is that Zavattini's social allegories are not the final examples of this symbolism, these symbols themselves being simply the allegory of love. Psychoanalysts explain to us that our dreams are the very opposite of a free flow of images. When these express some fundamental desire, it is in order perforce to cross the threshold of the super-ego, hiding behind the mark of a twofold symbolism, one general, the other individual. But this censorship is not something negative. Without it, without the resistance it offers to the imagination, dreams would not exist.

There is only one way to think of *Miracle in Milan*, namely as a reflection, on the level of a film dream, and through the medium of the social symbolism of contemporary Italy, of the warm heart of Vittorio De Sica. This would explain what seems bizarre and inorganic in this strange film: otherwise it is hard to understand the gaps in its dramatic continuity and its indifference to all narrative logic.

In passing, we might note how much the cinema owes to a love for living creatures. There is no way of completely understanding the art of Flaherty, Renoir, Vigo, and especially Chaplin unless we try to discover beforehand what particular kind of tenderness, of sensual or sentimental affection, they reflect. In my opinion, the cinema more than any other art is particularly bound up with love. The novelist in his relations to his characters needs intelligence more than love; understanding is his form of loving. If the art of a Chaplin were transposed into literature, it would tend to lapse into sentimentality; that is why a man like André Suarès,[4] a man of letters *par excellence*, and evidently impervious to the poetry of the cinema, can talk about the 'ignoble heart' of Chaplin when this heart brings to the cinema the nobility of myth. Every art and every stage in the evolution of each art has its specific scale of values. The tender, amused sensuality of Renoir, the more heart-rending tenderness of Vigo, achieve on the screen a tone and an accent which no other medium of expression could give them. Between such feelings and the cinema there exists a mysterious affinity which is sometimes denied even to the greatest of men. No one better than De Sica can lay claim to being the successor to Chaplin. We have already remarked how as an actor he has a quality of presence, a light which subtly transforms both the scenario and the other actors to such an extent that no one can pretend to play opposite De Sica as he would opposite someone else. We in France have not hitherto known the brilliant actor who appeared in Camerini's films. He had to become famous as a director before he was noticed by the public. By then he no longer had the physique of a young leading man, but his charm survived, the more remarkable for being the less easy to explain. Even when appearing as just a simple actor in the films of other directors, De Sica was already himself a director since his presence modified the film and influenced its style. Chaplin concentrates on himself and within himself the radiation of his tenderness, which means that cruelty is not always excluded from his world; on the contrary, it has a necessary and dialectic relationship to love, as is evident from *Monsieur Verdoux*. Charlie is goodness itself, projected onto the world. He is ready to love everything, but the world does not always respond. On the other hand, De Sica the director infuses into his actors the power to love that he himself possesses as an actor. Chaplin also chooses his cast carefully but always with an eye to himself and to putting his character in a better light. We find in De Sica the humanity of Chaplin, but shared with the world at large. De Sica possesses the gift of being able to convey an intense sense of the human presence, a disarming grace of expression and of gesture which, in their unique way, are an irresistible testimony to man. Ricci (*Bicycle Thieves*), Totò (*Miracle in Milan*), and *Umberto D.*, although greatly differing in physique from Chaplin and De Sica, make us think of them.

It would be a mistake to believe that the love De Sica bears for man, and forces us to bear witness to, is a form of optimism. If no one is really bad, if face to face with each individual human being we are forced to drop our accusation, as was Ricci when he caught up with the thief, we are obliged to say that the evil which undeniably does exist in the world is elsewhere than in the heart of man, that it is somewhere in the order of things. One could say it is in society and be partly right. In one way *Bicycle Thieves, Miracle in Milan,* and *Umberto D.* are indictments of a revolutionary nature. If there were no unemployment it would not be a tragedy to lose one's bicycle. However, this political explanation does not cover the whole drama. De Sica protests the comparison that has been made between *Bicycle Thieves* and the works of Kafka on the grounds that his hero's alienation is social and not metaphysical. True enough, but Kafka's myths are no less valid if one accepts them as allegories of social alienation, and one does not have to believe in a cruel God to feel the guilt of which Joseph K. is culpable. On the contrary, the drama lies in this: God does not exist, the last office in the castle is empty. Perhaps we have here the particular tragedy of today's world, the raising of a self-deifying social reality to a transcendental state.

The troubles of Bruno [Ricci] and Umberto D. have their immediate and evident causes but we also observe that there is an insoluble residue comprised of the psychological and material complexities of our social relationships, which neither the high quality of an institution nor the good will of our neighbors can dispose of. The nature of the latter is positive and social, but its action proceeds always from a necessity that is at once absurd and imperative. This is, in my opinion, what makes this film so great and so rich. It renders a two-fold justice: one by way of an irrefutable description of the wretched condition of the proletariat, another by way of the implicit and constant appeal of a human need that any society whatsoever must respect. It condemns a world in which the poor are obliged to steal from one another to survive (the police protect the rich only too well) but this imposed condemnation is not enough, because it is not only a given historical institution that is in question or a particular economic setup, but the congenital indifference of our social organization, as such, to the fortuitousness of individual happiness. Otherwise Sweden could be the earthly paradise, where bikes are left along the sidewalk both day and night. De Sica loves mankind, his brothers, too much not to want to remove every conceivable cause of their unhappiness, but he also reminds us that every man's happiness is a miracle of love whether in Milan or anywhere else. A society which does not take every opportunity to smother happiness is already better than one which sows hate, but the most perfect still would not create love, for love remains a private matter between man and man. In what country in the world would they keep rabbit hutches in an oil field? In what other would the loss of an administrative document not be as agonizing as the theft of a bicycle? It is part of the realm of politics to think up and promote the objective conditions necessary for human happiness, but it is not part of its essential function to respect its subjective conditions. In the universe of De Sica, there lies a latent pessimism, an unavoidable pessimism we can never be grateful enough to him for, because in it resides the appeal of the potential of man, the witness to his final and irrefutable humanity.

I have used the word love. I should rather have said poetry. These two words are synonymous or at least complementary. Poetry is but the active and creative form of love, its projection into the world. Although spoiled and laid waste by social upheaval, the childhood of the shoeshine boy has retained the power to transform his wretchedness in a dream. In France, in the primary schools, the children are taught to say 'Who steals an egg, steals a bull.' De Sica's formula is 'Who steals an egg is dreaming of a horse.' Totò's miraculous gift which was handed on to him by his adopted grandmother is to have retained from childhood an inexhaustible capacity for defense by way of poetry; the piece of business I find most significant in *Miracle in Milan* is that of Emma Grammatica rushing toward the spilled milk. It does not matter who else scolds Totò for his lack of initiative and wipes up the milk with a cloth, so long as the quick gesture of the old woman has as its purpose to turn the little catastrophe into a marvellous game, a stream in the middle of a landscape of the same proportion. And so on to the multiplication tables, another profound terror of one's childhood, which, thanks to the little old woman, turns into a dream. City dweller Totò names the streets and the squares 'four times four is sixteen' or 'nine times nine is eighty-one,' for these cold mathematical symbols are more beautiful in his eyes than the names of the characters of mythology. Here again we think of Charlie; he also owes to his childhood spirit his remarkable power of transforming the world to a better purpose. When reality resists him and he cannot materially change it – he switches its meaning. Take for example, the dance of the rolls, in *The Gold Rush*, or the shoes in the soup pot, with this proviso that, always on the defensive, Charlie reserves his power of metamorphosis for his own advantage, or, at most, for the benefit of the woman he loves. Totò, on the other hand, goes out to others. He does not give a moment's thought to any benefit the dove can bring him; his joy lies in his being able to spread joy. When he can no longer do anything for his neighbor, he takes it on himself to assume various shapes, now limping for the lame man, making himself small for the dwarf, blind for the one-eyed man. The dove is just an arbitrarily added possibility, to give poetry a material form, because most people need something to assist their imaginations. But Totò does not know what to do with himself unless it is for someone else's benefit.

Zavattini told me once: 'I am like a painter standing before a field, who asks himself which blade of grass he should begin with.' De Sica is the ideal director for a declaration of faith such as this. There is also the art of the playwright who divides the moments of life into episodes which, in respect of the moments lived, are what the blades of grass are to the field. To paint every blade of grass one must be the Douanier Rousseau. In the world of cinema one must have the love of a De Sica for creation itself.

Notes

1 EDITORS' NOTE: Bazin is perhaps referring to American films of the documentary-influenced thriller genre, which might include such almost *film-noir* pieces as *Panic in the Streets* (1950) or *Call Northside 777* (1948), as well as documentary dramas such as *The Quiet One* (1949), which won an award at the Venice film festival. Its neorealist style re-emerged briefly in the Ruth Orkin

and Morris Engel film *The Little Fugitive* (1953), which postdates Bazin's essay but nevertheless serves as an example of the limited scope of neorealism in America.

2 EDITORS' NOTE: Bazin is probably referring to the episode at the end of *Bicycle Thieves* in which Ricci is caught, and nearly beaten, after trying to steal a bicycle.

3 TRANSLATOR'S NOTE: The three theological virtues are faith, hope, and charity.

4 EDITORS' NOTE: André Suarès (1868–1948), a French poet, dramatist, and essayist who prefigures existentialist engagement in his eclectic writings.

Umberto D. and Realism

GILBERTO PEREZ

Gilberto Perez is the author of a number of essays on Italian film which have appeared in Raritan *and the* Hudson Review. *The following discussion of realism and the cinema is from his book* The Material Ghost: Films and Their Medium *(1998). Part of what Perez is suggesting is that the criticism of realism in terms of its failure 'really' to be 'reality' is irrelevant insofar as realism recreates reality and in fact sends one into one's own world with an altered sensibility. Perez's discussion has a spiritual tie to the later writings of Roland Barthes, especially perhaps* A Lover's Discourse *(1978), in which Barthes examines the function of photographic images in a non-semiological way.*

An imprint gives evidence of what has been; an image gives presence to what it depicts. A photograph gives evidence of what it depicts and gives presence to what has been. It is a documentary image as a painting can never be: not because it is necessarily more realistic than a painting but because it has a necessary material connection with reality.

What a photograph depicts has been; what a painting depicts comes into being in the picture. What a movie depicts can, in each of its details, be said to have been: each thing we see must have been there before the camera, which has no imagination and 'infinite appetite for the material.' But the movie as a whole, the world of the movie, comes into being on the screen. What has been is documentary, what comes into being is fiction; a movie is a fiction made up of documentary

Gilberto Perez, *The Material Ghost: Films and Their Medium* (Baltimore: Johns Hopkins University Press, 1998), 34–7 details. The camera doesn't make things up, it receives their light from reality; but the projector has its own light. One camp of film theory, the camp that stresses photographic realism, subordinates the projector to the camera's documentary image; the other camp, the camp that stresses fantasy and the imaginary, subordinates the camera to the projector's illusory image. But the film image is both the camera's and the projectors's: the material ghost.

A still from Lumière's movie of a train arriving at a station gives presence to what has been. Projected on the screen, the movie animates that presence, brings it to life, we say; and many would say that it brings it into a present, a now rather than a then. The early spectators who got out of the train's way seem to have taken the movie as the present. But we don't get out of the way. We don't take a movie as the present, for the present is where we are, and a movie, even if it is a world animated into a now, is a world elsewhere. Hence Stanley Cavell has disputed that a movie is a present and maintained that it is a world past. But Cavell, like other theorists, confounds the photographic and the cinematic image. Still photographs are clearly of the past. The tense of the movies is not so clear.

Documentary is what has been, and yet it is often the more documentary movies that seem to give the stronger impression of the present. The newsreel immediacy of Rossellini's movies in the pioneer years of neorealism won praise from James Agee for 'giving the illusion of the present tense.' The death of the Anna Magnani character in *Roma città aperta / Rome, Open City* (1945) is justly famous for its moving immediacy. It is a death designedly not prepared for. The dramatic tension in the scene Rossellini had cunningly diverted in another direction, and it seemed to have subsided when suddenly the woman rushes out into the street after her boyfriend is taken prisoner and the Nazis shoot her dead: the tragedy bursts upon us unexpectedly, with the force of something real that the camera itself had not anticipated and photographed as best it could in the rough manner of a newsreel. But the urgency of a newsreel is the urgency of the right then and there, not the right here and now: the camera may speak in the present, but it is a present now past when we watch it on the screen. The poignancy of such a scene – even if it is not a death scene it is always the poignancy of death – is the poignancy of what reaches us from the past with the urgency of the present.

De Sica and Zavattini's brand of neorealism does not adopt the look of a newsreel; it does not look at the kind of thing that appears in the news but at the ordinary things of everyday life. And yet its closeness, its transparency to the ordinary has also been taken as a presentness; its attention to the time of everyday life led Bazin to call Zavattini 'something like the Proust of the indicative present.' Bazin specifically had in mind *Umberto D.* (1952), one of the last and perhaps the finest of the neorealist films (written by Zavattini, directed by De Sica, with the great G.R. Aldo as cinematographer). Umberto D. is an old man, a retired government clerk living alone on a meagre pension and owing back rent on the room where he has long resided to a landlady who now wants to evict him. Nobody will help him out. His few friends back away; aside from his dog, only the landlady's housemaid, a young woman from the country with troubles of her own, shows any concern for him. But then there is De Sica's camera. It is a camera that, as Bazin said, shows affection for the characters as no other means of representation can, for no other means can represent human beings so concretely, so particularly, with such exact attention to their singularity. De Sica's camera loves his characters not because they are good or beautiful or admirable but because they are. The love it shows is not eros, the love of the desirable, but agape, the kind of love God bestows on His creatures. And it shows this love by staying with the characters through the details of ordinary experience, savoring the time of daily existence like a Proust delving into the present.

Umberto D. is a picture of alienation: alienation countered by affection. The affection of the portrayal, the camera's and ours, counters the alienation portrayed, the breach Umberto D. feels between him and just about everyone and everything around him. The world is distant but we feel close; the world is cold but there is warmth that may kindle it. Yet when the old man at last despairs of life and, intending to do himself in, leaves the room where he is not wanted, says good-bye to the maid, gets on a streetcar and sees her receding from him at an upstairs window, something remarkable happens: suddenly the whole world seems to recede irretrievably, suddenly what had seemed close at hand seems far away, suddenly the illusion of presentness gives way to a vertiginous pastness. No other work so chillingly conveys the mood of suicide. If the materiality of the film image, its closeness to concrete reality, enables De Sica to express love as no other medium can, the ghostliness of the image on the screen enables him to express death as no other medium can.

The lifelike image is also the ghostlike image: the vivid harbors the vanished. The vivid that at any moment may vanish, all the more vivid because we fear it may vanish, is the theme of Humphrey Jennings's great documentary of Britain at war, *Listen to Britain* (1942). 'Humphrey Jennings worked best,' wrote Eric Rhode, 'when the things he loved were most under threat.' *Listen to Britain* focuses not on the war but on the everyday life of a people in wartime, the ordinary manifestations of existence made extraordinary under threat of destruction. Like *Umberto D.*, Jennings's documentary depends for its tenderness and its pathos on the combination of presentness and pastness peculiar to the film image. Perhaps the most eloquent moments in his cinematic orchestration of the 'music of Britain at war' are moments of synchronized sound: the comedians Flanagan and Allen singing into a microphone at a factory workers' playtime, the pianist Myra Hess striking the keyboard at a lunchtime concert at the National Gallery. The image with synchronized sound feels more present, more attached to the concrete, a more vivid affirmation of life not yet vanished.

A photograph is past, a painting is present; a play is present, a novel is past. The tense of the film image is dual, one might say: sometimes it acts like the past. Is light a wave or a stream of particles? Sometimes it acts like a wave, sometimes like particles, as modern physics has discovered: particle and wave, matter and energy, are not two different things but two different aspects of the same thing, two different ways in which the thing behaves. Present and past, icon and index, fiction and documentary, drama and narrative: these are different aspects of the film medium, different ways in which it can behave.

Beyond the Movement-Image

GILLES DELEUZE

Although Gilles Deleuze in his books Cinema 1: The Movement-Image *(1988) and* Cinema 2: The Time-Image *(1989) addresses specific De Sica films only peripherally, he provides a radically different starting point for understanding neorealism. Deleuze, here and elsewhere, focuses upon motion and image as determining elements of value or signification in cinema. For Deleuze it is the 'optical situation' more than 'reality' that defines the essence of neorealism. Neorealism is a construction of a reality that is itself a kind of construction of textual laminations.*

Against those who defined Italian neorealism by its social content, Bazin put forward the fundamental requirement of formal aesthetic criteria. According to him, it was a matter of a new form of reality, said to be dispersive, elliptical, errant or wavering, working in blocks, with deliberately weak connections and floating events. The real was no longer represented or reproduced but 'aimed at.' Instead of representing an already deciphered real, neorealism aimed at an always ambiguous, to be deciphered, real; this is why the sequence shot tended to replace the montage of representations. Neorealism therefore invented a new type of image, which Bazin suggested calling 'fact-image' (see Bazin, 35–9). This thesis of Bazin's was infinitely richer than the one that he was challenging, and showed that neorealism did not limit itself to the content of its earliest examples. But what the two theses

From Gilles Deleuze, *Cinema 1: The Movement-Image; Cinema 2: The Time-Image*, trans. Hugh Tomlinson and Barbara Habberjam (Minneapolis: University of Minnesota Press, 1988; 1989)

had in common was the posing of the problem at the level of reality: neorealism produced a formal or material 'additional reality.' However, we are not sure that the problem arises at the level of the real, whether in relation to form or content. Is it not rather at the level of the 'mental,' in terms of thought? If all the movement-images, perceptions, actions and affects underwent such an upheaval, was this not first of all because a new element burst onto the scene which was to prevent perception being extended into action in order to put it in contact with thought, and, gradually, was to subordinate the image to the demands of new signs which would take it beyond movement?

When Zavattini defines neorealism as an art of encounter – fragmentary, ephemeral, piecemeal, missed encounters – what does he mean? It is true of encounters in Rossellini's *Paisà / Paisan* (1946), or De Sica's *Ladri di Biciclette / Bicycle Thief* (1948). And in *Umberto D.* (1951) De Sica constructs the famous sequence quoted as an example by Bazin: the young maid going into the kitchen in the morning, making a series of mechanical, weary gestures, cleaning a bit, driving the ants away from a water fountain, picking up the coffee grinder, stretching out her foot to close the door with her toe. And her eyes meet her pregnant woman's belly, and it is as though all the misery in the world were going to be born. This is how, in an ordinary or everyday situation, in the course of a series of gestures, which are insignificant but all the more obedient to simple sensory-motor schemata, what has suddenly been brought about is a *pure optical situation* to which the little maid has no response or reaction. The eyes, the belly, that is what an encounter is ... Of course, encounters can take very different forms, even achieving the exceptional, but they follow the same formula. Take, for example, Rossellini's great quartet, which, far from marking an abandonment of neorealism, on the contrary, perfects it. *Germania anno zero / Germany Year Zero* (1947) presents a child who visits a foreign country (this is why the film was criticized for not maintaining the social mooring which was held to be a condition of neorealism), and who dies from what he sees. *Stromboli, terra di dio / Stromboli* (1949) presents a foreign woman whose revelation of the island will be all the more profound because she cannot react in a way that softens or compensates for the violence of what she sees, the intensity and the enormity of the tunny-fishing ('It was awful ...'), the panic-inducing power of the eruption ('I am finished, I am afraid, what mystery, what beauty, my God ...'). *Europa '51 / The Greatest Love* (1952) shows a bourgeois woman who, following the death of her child, crosses various spaces and experiences the tenement, the slum and the factory ('I thought I was seeing convicts'). Her glances relinquish the practical function of a mistress of a house who arranges things and beings, and pass through every state of an internal vision, affliction, compassion, love, happiness, acceptance, extending to the psychiatric hospital where she is locked up at the end of a new trial of Joan of Arc: she sees, she has learnt to see. *The Lonely Woman* [*Viaggio in Italia / Voyage in Italy* (1953)] follows a female tourist struck to the core by the simple unfolding of images or visual clichés in which she discovers something unbearable, beyond the limit of what she can personally bear. This is a cinema of the seer and no longer of the agent [*de voyant, non plus d'actant*].

What defines neorealism is this build-up of purely optical situations (and sound ones, although there was no synchronized sound at the start of neorealism), which are fundamentally distinct from the sensory-motor situations of the action-image in the old realism. It is perhaps as important as the conquering of a purely optical space in painting, with impressionism. It may be objected that the viewer has always found himself in front of 'descriptions,' in front of optical- and sound-images, and nothing more. But this is not the point. For the characters themselves reacted to situations; even when one of them found himself reduced to helplessness, bound and gagged, as a result of the ups and downs of the action. What the viewer perceived therefore was a sensory-motor image in which he took a greater or lesser part by identification with the characters. Hitchcock had begun the inversion of this point of view by including the viewer in the film. But it is now that the identification is actually inverted: the character has become a kind of viewer. He shifts, runs and becomes animated in vain, the situation he is in outstrips his motor capacities on all sides, and makes him see and hear what is no longer subject to the rules of a response or an action. He records rather than reacts. He is prey to a vision, pursued by it or pursuing it, rather than engaged in an action. Visconti's *Ossessione / Obsession* (1942) rightly stands as the forerunner of neorealism; and what first strikes the viewer is the way in which the black-clad heroine is possessed by an almost hallucinatory sensuality. She is closer to a visionary, a sleepwalker, than to a seductress or a lover (similarly, later, the Countess in *Senso*, 1954).

In volume 1 the crisis of the action-image was defined by a number of characteristics: the form of the trip/ballad,[1] the multiplication of clichés, the events that hardly concern those they happen to, in short the slackening of the sensory-motor connections. All these characteristics were important but only in the sense of preliminary conditions. They made possible, but did not yet constitute, the new image. What constitutes this is the purely optical and sound situation which takes the place of the faltering sensory-motor situations. The role of the child in neorealism has been pointed out, notably in De Sica (and later in France with Truffaut); this is because, in the adult world, the child is affected by a certain motor helplessness, but one which makes him all the more capable of seeing and hearing. Similarly, if everyday banality is so important, it is because, being subject to sensory-motor schemata which are automatic and pre-established, it is all the more liable, on the least disturbance of equilibrium between stimulus and response (as in the scene with the little maid in *Umberto D.*), suddenly to free itself from the laws of this schema and reveal itself in a visual and sound nakedness, crudeness and brutality which make it unbearable, giving it the pace of a dream or a nightmare. There is, therefore, a necessary passage from the crisis of image-action to the pure optical-sound image.

From *Cinema 2: The Time-Image*, 1–3

These are the five apparent characteristics of the new image [neorealism]: *the dispersive situation, the deliberately weak links, the voyage form, the consciousness of clichés, the condemnation of the plot.*

...

The Italians were able to have an intuitive consciousness of the new image in the course of being born. This explains nothing of the genius of Rossellini's first films. But it does at least explain the reaction of certain American critics who saw in them the inordinant pretension of a defeated country, an odious form of blackmail, a way of making the conquerors ashamed. And above all, it is this very special situation of Italy which made possible the enterprise of neorealism.

It was Italian neorealism which forged the five preceding characteristics. In the situation at the end of the war, Rossellini discovered a dispersive and lacunary reality – already in *Roma, città aperta / Rome, Open City* (1945), but above all *Paisà* – a series of fragmentary, chopped up encounters, which call into question the SAS form of action-image. (As the action-image on all its levels always brings together 'two,' it is not surprising that it should have two different aspects itself. The large form – SAS' – moved from the situation to the action, which modified the situation. But there is another form, which, on the contrary, moves from the action to the situation, towards a new action: ASA'. This time it is the action which discloses the situation, a fragment or an aspect of the situation, which triggers off a new action.) It is the post-war economic crises, on the other hand, which inspires De Sica, and leads him to shatter the ASA form; there is no longer a vector or line of the universe which extends and links up the events of *Bicycle Thieves*; the rain can always interrupt or deflect the search fortuitously, the voyage of the man and of the child. The Italian rain becomes the sign of idle periods and possible interruption. And again the theft of the bicycle, or even the insignificant events of *Umberto D.*, have a vital importance for the protagonists.

From *Cinema 1: The Movement-Image*, 210–12

In fact the most banal of everyday situations release accumulated 'dead forces' equal to the life force of a limit situation (thus, in De Sica's *Umberto D.*, the sequence where the old man examines himself and thinks he has a fever). In addition, the idle periods in Antonioni do not merely show the banalities of daily life, they reap the consequences or the effect of a remarkable event ...

From *Cinema 2: The Time-Image*, 7

Note

1 TRANSLATOR'S NOTE: Deleuze uses the word 'bal(l)ade,' an untranslatable pun on the words *ballade* (ballad) and *balade* (trip or voyage).

References

Bazin, André, *What is Cinema?* vol. 1, trans. Hugh Gray (Berkeley: University of California Press, 1967)

Ideological Continuity and Cultural Coherence

PHILIP V. CANNISTRARO

Philip V. Cannistraro's essay is from a 1975 issue of Bianco e nero *that was devoted entirely to De Sica. Cannistraro's discussion perceptively links De Sica the actor to his historical moment, and that role and that moment to De Sica the neorealist filmmaker. This essay is the only one in this volume that treats De Sica's acting career in connection with his directorial career, although we have expanded upon Cannistraro's discussion in our introduction (13–15 above). There is at least one book in Italian, Francesco Bolzoni's* Quando De Sica era Mister Brown *(1985), that deals with De Sica's early acting career in detail.*

The passing of Vittorio De Sica will undoubtedly initiate a series of critical and scholarly efforts to re-evaluate the many-faceted contributions of this great figure of the Italian cinema; perhaps the time will soon come when, after the deserved praise and anticipated eulogies have been made, it will be possible to recast both his contributions and his impact in a broader, more objective socio-cultural perspective. This special issue of *Bianco e nero* dedicated to De Sica may represent a first step in that direction. I would therefore like to offer here a series of observations – or rather impressions – from the viewpoint of an historian and to suggest a possible line of inquiry which may, at best, help us to better understand this complex figure, and, at worst, act as an exchange of ideas.

To begin with, the obvious point must be made that no one who

Philip V. Cannistraro, 'Ideological Continuity and Cultural Coherence,' *Bianco e nero* 36:9–12 (September–October 1975), 14–19

worked in the Italian cinema during the dark years of the Fascist dictatorship, whether as actor, script writer, director, or technician, could
have remained isolated and unaffected by that experience. The broad
outline and much of the details regarding the cultural policy of the
Fascist regime have been well-enough established to demonstrate this
point. What has not been fully investigated yet is the nature of the
multiformed reactions to that policy by artists and creative intellectuals
of various kinds. Certainly in the world of motion pictures, critics and
historians of film must begin to replace general assumptions with particular analysis and evidence. The repressive and culturally restrictive
influence of the Ministry of Popular Culture reached into every area of
cultural endeavour in a systematic attempt to impose a regimented,
conformist discipline upon the life of the nation. In regard to the mass
media, the regime's policy was perhaps most clearly developed; since
the most intransigent leaders and the most acute Fascist intellectuals
alike eventually came to realize that their hopes of creating an authentic
and explicit Fascist culture had met with failure, the regime's cultural
bureaucrats reconciled themselves to achieving two less ambitious
goals: a rigid administrative control over all stages of the production
and distribution of media messages, and the elimination of all themes
and subjects which might have confounded or counteracted official
propaganda values. In motion pictures these policies were carried out
with varying degrees of success by the Direzione Generale per la
Cinematografia. As had been the practice before 1922, and would be
again after the fall of the regime, during the Fascist period producers
continued to make films that would achieve the greatest possible commercial success – in spite of, or perhaps because of, Fascist policies,
Italian film companies aimed their products at the widest common
denominator of audience. In a dual effort to achieve both a narrow policy of film 'autarky' [economic self-sufficiency] and at the same time
to encourage the making of films that conformed at least minimally to
the regime's propaganda values, the Direzione Generale resorted to
the practice of awarding monetary prizes to those companies that
produced the most commercially successful motion pictures. The result was that the bulk of Italian commercial films made between 1922
and 1943 were either a popular escapist genre of comedy-adventure-
historical-costume cinema, or films which more blatantly glorified officially favoured themes such as war, patriotism, and sacrifice for the
greater good of the nation. Films directly financed or produced by
the government – with the notable exception of the [Henry] Luce news-

reels and documentaries – that were directly propagandistic in nature were few.

Within the restricted limits imposed on cinematography by the regime, commercial film directors and producers were confronted with a narrow choice of options, and while the artistic and technical quality of each particular product varied considerably, none ventured to go beyond the officially accepted confines of subject and theme. For an actor and director of De Sica's experience and temperament, the choice was almost natural – one is tempted to say instinctive. Indeed, the problem of 'choice' in connection with De Sica's cinema seems almost artificial. De Sica, who was barely twenty-one years old when the March on Rome took place, certainly could not remain unaffected by the cultural climate and social priorities forced upon Italy by the Fascist dictatorship, but he could mirror them and comment upon their meaning in his own special way while remaining himself. Then, too, immediately after the collapse of Fascism, De Sica did not remain aloof from the climate produced by the anti-Fascist resistance and its moral-social imperatives, just as in the years following the initial stages of national reconstruction and recovery, and especially during the economic boom of the 1960's, De Sica once again reoriented his work to the changed conditions and atmosphere of Italian society. These shifts in theme, subject, and style – represented perhaps by the films *Gli uomini, che mascalzoni! / Men Are Such Rascals* (1932), *Ladri di biciclette / Bicycle Thieves* (1948), and *Matrimonio all'italiana / Marriage Italian Style* (1964) – were startling and disturbing and, to film historians, perplexing. In view of the apparent ease with which De Sica moved from one genre to another, it is natural that critics would pose serious questions regarding the nature of his motivations and purpose. In retrospect, it is certainly this fluctuating evolution of interests that is the keynote of his legacy to film critics. Once they overcome the brilliance and poignancy of his neorealist achievement, critics are constrained to ask the disturbing question of whether it is possible to find any secure, clear lines of ideological continuity and cultural coherence in De Sica's career. To pose the problem in even more direct terms, was the neorealist phase little more than a temporary aberration lacking in genuine commitment and born out of stylish opportunism or ideological conformism?

It has been suggested above that De Sica's role during the Fascist period was an instinctive one, but a judgment as to both the precise nature of that role (a judgment cannot be formed without reference to the general condition of Italian society during the Fascist period) and as to whether his activity transcended and extended beyond the Fascist experience remains unformulated. De Sica's social background and the nature of his early success must have contributed significantly to the line of coherency that is discernible in his cinema: that of an impoverished bourgeois office clerk who rose quickly to the height of popular fame. Years before he entered motion pictures, De Sica had achieved great success in musical comedy, vaudeville, the music hall, and in radio. The combination of a brilliant, comic-sentimental stage talent with an instinctual élan, a deep-rooted humanitarian personality, made him an unparalleled portrayer of the social aspirations and fanciful expectations of the petty bourgeoisie and of that middle class of Italian society that was struggling to emerge out of the ruins of the great depression under Fascism. Shows such as the 'Za-Bum' spectacles in 1927 had already made De Sica the favourite of audiences composed to a large extent of shopgirls, office workers, small merchants, and lower-level government employees.

To transfer this talent to the movie screen and to develop it even more fully was for De Sica an easy matter, and indeed an almost logical progression. For it may be argued – without making political associations or casting moral aspersions – that De Sica's rise to stardom and his role as one of the first cases of 'divismo' in Italian sound films was perfectly in accord with the cultural policies and social propaganda of the Fascist regime. We can see in De Sica's acting career a confluence of his own personal instincts with some aspects of the broad social-cultural atmosphere of the regime of the 1930's, an atmosphere characterized by an emphasis on the mass media as the cultural focus of the anonymous masses, an attempt to escape by pretence the crushing effects of the depression, and a distinct anti-bourgeois propaganda which hailed the petty bourgeoisie as the real 'people' of the nation and the essence of the Fascist revolution. Although many films of the 'White Telephone'[1] variety provided audiences with glimpses of the plush world of the idle rich, it was the De Sica type of film that was enthusiastically favoured by the Direzione Generale per la Cinematografia. At the same time that it sought to avoid the dangerous implications of conflicting social aspirations, the regime publicly emphasized and reinforced a whole range of petty-bourgeois values against the established, snobbish, wealthy middle classes. But while Fascist propaganda championed the aspirations of the lower middle classes, it also was forced to confront the fact that these aspirations remained largely unfulfilled in spite of the Fascist revolution, with the result that the regime's propagandists reached the conclusion that such aspirations should not be fulfilled by people striving to reach beyond their status and social means. In essence, the contradictions implicit in Fascist social policy provided De Sica with the core of his contribution as a film actor in the 1930's.

If we consider briefly De Sica's major roles in the prewar period, this argument becomes clearer. De Sica excelled in portraying with sympathy and humour the strivings of the 'little man' in the big city, roles which won him wide acclaim especially in the films of Mario Camerini. The awkward efforts of the shy delivery boy to meet the pretty blond department store clerk in *Men Are Such Rascals* (1932) are resolved with humorous success against the background – filmed on location – of the commercial world of the Milan fair. The message of unfulfilled social aspirations conquered by love is even more effectively developed in a satirical film called *Il signor Max / Signor Max* (1937), in which a young newspaper seller played by De Sica is caught in a conflict of choices between the unreal, snobbish world of the wealthy and the real life of the humble, and ultimately chooses the latter. Perhaps most symbolic of all was the popular song 'Se potessi avere mille lire al mese' ['It's possible to have a thousand-lire meal'] made popular by De Sica in 1938 in the show 'Le lucciole della città' ['The Lights of the City'], in which a 'simple employee with no pretensions' expressed his modest dreams of simple comfort.

De Sica's performances in Camerini's films and his own later direction of comic movies like *Maddalena zero in condotta / Madeline, Zero in Conduct* (1940), *Teresa venerdì / Mademoiselle Friday* (1941), and *Un garibaldino al convento / A Policewoman in the Convent* (1942) were, in today's perspective, perfect expressions of the hopes and aspirations of those segments of the Italian middle classes that were hoping to emerge under the aegis of Fascism. It seems clear, however, that De Sica played these roles out of natural instinct and not because they reflected a conscious adoption of Fascist rhetoric. Indeed, one can trace a continuous but subtle line of satirical critique of the bourgeoisie in De Sica's films of the 1930's and 1940's; and while the critique may have found favour in official film circles, it also reflected De Sica's own impulse: these social aspirations were real and widespread in the Italy of the depression decade, but in De Sica's talented, human, funny, and 'populist' hands they were transformed into intensely popular, wistful and sentimental, external treatments of a fundamental aspect of the social environment of the period.

It is only against this background that a final critical and historical judgment of De Sica's role in the Italian cinema can be made, for to isolate the neorealist phase of his activity from what came before or later, to speak only of a segment of time that runs from *I bambini ci guardano / The Children Are Watching Us* (1942) to *Umberto D.* (1952), as a newly discovered inspiration 'tout court' [all at once], after which De Sica's 'impegno' [imprint] declines, is to distort his meaning and his art. To arrive at such a conclusion is to give to Italian neorealism a mythic quality which De Sica would surely have rejected. The tragic and tortuous, yet momentous and triumphal, period of Italian history that opened in 1943 could obviously not remain outside the compass of De Sica's human sentiment and artistic perception, but to read into his films of the period an ideological commitment of 'resistance' is to seek for that which does not exist and to substitute unreasonable disappointment for the deserved admiration of a profound artist.

The crisis and collapse of Fascism represented for De Sica an opportunity to liberate himself from the restrained, artificially controlled external portrayal of social aspirations that Fascism had permitted to a more natural, freer, and emotive internal critique for which the liberation provided the necessary conditions. De Sica's cinema both before and after Fascism is not one of resistance but of depiction; his concerns as an artist are those of revelation through human-emotional identifications rather than the ideological education of the social consciences of his audiences; he does not condemn or proselytize, but seeks rather to express the most immediate, tactile level of social consciousness: the heart of De Sica's relationship to his audience is, as Tino Ranieri has properly observed, 'per spiegare problematicamente il proprio mondo a se stessi' [to explain problematically my world to myself]. De Sica's cinema is designed not to create militant cadres or indoctrinate political-social attitudes, but to permit the audience to understand, to participate emotionally in and to reflect upon, the existing social relationships of the moment, and to do this on an immensely human level.

These observations, general though they may be, are applicable to De Sica the artist of cinematography, not to De Sica of the pre-Fascist period or De Sica the neorealist. For below the surface of each of the phases of his development there remained always the fundamental, immutable sentiment that reveals him as a 'social' pessimist. With the new political-cultural freedom that the liberation brought and with the aid of the tremendously powerful techniques of neorealist cinematography, De Sica could unleash his emotive pessimism in a series of films

that portrayed the convergence of social tragedy and individual aspiration; in the days of the Fascist regime this instinct had to be content
with its resolution in terms not of tragedy but of satirical disappointment and the comforting realization that the social condition which we
cannot change is, after all, the one best fitted to us. For De Sica the neorealist, the social condition is still filled with disappointment and futility, but now expressed in tragedy rather than comedy. For De Sica the
actor – and he always remained an actor – understood the temper and
sentiment of his audience, whether on the stage or on the screen, and if
in the gray, conformist days of Fascism the lower middle classes found
comfort in fantasy and comic-sentimental love, in the crushing
destruction and poverty of the immediate postwar world, those same
audiences found 'escape' in the unrestricted release of sentimentalized
anguish born of human despair in the face of social tragedy.

Nevertheless, when all is said, De Sica remains something less than a
resistance fighter and considerably more than a 'cinematografaro pic-
colo borghese' [a little bourgeois cinematographer]. Throughout his
work it is not difficult to find beside De Sica the social pessimist
another De Sica, that of the human optimist. In this context, De Sica
argued always that in the face of a destructive social environment men
and women can find sustenance and happiness in a personal contact
that leads to understanding and love, in the individual resolve to
struggle, to work, to live and to survive against all the disappointments and brutalities of social existence. If De Sica's films have posited
an image of society in a general configuration, it is unquestionably one
in which the dehumanization and tragic cruelties of social groups can
be tempered and overcome only through the recognition and actual-
ization of the moral premise upon which society is based. If, in effect,
De Sica's cinematographic achievement is to be judged in terms of the
encounter between the cultural wasteland that was Fascism and the
cultural revival that was the resistance, then perhaps it may be said
that he acted the role of jester who, with his laughter and tears,
bridged the gap between social myth and human reality. Surely in
looking back upon a half-century of life in the world of cinematography, De Sica might have agreed that, after all, there is not such a great
difference between his fortuitous bicycle ride in *Men Are Such Rascals*
and the futile search for one in *Bicycle Thieves*: like many of his generation, De Sica had made the difficult voyage through tyranny to freedom by keeping faith with the belief that social aspiration must be
nurtured by human dignity.

Editors' Note

1 'White Telephone' films were so named because such telephones denoted upper-class society, the mileu of these bourgeois melodramas.

Remembrance of Things Past

MARCIA LANDY

Marcia Landy's discussion of De Sica is taken from her extended study of the themes of Italian cinema in her book Fascism in Film: The Italian Commercial Cinema, 1931–1943, *which was published in 1986. She views De Sica's early directorial efforts in their ideological relationship to other films of the period. Some may find problematical Landy's conflation of the image of innocent youth in De Sica's Fascist-period films with those of his later films, neorealist and beyond. Landy's book discusses at length the shaping power of Fascist ideology on the sort of character who could be represented in an Italian film, a character formed by the concept of health and strength inherited from the writer Gabriele d'Annunzio, whose philosophy of naturalism and the superman and celebration of war resulted in his nomination to the Accademia in 1937. It is to some degree the d'Annunzian human figure we see in Fascist films and the anti-d'Annunzian figure in the films on which De Sica and Zavattini collaborated.*

Presenting a less puritan vision of the rewards of renunciation, Vittorio De Sica's 1940 film, *Maddalena zero in condotta / Madeline, Zero in Conduct*, a popular film at the time, is a comedy set in a young girls' school that plays with oppositions between repressive and authoritarian institutions and those who subvert authority. Structured around the classroom and the home, the classroom episodes stress the attempts of the teachers to impose discipline and the young women's energetic attempts to disrupt and frustrate institutionalization. For the most

From Marcia Landy, *Fascism in Film: The Italian Commercial Cinema, 1931–1943* (Princeton: Princeton University Press, 1986), 51–5, 66–7 part, the teachers are caricatured in the portly male professor who is intent on asserting his dominance, the severe female principal who is responsible for maintaining order and continuity, and the inept male gym teacher who cannot perform the exercises he sets for his students. The young female teacher of commercial writing, Signorina Malgari, like her students, is oppressed by this environment. The students are portrayed as unruly, seizing every opportunity to play tricks on the teachers and on the teacher's pet.

Maddalena, the ringleader in insubordination, succeeds in disrupting the normal functioning of academic life and, in the process, of liberating the oppressed Signorina Malgari. Taking advantage of the teacher's absence from the classroom, she and her colleagues rummage through the teacher's papers where Maddalena finds a love letter inserted into a book on commercial correspondence, written by Signorina Malgari to an imaginary person. Maddalena reads it and mails it to Hartman, the author of the book. The letter arrives in Vienna where it is delivered to the firm of Hartman. The letter is brought first to an old man, then to a middle-aged man, and finally to a young man, each representing a different generation of the Hartman family. De Sica plays all three roles. This metamorphosis highlights the film's concern with generational differences and the emphasis on youth. While the grandfather and father reject the letter, the son decides to be adventurous and locate the writer. With a companion, he travels to Rome and to the Audax School where, after much confusion, the two men become romantically involved with Maddalena and the teacher.

The scenes in Malgari's house and Maddalena's are the setting for the courtship sequences, while the school setting becomes the locus for elaborate scenes of investigation, misidentification, and confessional. The final sequences in the film reveal order restored as a new teacher appears to assume Malgari's position and the cycle of repetition asserts itself.

De Sica gently satirizes the institution of the school and provides a fantasy of liberation from its strictures cast in the mold of romantic comedy. Sexual fantasy provides the escape from dreary routine and repression. The letter that brings an imaginary love object to life who is willing to drop his business affairs to seek romance is the signifier for the film itself as the vehicle for transforming the oppressive structure of quotidian existence. The young female students' attempts to resist banality are linked to the film's similar attempts to transform the immediate surroundings by evoking and invoking liberatory fantasies.

Like *Addio giovinezza*, *Maddalena* portrays youth as energetic, adventurous, and rebellious in contrast to the staid, pompous, and incompetent older generation, but unlike the Poggioli film, *Maddalena zero in condotta* is not based on renunciation and an acceptance of the world of work and responsibility. The tricks the students play on their teachers can be read as the film's playful agenda, though its 'subversive' alignment with the young people seems consonant with the film's critique of repressive institutions. The comic resolution is the restoration of social relations through love.

De Sica's *Teresa Venerdì / Mademoiselle Friday* (1940) takes place in a girls' orphanage rather than a school. Using Hollywood images and character types, the film makes the young girl, Teresa, the agent of social change. Steven Harvey, commenting on this film, finds that

> ... the characters ... are all seemingly based on contemporary Hollywood prototypes. The wishful ingenue heroine is strongly reminiscent of the American Anne Shirley, and De Sica resembles Cary Grant at his most antic; Magnani's other woman, a coarse and pretentious golddigger, is blood kin to Gypsy Rose Lee who struggled vainly to entice Tony Martin away from Alice Faye in all the thirties Fox musicals. Flanking these characters are such archetypes as the whimsically incompetent butler, the giddy heiress, the scatterbrained mother and vulgar parvenu father.   (Harvey, p. 2)

Similar to the Hollywood ethos, *Teresa Venerdì* holds out the possibility of upward mobility through merit.

In classic narrative fashion, the young orphan becomes the instrument of the rake's transformation. Teresa (played by Adriana Benetti), innocent, unspoiled, altruistic, and self-sacrificing, is able to reclaim the roué doctor played by De Sica. Dr. Pietro Vignalli is a disappointment to his father. He squanders his money, plays around with women, and refuses to take his profession seriously. Again, we have a film that, in spite of its title, makes the man's transformation the central issue. He is the object of the young women's competition and the good woman wins him.

The doctor meets Teresa at the orphanage where, as a result of his father's arrangements, he has become the institution's physician. As in De Sica's other films (and in Camerini's, his mentor), there are sentimental scenes involving children. The children's obedience, gratitude, humor, and bravery are highlighted, and Teresa herself is the paragon of virtue. Of course, there is also the troublemaker who tries to create difficulties for Teresa with the doctor, but her plans fail. At first the physician balks at his responsibility for the children, but gradually Teresa's beauty and competence involve him in spite of himself, though he is pulled in several directions.

The denouement occurs when Teresa, having run away from the orphanage, comes to the doctor's house for protection. Conflicted over her presence but drawn to her, Vignalli reluctantly reports her presence to the headmistress. Teresa returns to the orphanage but Vignalli finally comes and takes her away with him. An exchange has occurred. Teresa has 'saved' him from Lolita (Anna Magnani), a chanteuse, and from financial ruin, and he in turn 'saves' her by taking her out of the orphanage and giving her a home. Significantly, her redemption of him corresponds to his father's wishes, and it was his father who found him the position in the orphanage that enabled him to meet Teresa. Thus, Pietro's acceptance of conformity is consonant with the father's expectations of the son. In a sense, too, Pietro becomes the orphan's, Teresa's, father.

The element of performance is important in this film as an index to 'proper' social roles. We learn that Teresa's parents were artists, and she herself performs for the younger children. In one scene, she recites the part of Juliet to her eager and admiring audience. Lolita, too, is a performer, and she is shown singing with a band. Lili, the spoiled young heiress whom Pietro rejects, is addicted to role-playing, though her audience is limited to her family and Pietro. In a sense, then, Pietro chooses the best performer, whose role-playing accords with socially desirable attitudes. Teresa's role, like Juliet's, is chaste, devoted, dependent, and self-sacrificing, whereas the other two women are portrayed as self-indulgent and self-aggrandizing.

In renouncing the rich heiress, Pietro chooses service over wealth and Teresa's removal of Lolita (confirmed by Pietro) seems to signify a choice of familial responsibility, of parenthood over sexuality. What does Teresa gain? She gains a home, a parent, and the opportunity to continue to nurse and parent others, especially Pietro. Like De Sica's later films, the film's rhetoric turns on sentiment developed through the images of youth and innocence, which are at first threatened but later affirmed. Sexual and class conflict are suppressed or ignored.

As in *Seconda B* [a 1934 film by Goffredo Alessandrini, a pro-fascist director], the antibourgeois element is present only to elevate the sturdier working-class values that are universalized in psychological fashion: merit, responsibility, loyalty, family integrity, and benevolent authority. In many ways, De Sica's film reproduces the Camerini formulae: wealth is corrupting; businessmen are vulgar and to be ignored; happiness is with your own kind; inflated aspirations lead to difficulties. The film's formal qualities depend on certain conventions, too, that can be found in Mario Camerini's films and in the Hollywood cinema. The film's unity is dependent on a fairly tight editing of sequences that use locale and character contrast for thematic purposes. Characters are not highly individuated. Comic elements are introduced by means of ironic contrasts and physical gesture. In all its aspects, the film seems geared to appeal to a broad audience and to reinforce familial sentiments.

...

Vittorio De Sica's *I bambini ci guardano / The Children Are Watching Us* (1942), often cited as one of the important pre-neorealist texts (Bondanella, p. 53), uses a young boy to involve the audience in the film's judgments on a moribund society. While sharing stylistic characteristics with the neorealist film, it can be understood more appropriately within the context of the other melodramas of the later years of the Ventennio. The film is drawn from a novel, *Prico*, by Cesare Giulio Viola, who worked on the film script with De Sica, Adolfo Franci, Margherita Maglione, Gherardo Gherardi, and Cesare Zavattini, one of the architects of neorealism. De Sica's *Ladri di biciclette / Bicycle Thieves* (1948) and *Sciuscià / Shoeshine* (1946) also feature young children.

The plot of *The Children Are Watching Us* is simple. A young child is the victim of marital conflict between his parents. Prico's father, a petty-bourgeois bureaucrat, is jealous of his wife. Having discovered that she is having an affair with another man, he insists that she leave the child. He takes Prico to his own mother's house but she is unable and unwilling to care for him. Prico becomes ill and the father takes him home where, after a visit from the mother, the father relents and a reconciliation is effected by the couple. At vacation time, the family goes to a seaside resort where the wife (Isa Pola) tries to enjoy herself despite the constant surveillance of her husband, who seeks to guard her from potential seducers. Prico has a semblance of family life until the time arrives for his father to return to work in the city, leaving his wife and child to remain on holiday a while longer. The mother's former lover arrives, and they resume their relationship. Prico is again neglected. He tries to run away, attempting to return home, but he has no money and is sent away by the ticket agent at the railway station. Dejected, he walks along the railroad tracks. He is almost hit by a train, frightened by a railway worker, lost on the beach, and eventually found by the police who return him to his mother.

At home again, Prico refuses to tell his father what has happened, fearing to betray his mother. After a letter from the mother, indicating that she is not planning to ever return home, the father makes arrangements to send Prico to a boarding school. The father outfits the boy, takes him to the school, and when he returns home commits suicide. The final sequences of the film involve the housekeeper's visit to the school to inform Prico of his father's death. The mother arrives too, but he ignores her, only acknowledging the housekeeper's presence.

The film is unrelenting in its movement from one disaster to the next. From the very beginning, Prico's resentment against his mother is made obvious. She takes him to the park ostensibly for him to play but she also uses this as an opportunity to meet her lover. Prico watches his mother as she greets the man, and the child sullenly refuses to have anything to do with him. His playtime is spoiled as he stands alone at a distance watching the two. Life at home is not any more satisfactory. The father, preoccupied with his obligations at work and with his dissatisfactions at home, is unable to talk to the child. The housekeeper, Agnese, is kind to the child but unable to compensate for his loneliness and sense of injury. While the women in the film are associated with experiences of violence, rejection, and abandonment, the father emerges as the nurturant figure. The film plays with the reversal of traditional male and female roles. Ultimately the father is associated with home and tending the child, in a society where such care is expected from the woman. The mother is the philanderer, the one who runs off with a lover, who is restless and unable to assume responsibility for the child.

Prico is presented as a sensitive child, forced prematurely to confront conflict. He is not shown as interested in sports but in puppet shows and magic. He lives in a world of women: Agnese (the housekeeper), his mother, his grandmother, and Paolina, but his encounters with them are disillusioning, as he is torn between anger and loyalty. He is compelled to maintain secrecy to protect his mother which creates conflict between him and his father. The father's suicide marks the complete disintegration of the family. Prico's only friend now is a priest, Father Michele, whom Prico has learned to trust. The final shots in the film show Prico walking slowly away from the women, Agnese and his mother, toward the priest standing in the doorway. In a long take, the camera films Prico as he joins the man and the scene fades.

As with *Shoeshine*, De Sica's use of the child as the film's central figure and focus is highly rhetorical. The adult world as mirrored through the child's look is harsh, alienated, and ungenerous, but the problems stem not from economic but from psychic deprivation. The critique of the family, of immediate and extended members, seems to be the film's central concern. The child, along with the audience who inhabits his perspective, becomes the judge of the domestic failure. Like other melodramas made during the war years, the film examines the disintegration of the family. The father's weakness, the mother's restlessness, the child's vulnerability call into question images of authority, respectability, loyalty, and the efficacy of hard work, and the film seems to reproach their absence.

In its evasion of overt politics, the film seems most political. Like Visconti's *Ossessione / Obsession* (1942), the politics of the time are here seen in private, not public, fashion, as if acknowledging that the reproduction of social relations takes place in the immediate arena of the neighborhood and the family. *The Children Are Watching Us* can be seen as a nostalgic text, lamenting the loss of social bonds. It can also be seen as a critical text, exposing the fundamentals of fascist ideology: heroic male sacrifice, female service and subordination, and youthful enthusiasm, by portraying the breakdown of these 'values.' The image of the child thus functions, as it does in *Shoeshine*, as a safe strategy for an innocent unmasking of political structures. The implied prescriptions – love and responsibility – are almost irrelevant to the excess of negative affect generated by the narrative.

References

Bondanella, Peter. *Italian Cinema: From Neorealism to the Present*. New York: Frederick Ungar, 1983.

Harvey, Steven. *'Teresa Venerdi.'* New York: Museum of Modern Art, 1978. Mimeographed.

On a Train to the Kingdom of Earth: Watching De Sica's Children

GEORGE TOLES

I bambini ci guardano / The Children Are Watching Us (1942) *was regarded at the time of its release as being sufficiently dangerous to Italian morale to be banned from screening outside Rome. In the October 1964 issue of* Films and Filming *Douglas McVay comments that the narrative method of* The Children Are Watching Us *resembles that of* The Fallen Idol (1948) *by Carol Reed, in that the dramatic events are observed through the 'uncomprehending eyes of the person they predominantly affect.' Indeed, notes McVay, throughout the film De Sica uses a most imaginative combination of images to stress the significance of the title. He adds: 'For once in a De Sica film there is no "moral recompense," not even the austerely implied one of a* Bicycle Thieves *or* Shoeshine' (McVay, 16). *George Toles's original essay discusses De Sica's use of cinematic space as an extension of the issue of see-ing in the film and as a particularly successful contribution to the corpus of discourses on childhood. Unlike some critics who have seen De Sica's use of childhood perspective as sentimentally exploitative of the audience, Toles argues that such a perspective is absolutely essential and correct for De Sica's aesthetic / moral vision.*

They drop bombs because they say: I am dropping a bomb; nobody would drop it if he had the patience to say: I am dropping a bomb which will fall on that square yard of that town x and will hit the home of c. and of p., of t. ... and blow three fingers off n.'s hand, shatter p.'s left breast, c.'s neck, the teeth of s. who was saying to m. that r. is etc. There is no patience.

CESARE ZAVATTINI

I

While doing research on Vittorio De Sica's film-making activities during World War II, I discovered an intriguing plot outline of his virtually forgotten film *La porta del cielo / The Gates of Heaven* (1945). The unadorned account of the narrative situation nicely frames many of the elements that give De Sica's work its distinctive form and ethical direction during his neorealist decade. A group of invalids and religious pilgrims are journeying by train to the shrine of the Blessed Virgin Mary at Loreto, on the Adriatic coast. A large number of the passengers are afflicted with some form of paralysis; the sufferers and their companions, nearly all city dwellers, come from every class and age group. Naturally, some of those making the journey lack strong religious convictions and have little hope of a cure, but for a variety of reasons they have seized the chance to escape briefly from their onerous present circumstances. The film ends at the shrine, where an impassioned ceremony invoking the Blessed Mother's healing powers is in progress. We leave the pilgrims before we have witnessed either their desperately awaited miracles or their disappointed return to outwardly unaltered lives.

Five structural and thematic features of this tantalizing, unseen film are central to my reading of De Sica's work: 1 / We are presented with an open-ended journey that is also a search. 2 / Children form a crucial segment of the company of pilgrim sufferers (a frail, paralysed boy is one of the main figures in the narrative; he is accompanied by a young girl, otherwise alone in the world, who has pledged herself to assist him). 3 / Paralysis, spiritual as well as physical, is a shared condition of those making the journey to the shrine. It is the obvious general term for what is most in need of cure. 4 / The initially expected transformation of circumstances (miraculous healing) is gradually replaced by less easily identified 'openings' for vision. The experience of waiting becomes ever more closely linked with the process of meeting and finding one's world (one's fulfillment?). 5 / The search depicted here, as in other De Sica films – whether it be for a literal miracle, an absent parent, a stolen bicycle, a lost dog, or a white horse bearing an estranged friend – eventually leads us to borders between the material and metaphysical realms, borders of 'sacred longing' where we (like De Sica's characters) are confronted with what John Stuart Mill has termed 'the permanent possibility of experience.'

The brief plot summary, coupled with the title, *The Gates of Heaven,* suggests that the viewer's destination in this narrative is the threshold or gate of potentially redemptive vision. As so often with De Sica, the means to a solution of the characters' distress is shown to be out of their hands – beyond their imaginative reach and, to a similar degree, beyond the reach of the film-maker and implied viewer. Yet we are invited nonetheless, for furtively mystical reasons, to contemplate the physical/emotional environment that the characters are left with in the 'here and now' as something more than an impasse. Love, conceived of as a surge of vision entering a human space torn open by enormous, acutely exposed need, is the integrating miracle that nearly every De Sica film of the neorealist period aspires to. The purging of despair, or what Irving Massey calls 'the potential for nothingness in the things that we look at' (Massey, 33), takes place, if at all, through an act of illumination in which objects and human souls are somehow lifted up and beheld in the light of love. The Austrian writer Hugo von Hofmannsthal describes in his celebrated 'Letter of Lord Chandos' a state in which every common experience, however worn by repetition or clouded by pain, 'rises toward me with such an abundance, such a presence of love, that my enchanted eye can find nothing in sight void of life. Everything that exists, everything I can remember, everything touched upon by my confused thoughts, has a meaning. Even my own heaviness ... seems to acquire a meaning; I experience in and around me a ... never-ending interplay, and among the objects playing against one another there is not one into which I cannot flow' (Hofmannsthal, 138).

Needless to say, a fictional effort to make 'ordinary' tragedies, full of hurt and helplessness and loss, less terrible through an inexpressible deus-ex-machina force of love is rife with danger and temptations to falsity. The vision that De Sica attempts to make real for us is not spiritually consoling in any familiar sense, nor is it politically consoling. There is no ready-made rhetoric to guide us to a correct response or to a reliable higher authority. What De Sica does repeatedly endeavour to attain (and again there are parallels with Hofmannsthal's ethic of integration) is the greatest possible degree of self-suppression, which may allow 'the real' to awaken and begin speaking in the film-maker's place. Theorists repeatedly point out, with mantra-like confidence, that any attempt to document 'reality' in film is naive and doomed to failure. And yet the distinctiveness of De Sica's 'hold' on the vibrant surfaces of *his* reality must still somehow be accounted for. De Sica and his most influential collaborator, the screenwriter Cesare Zavattini, see the road to knowledge and love leading us towards a complete identification with the world and all it contains. The unique properties of the camera as recording instrument allow maximum respect for the ever-fluctuating world-object and ceaseless opportunities to renew the act of identification. The nature of the photographic medium, as De Sica and Zavattini apprehend it, makes the desired harmony of ego and world conceivable, if not in any respect easy to accomplish.

What might De Sica regard as the ideal result, the perfect fulfillment of the camera's encounter with reality? Here is how Hofmannsthal evokes the weaving together of perceptual spirit and the forces of nature and human life in his essay 'Colours':

> I do not want to strengthen anything in myself which would isolate me from mankind. But truly in no moment am I more a human being than when I feel myself living with hundredfold strength, and this happens to me when that which has always lain mute and closed before me and is nothing but massiveness and strangeness, when this opens and, as in a wave of love, entwines me with itself. And am I not then at the inner core of things as much a human being, as much myself, as ever I could be – nameless, alone; not, however, petrified in aloneness, but as if there flowed from me in waves the strength that makes me the chosen mate of those strong, silent powers which sit around me mutely as on thrones? And is this not the spot you always reach on dark paths, when you live active and suffering among the living? Is this not the mysterious heart-kernel of personal experience, of dark deeds, dark sorrows, when you have done what you should not and yet had to do, when you had experienced what you had always divined but never believed, when everything had collapsed around you and the Frightful could nowhere be undone? Did not the embracing wave then wind itself out of the innermost centre of experience and draw you into itself ... ? Why should not silently wooing Nature, who is nothing but life lived and life that wants to be lived again, impatient of the cold glance with which you greet her, draw you into herself at rare hours and show you that she, in her depths, also has secret grottoes wherein you can be one with yourself, you who were estranged from yourself in the outer world?   (Hofmannsthal, 153–4)

The mystical fusion so strikingly envisioned here is, we are reminded, the unpredictable beneficence of 'rare hours' (or, less optimistically, rare moments) when the mood of the so often frustrated seer offers no impediment to a full encounter. In the ordinary course of things both the observing eye and the waiting world seem veiled, closed in many ways to the desired effortlessness of presence. Who knows what makes it possible for love sometimes to forge ahead and enter freely into 'the open,' a relationship with things in which no barriers assert themselves? Hofmannsthal's times of entering in come about, as a rule, in the kinds of places where the visions of nature poets typically arise – in the solitude of a forest, in the silence of a field, garden path, or high mountain, on the deck of a ship in the early morning. When he talks about obstructions to identification, he returns us to the teeming, multifarious ground of the gloomy city, where he lives (or fails to live) 'surrounded by faces ravaged by money which they owned or by money which others owned. Their houses ... their streets were for me [in a moment of disgusted recoil] the thousandfold mirrored grimace of their spookish Non-Existence' (Hofmannsthal, 145). For De Sica and Zavattini, by contrast, the experience of world identification must take place in the very midst of such a city, or nowhere. The impoverished, paralysed, and fear-burdened multitude replaces the isolated natural setting as the realm for purifying encounters. The mystery of the crowd must penetrate us as fully as the waves heaving towards one on the lonely deck of a ship. The crowd, as much as anything, is the beckoning 'whole' of our existence, rolling towards us (wave upon human wave) and 'foaming up in inexhaustible presence.' World identification must reckon with the totality of the city and never seek to exchange the city's true qualities, whether they be scatteredness, greed, starvation, or overt hostility, for ones more amenable to the progress of love. The role of imagination in De Sica's best films adheres scrupulously to Shelley's definition of the chief purpose of poetry: imagination enables us to identify with another person's suffering, without the necessity of explaining it, resolving it, or making it exemplary (Shelley, 'A Defense of Poetry,' 487–8).

In 1944 Zavattini wrote of his conviction that 'only in this moment' of the final phase of the war of liberation in Italy do people possess 'a power of sincerity that they will lose again very soon. Today a destroyed house is a destroyed house; the odour of the dead lingers; from the North we hear the echoes of the last shellings; in other words our stupor and our fear are whole' (Zavattini, 9). If cinema is to document this 'moment' of sincerity without the customary level of distortion, it must 'abandon its usual narrative methods and adapt its language' to the not yet covered-over revelations in the city streets. The camera, Zavattini believed, would have less difficulty than formerly in finding the truth of the city's life by attending patiently and with vigilant expectancy to how everything, right now, appears. The surface of life suddenly seems to go deeper, thrown open to the camera's power by the rent in the social fabric brought on by the still fresh catastrophes of the war.

Discussions of neorealism devote too little attention to this phenomenon of the ravaged city world stepping out (like a ghost of itself) from its everyday condition of deep concealment. This is what I take to be the substance of the 'sincerity' to which Zavattini alludes. In its stunned efforts to awaken to its unreckoned losses, the city surrenders all the pride and instinct for deception that might defend it from the camera's scrutiny. Something previously withheld from view now reaches out to us for a brief interval and bids us contemplate it, freely, without the usual preparatory labour required for meaningful discovery. The neorealist opportunity emerges with the realization that in the hyperexposed present of the war's end it would require more work to keep one's eyes closed than fully open. The common sights recompose themselves in the collective gaze of the populace with a painful intensity of being that seems natural. Is it not natural for Italians to greet the urban landscape as it is being given back to them, pitted with scars and burns and corpse-strewn rubble, and to see in it an extension of their own bodies and consciousness? Are not the boundaries of what might still survive for them to know and love so tenuous that they do not yet need to determine where any one person's property ends and another's begins?

Jean Vigo, the director of *L'Atalante*, once spoke with plaintive force about the near impossibility of gaining adequate knowledge of other lives: 'About a human being, however much one can love and want to understand, one must, I believe, renounce ever reaching the reality of them ... What anguish one feels in this race before a maze of mirrors, which only yield up the image of our own image, always of our own image' (Warner, 77). Although no more confident of their capacity to know others, De Sica and Zavattini turn Vigo's metaphor of the mirror into a positive potential source of contact with neighbouring destinies. Everything is everywhere, if we can be made to see it. Everything reflects us, which we remember in the act of waking up. Wherever we find our own image in the face of another, we are enlarged by the recognition and possibly less surprised and fearful to consider that our responsibility dwells here as readily as with the things that stand closest to us.

Another entry from Zavattini's war journal: 'De Sica tells me he saw a woman with a decapitated girl in her arms. What is the difference between De Sica who saw her and me who didn't? Between events known and events seen?' (Zavattini, 218). He goes on to express his distrust of seeing as an automatic form of knowing. The decapitated child, as a fragment of a scene, a glimpse of horror without sense or remedy, can do little except entangle us in nothingness. 'We tend to make everything definitive,' Zavattini observes elsewhere, 'but since nothing stops, our stopping is changed continually as it stops' (Zavattini, 227). This statement helps to clarify Zavattini and De Sica's passionate commitment to the ideal of portraying suffering and other forms of experience 'in their actual duration.' The flow of things in a time that is not sensationalized by the overemphasis and isolation of shocking particulars is a way for film to keep a sense of the whole, and a respect for the sheer quantity of significant relations that persist even at the dead centre of what is tragic. An old woman is buried under debris after the collapse of her dwelling; her children arrive, embrace one another desperately; 'they hope in desperation that something will change ... A short time after the catastrophe a door that gave on the void came open every now and then and somebody looked out.' Off to one side, to calm himself, someone eats a cake. Eating a cake 'might evade, especially in this moment, the law that all is either good or bad' (Zavattini, 215, 216). Where in all of this forward action does the tragic event, as a privileged single entity, reside? Paralysis, in all of its guises and manifestations, serves to express the naturalness, but not the necessity, of our separation (or withdrawal) from experience. Paralysis is the tempting, reasonable halting place before the unknown forces that may destroy or rekindle us. The search, as the logical opposing movement to paralysis and capitulation, somehow puts us in contact with the 'far distance' as a vital dimension of our life in the present. In De Sica's hands the search does not empty out the present in favour of some chimerical future goal, but rather enlarges the present's powers of attraction. As with the train journey in *The Gates of Heaven*, one seems so often in De Sica's world to be moving at unaccustomed speed towards the far distance, so characters can feel its influence and linkage with them long before any actual arrival.

Perhaps the images in De Sica that most fully convey to me the force of distance in its decisive relation to the near at hand occur in *Bicycle Thieves*. Ricci, having been separated from his son Bruno after a brief, fatigue-induced quarrel, hears at some remove cries that a child has drowned. As he runs towards the frantic, disjointed activity of defeated rescuers and hovering witnesses, he tries to make out whether the small body being lifted out of the water in the distance is his son. Almost at the moment that Ricci realizes, with trembling relief, that this boy's death is someone else's tragedy (and just as the need to see his own son alive and well replaces all else as a sign of highest earthly good) Bruno appears, silhouetted on a flight of steps high above him. The child, still mindful of his own hurt and isolation, cannot see that the father crying out to him from below has been shaken and transformed in the short time they have been apart. He moves somewhat tentatively towards the familiar shape summoning him by name, a presence as well known to him as any in the world, but who in the trifling space of a few moments' absence has turned mysterious. All the love and gratitude Ricci has in his possession are now spontaneously released towards his child.

The implicit question raised in this episode (raised, perhaps, just as we see the image of the boy raised at the top of those actual steps, against the sky) is how long the recovered son can be a sufficient good in itself to alter the reality represented by the still-lost bicycle. Behind the boy, in other words, if one must look past him, is a vanishing point where the struggling worker's entire means of livelihood is still gone, still hopelessly hidden. If Ricci chooses, the boy himself can be re-imagined instantly as a bearer of luck in an otherwise frightening world of pure contingency: *'Because my boy has come back to me, other valuable things may come back through him. He may be showing me, through his safe return, that I have as much right as anyone to find what has been unjustly taken away. This moment's reunion is a preparatory experience for the full joy of going home with my child and bicycle.'* Where one opening is revealed to the seeker, others may naturally follow. But the idea of searching in De Sica is always complicated by the suggestion that the numerous acts of incidental recovery along the way are the true sum of what will be shown to us. Only this much; is it enough? In Loren Eiseley's suggestive phrase, by way of answer: 'Anywhere along the way it could have been different' (Carrithers, 81). We need to make our reckoning of gain from 'returns' as ill-sorted and unfitted to our pressing concerns as the oddments that the distant sea continually washes up on the shore. The water, like every other carrier of experience, seems either to live or to die at our feet with its enigmatic postings from far away.

Another episode from De Sica, nearly as resonant as that from *Bicycle Thieves* in its manner of investing remote things with kinship and of unsealing a possible avenue to love, occurs late in *Umberto D*. The old man Umberto is taking an early-morning streetcar ride as he prepares himself for suicide. On the almost empty vehicle he is abstractedly in the company of the beloved dog he must still find an adequate home for and one other man, a stranger, whose age, solitude, and air of bereftness are a mirror of his own. Umberto is barely cognizant of either mute, adjoining presence as the streetcar pulls away from the building where he has lived for so many years. In some strange way the viewer feels compelled to fasten onto these overlooked companions in misfortune and make something of them, as the strongest immediate evidence of what mere existing consists of. Perhaps it strikes us as a limitation of Umberto here that he cannot see himself in the man beside him, or offer him the slightest passing acknowledgment. As has often been the case, Umberto is so taken up with the immensity of his own privation that he evades contact with any being, other than his dog, which he cannot appeal to for assistance. The film grants us no explanation of the forces that have shaped him, of how he has come to be harsh and self-enclosed, though he does not seem markedly less responsive than the ordinary others in his environment. Nor does De Sica encourage us to imagine that a more yielding and compassionate disposition would provide a remedy for his terrible (and common) plight.

What we are shown, unexpectedly, is a window: as Umberto stares blankly out his own streetcar window at the passing forms of the apartment buildings on the street where he has lived, we notice that high above him Maria, a servant girl in his lodging house, has lingered to watch his departure from an open window. She appears very briefly (the streetcar is in motion and soon leaves her image behind) but the mere fact of her watching is quietly arresting. Her persisting presence somehow intimates the elusive ways that we are connected to the world, in spite of the countless times and places where the world seems to refuse us. De Sica has the good sense to treat this detail as if it were minor; we cannot be sure what value, if any, Umberto assigns to it, or how the act of attending to it might lessen his resolve to end his life. But there is something about this image, like so many ephemeral 'noticings' in De Sica scenes, that enjoins the viewer to remain in it, and to inquire into its seemingly disproportionate capacity to make a difference.

I am reminded of a streetcar ride in Jiri Weil's novel *Life with a Star* in which the narrator, Josef, a Jewish ex-bank clerk in Prague during the

Nazi occupation, is travelling with a group of fellow-Jews (all of them strangers to him) after a lengthy interrogation by Nazi-appointed officials. They are still, nominally, free to go back to their homes. The narrator observes as he listens to snatches of the passengers' conversation that 'everyone seemed to be learning something or wanted to learn something. They were excited, as though their lives depended on learning something. I felt left out because I wasn't learning anything and didn't want to learn anything' (Weil, 23). This repudiation unconsciously brings him closer to the psychology of those in charge of arranging the Jews' transport to the camps, for whom 'it was imperative to forget everything quickly and never see anything' (Weil, 114). The dog at Umberto's feet, the old man at his side, and, most expressively, the young woman watching from the distant window are all silent and separate, yet the film threads them together, nearest point connected to the farthest, as though they were part of one injunction: to draw the things you might experience around you, like a coat against the wind, and seek, if possible, to learn something from the mere readiness to experience. Umberto, who has much cause not to wish to take in anything, appears, like Josef in *Life with a Star*, to be left out by his decision to repudiate the flow of meaning. He absents himself from conversation with the particulars of his own existence. In facing facts he believes he has come to the end of learning, so he turns his face away from possibilities.

Zavattini records the following experience in his war journal:

> I met a friend in Via Bertoloni, ciao, ciao. He interrupted me; I was counting the paces that separate my house from Piazza Verdi, probable target of airplanes. They miss by no more than five hundred yards, no more, I thought: a thousand and one, a thousand and two, a thousand and three, as the number of paces increased my family became safe and therefore I was scattering dead bodies for a radius of three or four hundred yards.   (Zavattini, 218)

Zavattini carefully measures out, in even steps, the distance separating probable life and safety from death. In imagination he purchases a reprieve for his loved ones, on the tangible edge of projected calamity. But his imagination also pays the price of identification with the faceless pilot-executioner. In the process of counting out his family's precise degree of removal from peril, he seems in his own mind to be sowing the intervening ground with corpses. Part of him glories in such necessary fantasy stratagems for outwitting disaster. He delights in securing a modest space for likely survival (where every detail that persists, even a damp circle on a bedroom ceiling, can be loved because it is clearly his – saved, as it were, for him). Another part of Zavattini abhors the idea of distance as disconnection from other lives, as though it were all moral crimes in embryo. Notice how even in this short anecdote we begin with an interruption of self-absorption by a chance encounter with a friend. As one attempts in isolation to chart a protective distance within from a real distance outside, a figure who is known felicitously emerges. He recognizes and approaches, bringing news from another quarter, or perhaps simply the same story he always tells. There are always interruptions, thank goodness, Zavattini means to remind us. Yet he also knows that we must persist in the essential inward labour of fortifying ourselves against interruptions (the wrong kind), of building something apart from others that is strong and large and inviolate. It is a matter of survival, what we posit against the awareness of 'how accidental we all are.' This withheld force is anything we dare not entrust to the world's keeping, for fear that we will be placed too much at its mercy. Call it, in the broadest sense, our right to say *no*. It is what we hold in private, ironically, that enables us to face the world lovingly, that gives us quick, attentive eyes and the urge to seek unity of ego, expression, and world object. It is only from the ongoing tension between one's self and the world that perceptual strength springs. This tension is 'the very structure of our conscious life and the source of all articulated orderliness' (Bennett, 118).

The often demoralized and debilitated figures we encounter in De Sica's films, I suggest, are shown to be suffering from a bewitchment of vision (perhaps identical with our own). It is the nature of this bewitchment that the eyes find it easier to turn away from possible experience than towards it, and to approach life situations chiefly in terms of what is missing from them, what they do not yet contain. To look past the immediate particulars is, of course, the essence of imaginative freedom, as well as the beginning of every attempt at social reform. But the danger always bordering on this freedom is the loss of relation with what is already at hand, always in some simple, baffling sense already ours to claim if we could but know it. Is it possible (and revivifying) for our vision to go, in effect, on holiday from the pain and misfortune in our lives? Or is vision as bound to the facts of distress as our knowledge is to mood? According to William James, 'having reached the limit of its possible competence,' knowledge goes on holiday, and there philosophy (for the pragmatist) begins. James is concerned to find in every supposition and belief 'what works best in the way of leading us, what fits every part of life best.' And where the absence of certain knowledge seems a barrier to belief, we need not look to knowledge to set our limits. (For the linking of James's *Pragmatism* with Wittgenstein's idea of language 'going on holiday' see Danto, 12.)

The recurring questions implicit in De Sica's early films seem to be these: What is it in a given predicament that prevents the world from remaining fully present and connected to those who are involved in it? How does privation keep one not merely hungry or cold or alone but also unseeing? And if feeling-filled sight is restored by some propitious act or by the pressure of circumstances (let us say in the absence of other, more urgently sought relief), what is it that has been gained? The nature of these questions, and the aptness of the term 'bewitchment' to characterize the malady of eye and spirit awaiting cure, leads me to describe De Sica's neorealist films as fairy tales, in the highest, most dignified sense of that frequently belittled form of expression. It is the utopian drive towards spiritual transformation and the redemption of mislaid vital attributes of the human that I see De Sica suggestively sharing with Nathaniel Hawthorne, Gottfried Keller, Oscar Wilde, Goethe, Theodor Storm, and Hofmannsthal in their socially pointed, often tragic, tales of enchantment. For all of Zavattini's repeatedly expressed scorn for movie artifice and story, I find a gravitational pull in his scripts for De Sica towards moments of veil parting: a sudden recovery of lost time or world image; a soul reabsorbed by love into the force field of magically amplified, present being.

Though only one of the De Sica–Zavattini collaborations, *Miracle in Milan,* contains a prominent magical or supernatural dimension, there is almost always a passage or interlude in the other films that conveys a deep affinity with fairy-tale procedure: think of the fortune teller in *Bicycle Thieves* and the white horse in *Shoeshine.* Moreover, the whole problem of vision in a De Sica film returns us again and again to the mysteries of childhood. The search De Sica typically dramatizes invokes the child's salutary defencelessness before unaccustomed, nameless sensations and longings and also the child's admirable openness of gaze. It might almost be said that the children in De Sica films are called forth to repair and balance that other, reverse image of the murdered child, which Irving Massey has termed 'the key to the Holocaust' (Massey, 84).

II The Children Are Watching Us

At noon I was in Largo Argentina, in front of walls covered with drawings by children of the village of Nasino ... who paint suns, not the way Rouault sometimes does to create a luminous nail on which to hang a heavy picture, but whirling or dripping suns over the good and wicked (this phrase recurs often in the simple explanations the schoolchildren give their work on the back of the drawing). Once again I feel the desire to make a film in which the oldest character is seven ...

CESARE ZAVATTINI

We are once again on a train track, this time with a runaway five-year-old boy named Prico in De Sica's 1942 film *I bambini ci guardano / The Children Are Watching Us*. Prico is on his way to Rome to find his father, after coming upon his mother in the arms of her lover (the fearsome, inescapable 'enemy,' Roberto) during a vacation at a beach resort. Having been thwarted in his efforts to purchase a train ticket, Prico asks an elderly woman outside the station to point him in the direction of Rome, and with no more knowledge at his disposal than that the tracks will eventually arrive there, he compulsively sets out on the long journey 'home.'

Earlier in the film we saw Prico and his father as passengers inside a train compartment, bound for the same destination. Prico was ill with a fever throughout the first trip and had slipped into delirium while gazing at his reflection in the train window. The window was then transformed into an expressionist mind-space on which a nightmare barrage of feverish dream images was projected. This array of terrors culminated with Prico's mother's image darkening and dissolving into a landscape, abandoning the child in an all-encompassing departure for the inseparable mysteries of eroticism and death. When finally awakened from his traumatic dreams, Prico found himself in his familiar bed at home, with his mother once again present and gazing at him in a 'language' he recognized. Her look and manner conveyed her best intentions to take care of him and stay close. The mere fact of being returned to his room on that prior occasion had been enough to bring his world back to order. Now the child, back on the train tracks, is trying to regain that remembered place of 'getting well.'

What is the primary emotional colour of Prico's flight? Does the sight of the boy stumbling up the rock bed beside the rails to the smooth, clear path of the wooden ties stretching to the horizon yield more grief or astonishment at the size of the task this tiny figure has taken on? We feel no guarantee of safety in Prico's setting out, no magical dispensation from lasting harm of the sort that surrounds every young child's adventures in the very different country ruled by Disney. In fact, when a train blindly bears down at great speed towards the place where the boy is walking, and he does not immediately react to the danger, we believe equally that he could perish (summarily obliterated from his own narrative) or leap just in time into the clear. Even without the train tracks, the composition of the shots documenting his journey is reminiscent of Buster Keaton. A vast, impersonal environment fans out into the distance, and a single, small figure balances all the things that threaten him with his isolated attentiveness and bare will to proceed. In this unpopulated context the child does not, any more than Keaton, appear in the guise of a social being. Rilke has characterized this shedding of ordinary relations as one in which the human form is 'placed amongst things like a thing, infinitely alone, and ... all which is common to them both has withdrawn from things [and child] into the common depth' (Rilke, *Selected Prose*, 5).

Prico is restored to self-consciousness after he is almost killed by the train. A railway worker suddenly appears, yelling at him for being where he was not supposed to be (in danger of death), then, as a delayed second thought, inquires with genuine concern whether he has been hurt. It is perhaps the sole instance in the film where an adult assumes that Prico is capable of considering a specific injury he has received and reporting accurately on how it affects him. He has fallen and scraped himself as he ran from the train track (from which he has just been banished) back to the beach, a setting strongly associated in his mind with both his lost mother and her betrayal of the family with her lover. Prico comes to a halt and takes a momentary inventory of the damage to his clothes and general appearance, as if that might furnish him with clues about what his present feelings are. His short pants are dirty and he also discovers a tear in them, which he probes tentatively and with mounting visible agitation. The tear carries with it, by habit, the anticipated reprimand for carelessness, but now the additional possibility that there will be no one ever to provide the scolding. The tear swiftly acquires a potential dimension of permanence, something not to be fixed or put aside for a garment that is whole and washed. The rip that the child fingers extends to his days, his entire future, which he can actually feel as something ragged, dirty, and beyond notice. De Sica cuts from this pondering of tatters to the seashore at night, glittering under a moon rendered maternal in its fugitive, beautiful pouring out of reflected light. Prico encounters another version of his torn clothes in a hanging fishing net, and through its coarse threads and holes he observes the approach of a drunken elderly sailor. Another flight ensues. This time it appears as though the boy is pursued, as in his fever-dream, by bodies that have turned into shadows.

De Sica recalls the limitless expanse of the train tracks and the moon-lit beach at the end of the film in the mammoth interior space of the Jesuit boarding school, an environment that could equally well be the hollow marble heart of a Borgia palace. In the magnificent final scene, which contains one of the most complex series of revelations in any De Sica narrative, we are suspended not once, but twice, in the imposing vastness of the Jesuit academy's high-ceilinged reception hall. Prico slowly moves first into the hall (towards the camera) and then, after a brief interval that is dramatically unresolved, turns around and walks with equally measured gravity back to the door through which he first entered. (The camera's perspective is the same for both shots, repeating a set-up established in a previous scene when Prico watches his father travel the same course after he delivers his son to the Jesuits' care.) The reception hall functions most obviously as the architectural expression of the father's final parting from his son: the outward shape of abandonment. It is also the swelling-to-infinity experience of emptiness in the wake of the father's actual death. (He commits suicide not long after saying goodbye to his son.) Prico's return to this cold chamber occurs immediately after he has been told by one of the priests that his father has died. When we see Prico's slight form enter through a doorway in the remote depth of the frame and hesitantly make his way towards us, it seems as though each step that he takes is sharpening his realization of what his freshly absorbed loss encompasses. There is so much vacant space for him to traverse before his face is brought into focus that we have time to recall how his whole manner echoes (and continues) his previous journey on the train tracks. He appears utterly exposed and unaided.

Waiting for him at the other end of the room (in effect, by the viewer's side) are Prico's mother, Nina, the elderly family domestic, Agnese, and the priest in charge of the boarding school. In a film marked by a succession of closed doors imperfectly functioning to keep adult activity out of the child's view and hearing, and by an equal number of waiting areas where Prico is left to distract himself while his parents contend with difficulties they cannot help regarding as more urgent than his own, we are finally brought to a room where it seems that everything lies open to Prico. It is as if the boy's world has momentarily grown too weak and forgetful to shield itself from his painfully lucid inspection. Nina offers no protest when he refuses to embrace her and turns instead, briefly, to the less complicated solace offered by Agnese. Prico is also able to ignore the priest's demand that he observe the etiquette of family tragedy by going to his mother and allowing her the right to grieve with him. His face, when we finally see it, contains as much pure sorrow as it could visibly hold, and yet there is no destination for it, no place where it can meet with some relief, at least a partial disburdening. The most surprising feature of his encounter with the group is its brevity and inconclusiveness, given the length and held-breath quality of our wait for his arrival.

There is, of course, nothing ambiguous or muted about his refusal to accept any comfort from his mother, or about the lacerating reproach in his single, sustained look at her. One is strongly tempted to infer that his capacity for trust has been permanently blighted, and that even at the basic level of his ongoing need for maternal love (however imperfect), something irrevocable has occurred. There is, however, ambiguity in the mother's response to his rejection. On the one hand, she appears to revert to a familiar form of paralysis that both she and her husband have repeatedly manifested in the face of sudden, large demands and tormenting choices. On the other hand, her physical stillness and silence in response to her child's decision, however much they owe to guilt, nevertheless grant her son the right to his rage and his present disowning of their connection. There is a kind of bravery in her willingness to leave the child alone in this excruciating ordeal, to assert no claims on his attention (even though the priest encourages them). I credit her with an awareness that nothing in the immediate situation allows for either pleas for forgiveness or a self-serving explanation of her feelings. To impose herself in any way, even by unobtrusive efforts to move closer to him, would confirm our perhaps too facile judgment that she does not know him, that he is not merely estranged from her but, in some ultimate sense, a stranger as well. Instead I think De Sica wishes to emphasize her understanding that a five-year-old can declare himself a separate entity and be believed; he may already be as aware of what separateness means as she is, how it punishes and lies in wait in everything. Prico's face displays to her (and the viewer) a mourning in which, for now, there is no room for her, or for anything she may eventually, with his forbearance, find a means to give.

If Prico were older, let's say closer to the age of Chaplin's tramp, it would be far simpler for us to draw sustenance from his taking on a solitude that is, after all, our common legacy. We might then invoke Rilke's bracing injunction in *Letters to a Young Poet*: 'how much better it is to recognize that we are alone; yes, even to begin from this realization. It will, of course, make us dizzy; for all points that our eyes used to rest on are taken away from us, there is no longer anything near us, and everything far away is infinitely far' (Rilke, *Letters*, 87). The quotation perfectly captures a sense of how the expressionist environment works in De Sica's final shot. The unequalled insecurity of the child's abject departure is conveyed by the interior architecture's chill breath of worldlessness, a world taken away and placed at such a remote distance from the child that he is presently lost to the very possibility of its beckoning existence. But who would be so rash to presume that Prico, in losing his child's world, based on a faith in being with others and a dependency on these others that is both natural and good, is preparing to enter a better world by becoming a heroic solitary of the Rilkean sort, one who accepts everything that comes to him, as a confirmation of aloneness?

In 1957 Zavattini recorded some notes for a film scenario about the Chaplin tramp taking refuge on a mountain, where he lives for decades without encountering a single human being. Having become an old man who has grown afraid of people, he is at last drawn out of hiding by the 'heart-rending appeals' of a young girl. He reluctantly makes himself known to her but 'does not say a word because he has lost the habit of speech.' He begins a journey back to the city with her: 'little by little life comes toward him with its noise and all the rest.' Before very long, outfitted in a new overcoat and derby and holding the carefree cane of the adventurer, he remembers how to live in the streets: 'how he enjoys every little thing, how he savours the pleasure of greeting others and being greeted, of being in the crowd, of looking in shop windows, reading poetry. To recover lost time, greedy for everything, he takes part in everything; he runs from a funeral to a wedding, to a baptism, nothing is alien to him ... coming upon him, few ask who he is because he is so natural and his companionship seems so spontaneous.' The fable breaks off after the tramp, having regained his acceptance of the endlessly surprising world and his old, peripheral place in it, discovers that war once more has broken out. The 'invisible threads' by which he 'seemed bound to everyone else' seem to dissolve. He is alone in a different way (Zavattini, 115–16).

In Zavattini's lovely myth of Chaplin as the universal, resilient 'child' we have a picture of Prico's own continually disclosed adaptive skill, freshness of response, and eagerness to take part. How impressively he manages to right himself throughout *The Children Are Watching Us* whenever the state of emergency abates. Living so close to a foundering marriage whose daily tensions and upheavals profoundly threaten his stability, he can still find opportunities everywhere for brief truancies from agitation. He finds abundant rewards for his inquisitiveness and tiny free spaces in the general atmosphere of neglect and unhappiness where 'marvels' readily reveal themselves to him. One image that will stand for many is Prico's transfixed state in the presence of a magician at the beach resort who is drawing the usual assortment of birds and swirling fabrics from empty hats. The magician openly expresses annoyance at the boy standing so near to him, as though Prico's rapt concentration poses a close-range threat to illusion. An interesting tension is established between the man who works spells by rote, as if he were a carpenter hammering nails, and a child who has the audacity to remove all distance between himself and the healing powers of belief. The magician has oddly forgotten that wholehearted credulity is not an obstacle to his performance but its only justification. No one else in his audience is able to muster anything like full attentiveness. Behind Prico's back, as it were, a widening net of betrayal, seduction, and subterfuge of a drably routine sort spreads itself among the adult audience. In which direction is there more for the boy to learn? Is Prico less completely a part of his situation than those grounded in the reality behind him, who feel freer to flash their raw desire when Prico is not watching?

When a child is watching in what is considered to be the spirit natural to childhood (broadly speaking, whatever is meant by the term innocence), he or she is a kind of ideal mirror for a person or event's best intentions. I am reminded of Prico standing next to his father, Andrea, in a tailor shop late in the film, wearing the pinned together scraps of a military coat (still missing an arm) and gazing into a looking glass with him. Prico has told the tailor that he dislikes the cap that tops off his uniform. He is no doubt anxious at the thought of the school to which his finished costume will consign him. When Prico's father replaces the tailor at Prico's eye level in the mirror frame, going down on his knees to do so, he personalizes the cap by setting it on his own head: 'I used to wear a cap like that.' We see the boy immediately soften as he takes in his father's warmly reminiscent attitude. The father not only smiles but chuckles as he looks at himself in the cap, one of his rare concessions to openly shared satisfaction in his son's company: 'I was so happy ... Come, wear it.' The child's face is radiant with pleasure and expectancy as he transfers the now treasured object back to his own head. The cap becomes, on the instant, a charm strong enough to instil happiness in his profoundly melancholy, hard-to-reach parent. Prico's receiving the cap's meaning as it is reflected in Andrea's face, without the slightest intrusion of scepticism, is one of the most perfect renderings on film of a child's original openness to the world, that blessed, unforced fit between vision and the unspoiled offerings rising out of experience. Father, cap, and the intimation of lasting well-being are absorbed in one breath.

Included in the same scene is a shot of a child mannequin resembling Prico, neatly outfitted in a uniform like his, a tailor's forecast of the perfectly correct finished product. Andrea, in the irrationality of his own misery, is trying to build a secure, unchanging image of the son whom he will soon leave behind. If the boy acquiesces in his regimental makeover, he might learn to hold himself together like his contented frozen replica, in a void of steadfast forgetfulness. The father will enter the stasis of suicide; the child will be left in a stasis of priestly care, where he will get a new set of rules that will somehow manage his future and bring him repose (as though that were the only surviving goal for either of them).

Images of mannequins in black-and-white films nearly always seem to be a self-conscious admission of the deception and limitation inherent in film's attempts to lay hold of reality. Mannequins evoke the dead time of the single frame, where the trick of living motion is subtracted. They can remind us that the film-maker's commitment to process is equally a desire to make things appear this way and no other, once and for all. Images embalm actions in the course of attending, seemingly, to their free unfolding. Black-and-white film, more readily than colour, attunes us to this deathly undersong, in part because monochrome film sees things we do not see in a manner decisively at odds with ordinary perception. In Paul Coates's interesting formulation, black-and-white film 'insists on the existence of a phantom presence within reality, a world we cannot perceive' (Coates, 49). How effortlessly the well-designed mannequin stands up to the camera's scrutiny, as though it were the ideal film subject, and how smoothly it harmonizes with everything in the black-and-white world that is allied, to the slightest degree, with immobility. It is as if the space of film were suddenly able to confront, in the mannequin's gaze, the spectre of its own emptiness, which its noisy, borrowed life usually submerges. The mannequin is the unmasked death element in the black-and-white film's lordly conjuring of the appearances of life.

Prico's duplication in a resplendent, plastic alter ego hints, of course, at the child's fast-approaching enclosure in the static remoteness of absolute mourning. But I think it is also De Sica's declaration that he has authored the ending, in its potentially ostentatious, even heartless bleakness, and is as responsible as either of Prico's parents for the child's final placement in a space that reflects nothing back to him but loss. Who, after all, has set in motion the wholesale obliteration of an imaginative child's escape routes (the apparent sealing up of his responsive, mobile, capacious gaze)? If Prico, that quietest of boys, is unaccompanied in the last shot during his long walk towards a distant dark door, it is De Sica who has willed everything ('for the time being' of the ending) out of his reach. How would he have us respond to so much concerted erasure of elements that urge a possible sense of continuation?

I will return shortly to the details of the conclusion in order to demonstrate their congruence with what I take to be De Sica's ethics of integral presentness. The first precept of this ethics involves, in Roland Barthes's phrase about Antonioni, 'always leaving the path to meaning open' (Perez, 55). De Sica's images, at their representative best, stress what is emergent and thus undecided in a situation rather than what hastens us towards the desirable definite. An especially pertinent example from *The Children Are Watching Us*, which influences my reading of the ending, sets us once more by an open window, just after Andrea has realized that his wife has left him for the second time. Their marriage has run out of chances to be saved. In preparation for his wife's homecoming Andrea had purchased curtains for the window, which he knows she has wanted. He has just finished hanging them (a carefully planned surprise) before getting a surprise of his own: she will not be coming back. In a point-of-view shot belonging to Andrea we are shown the window containing the curtains. Interestingly, the buildings visible outside the window, warmed in the gentle city light of early evening, are more prominent in the shot than the curtains. We need to make a slight effort to recall the curtains and what they meant to Andrea (since a bit of time has elapsed in the scene after his work with them) in order to find them in the shot and identify them as the actual thought motivating Andrea's look. Our own inclina-

tion may be to savour the inviting reminder of a world still there
outside this problem, awaiting Andrea's willingness to recollect it as
well, rather than to share his concern with the wasted gesture of his
intended gift. His wife will never see the curtains; he in turn will never
regain the state of mind he so easily occupied when putting them up.
Customarily with point-of-view shots the viewer is directed to take on
the attitude or mood of the person looking. But De Sica, whenever possible, extends a choice. If your eye rests here, it will find an object that
proclaims futility, ignominious defeat, the ironic end of one set of
hopes. If the eye ventures further, over there, or forgets that the curtains are for Andrea the only point of looking, one will see a field of
action whose unknown solicitations are at the very least not identical
with the moment's searing pain.

The sheer duration of Prico's walking in the final shot: is this not De
Sica's nearest approach in the film to the heart of an as yet uncodified
neorealist aesthetic? That which cracks open the death-in-life mannequin (one symbolically complete version of Prico's ending) is the stub-
born persistence of the camera's interest in the fact of the boy's
walking, first, all the way forward, and then, all the way back. De Sica
intuits that a return over the same ground will not merely repeat a
meaning but rather, in a manner that resists paraphrase and complete
directorial control, will extend it. There is, to be sure, the coercively
expressionist architecture linked with dim, grandiose mausoleums
from which God and the warming traces of human fellowship have
alike been drained. In one respect, a child walking into such a 'prepared,' univocal setting is like a noun receiving the weight of a single,
heavy adjective (say, 'crushed'). But duration, for those of us who do
not need to rest our gaze, paralysed like Andrea's on the 'full stop' of
the window curtains, restores a hunger for details even in the face of
resolutely frozen situations. That barely discernible priest, for example, who appears at the door in the far distance, waiting for Prico: is he
to be understood as another figure cut from the same cloth as the cumbersome church official we have already met, someone almost unap-
proachable, thick with mechanical assurances and received ideas? Or
should we credit the official's words when he tells Prico's mother that
the boy 'loves Father Michel,' this otherwise purely mysterious presence in the background? It is he, we recall, who had been entrusted
with the delicate, wholly unwelcome task of informing Prico of his
father's death. As the shot continues, we may attach some modest
hope to the reappearance of this stranger who will accompany Prico

through the door once he has proven strong enough, in his own small selfhood, to arrive there. And, as I earlier suggested, from the other side of the room (where the mother, Nina, stands offscreen, watching her son choose to 'enact' his felt distance from her) I feel that a power approximating love is at work, keeping her from moving forward to thwart his will and impose herself, not for his sake but for her own. There is no way for her flawed but by no means valueless love to reach him, at present. But given the significant reality of the allowed open space behind him, she may, if she is fortunate, eventually succeed in narrowing the gap. She may in time partially repair the injury her weakness and her husband's have caused. My point then about the empty space revealed in Prico's wake as he walks away from us is that it is not, in spiritual or human terms, purely empty. Any more than the space that Zavattini counted off between likely bomb sites and his family's safety were empty of imaginatively authorized corpses.

Almost exactly contemporaneous with the birth of neorealism in the bombed cities and impoverished countryside of Italy, the style of *film noir* was devised to express an almost entirely antithetical response to urban malaise in the United States. *Film noir* is all about isolated egos falling out of a clearly lit picture in which traditional social values are seen as reasonably well aligned with individual needs and aspirations. The darkness and thrill of *film noir* come from a glamorous desertion of social accountability; the shadows bespeak a potent alternative landscape of the 'moral occult' in which normal routes to judgment or self-knowledge are of no use (Brook, 5). Neorealism, conversely, is about the peeling back of shadow, as in the aftermath of a detonation or a spray of random gunfire, when those who survive emerge from their places of hiding and take stock. Exactly who and what remains to us?

Elizabeth Bishop once created a lovely concord out of brute, meaningless succession with two plain pronouncements: 'The world is a mist. And then the world is / minute and vast and clear' (Bishop, 153). The proliferating horrors of senseless carnage and the stealthy, shameful compromises of the Occupation comprise Bishop's world as obscuring mist. Neorealism, the what-comes-after phase, strives to earn the right to a post-fascist vision by being 'minute and vast and clear' in its rendering of the harsh miracle of survival. Out of this jumble of inexplicably spared citizens, dwelling places, and landmarks, we must do our best to discover continuities, revived purpose, some basis for praising the literal, common stuff of dailiness that is not beholden to fascist rhetoric. The beguilingly shrouded city stage sets of *film noir* provide a fascinating visual-metaphysical tension with the Italian streets dreaming of a downpour of clarifying light. 'Only those who will be really different will survive,' Zavattini rather hopefully writes in his war journal, 'so one death or the other has to take place' (218). And in a memorable rough draft of the theology of 'open endings' as he and De Sica will pursue them, Zavattini conceives a nature of God that accords with the full weight of war disasters: 'God cannot have created anything of which he has to expect the outcome' (221).

At what point in *The Children Are Watching Us* does the plight of the individual child, Prico, seem to join up with the multitude of others alluded to in De Sica's haunting title? (The 1928 novel from which the film was adapted is merely called *Prico*.) The 'children' are unavoidably associated, given the date of the film's release (1942), with the young population formed within the environment of war. The war is never mentioned in the narrative, as though that reality were of a different time and place and character, unrelated to the conditions of this private family tragedy. But I would argue that there is a space reserved for the war in the immense, desolate interior which Prico passes through at the end of the film. His spiritually orphaned state summons up a ghostly company of others wandering aimlessly through city streets, peering out from the smeared windows of buildings and waste spaces where they forage for any kind of nourishment. The door towards which Prico moves, with the eerie dignity of one carrying the fragile remains of all childhood in his own person, opens out on a future larger than his, yet of course every bit as uncertain. It is important to know, in Ethan Canin's words, that 'there [are] as many worlds of anguish as there [are] doors' (151). Perhaps the clamour of child inmates in the prison-yard of *Shoeshine* is already faintly audible behind the door that belongs to Prico.

De Sica's customary tactic, in closing his later neorealist films, is visually to disperse the problems of the main characters' stories into the collective life of a crowd. One implicit question is always being posed: why should one arbitrarily chosen individual's experiences be privileged to rise above others and become more worthy of our attention? Visibility, in a higher, more consequential sense than we normally experience, is the goal in De Sica's films, but the limited narrative time for making things visible is always time besieged by what is excluded or neglected. De Sica's camera seems under a steady pressure to shift or extend focus, to secure more room, more light for observation on either side of an always too narrow aperture. The chosen centre of narrative vision dissolves into this wider field at the end of De Sica's best-known films, almost as an act of ritual sacrifice. The beloved particular, however much sympathetic awareness it generates, is never enough to carry us home. 'Home' is our world at floodtide, a selfless, *deluge* totality.

In *Children*, by contrast, the retention of the singular fate of Prico as final focus feels like an attempt to personify the essence of the periphery, the unnoticed casualty wandering at large, in its mute, intractable thereness. The title of the film reminds us that we live surrounded by the appraising witness of somehow overlooked beings, more often than not assigned to the vague outskirts of conflicts that adults (or anyone wielding power) regard as their private property. Again and again throughout this narrative the camera draws back to reveal the child's presence as the forgotten or lost component of a situation, which, when located, drastically alters our sense of its emotional boundaries. We are shown how experiential meaning is always a radius of possible influences, involving everyone who partakes of an event or its aftershocks, even when the sole connection is a weak thread of distracted or bewildered looking. And by what dreadful paradox does it happen that those least responsible for a terrible predicament, and perhaps least comprehending of its facts (the parts of the drama, in other words, that can be left out of our description of the main action), are elevated to first place in the order of suffering? Indeed, the thing left for them, as if it were their natural portion when the dinner plate was passed, is suffering, pure and simple. The resourceful or agreeably stoic adult embroiled in misery might find solace in the truth of discontinuity, when a brief respite arrives, like a character in Dostoevsky: 'It's funny, isn't it, Karamazov, all this grief and pancakes afterwards ... ? ' (Hass, 47). But can the child victim be ministered to by the reliable presence of irony in every serving of sadness? Where does the innocent go in the wake of violence that so often marks the final phase of wonder, when he intuits just how much can be taken away in life for good? Where does the innocent go, in the act of 'displacing the air of childhood'? Into the inconceivable spaces where his unlived life awaits, an existence possibly stripped now of marvels and the spontaneous spirit to embrace them. (Of course, it is the common lot to experience such losses.) What shape of love, De Sica's camera inquires with characteristic patience, might it take to bring the child Prico back from so formidable a space of absence, once so many bombs have dropped? As we wait for the child to leave our sight, it is our challenge to inhabit our own gaze more deeply, as if that were the child's best hope of recovering a fit world (De Sica's world) beyond his door.

References

Bennett, Benjamin. *Hugo von Hofmannsthal: The Theatres of Consciousness.* Cambridge: Cambridge University Press, 1988.

Bishop, Elizabeth. 'Sandpiper.' In *The Complete Poems.* New York: Farrar, Straus and Giroux, 1970.

Brook, Peter. *The Melodramatic Imagination.* New Haven, Conn.: Yale University Press, 1976.

Canin, Ethan. *The Palace Thief.* New York: Random House, 1994.

Carrithers, Gale. 'Loren Eiseley and the Self as Search.' *Arizona Quarterly* 50:1 (Spring 1994), 75–85.

Coates, Paul. *The Story of the Lost Reflection.* London: Verso, 1985.

Danto, Arthur. *Connections to the World.* New York: Harper & Row, 1990.

Hass, Robert. *Praise.* New York: Ecco, 1979.

Hofmannsthal, Hugo von. *Selected Prose.* Translated by Mary Hottinger, Tania Stern, and James Stern. Bollingen Series 33. New York: Pantheon, 1952.

Massey, Irving. *Find You the Virtue: Ethics, Image, and Desire in Literature.* Fairfax, Va: George Mason University Press, 1987.

McVay, Douglas. 'Poet of Poverty: Part I, the Great Years.' *Films and Filming* 11:1 (October 1964), 12–16.

Perez, Gilberto. 'A Man Pointing: Antonioni and the Film Image.' *The Yale Review* 82:3 (July 1994), 38–65.

Rilke, Rainer Maria. *Letters to a Young Poet.* Translated by Stephen Mitchell. New York: Vintage, 1986.

– *Where Silence Reigns: Selected Prose.* Translated by G. Craig Huston. New York: New Directions, 1978.

Shelley, Percy Bysshe. 'A Defense of Poetry.' In *Shelley's Poetry and Prose.* Selected and edited by Donald H. Reiman and Sharon B. Powers. New York: Norton, 1977. 'The great secret of morals is Love; or a going out of our own nature, and an identification of ourselves with the beautiful which exists in thought, action, or person, not our own. A man, to be greatly good, must imagine intensely and comprehensively; he must put himself in the place of another and of many others; the pains and pleasures of his species must become his own. The great instrument of moral good is the imagination; and poetry administers to the effect by acting upon the cause' (487–8).

Warner, Marina. *L'Atalante.* London: British Film Institute, 1993.

Weil, Jiri. *Life with a Star.* Translated by Rita Klimova and Roslyn Schloss. New York: Penguin, 1991.

Zavattini, Cesare. *Sequences from a Cinematic Life.* Translated by William Weaver. Englewood Cliffs, N.J.: Prentice-Hall, 1970.

Shoeshine

PAULINE KAEL

*Throughout her career as a popular movie critic Pauline Kael has been
unapologetically subjective, and, as in this 1961 essay on* Shoeshine, *she
often takes a bluntly autobiographical approach to the movie-going experience.
De Sica is one film-maker for whom Kael seems to have had a good eye. Many
of her remarks on De Sica's works, made throughout her career, have either
defined perspectives on him or opened up new dimensions of his work, as her
1971 essay in the* New Yorker, *'The Fall and Rise of Vittorio De Sica,' and
reviews elsewhere make clear. Our thesis that De Sica scripted for himself the
role of film-maker as physician would find some resonance in Kael's view of*
Shoeshine, *which may be described as 'therapeutic.'*

When *Sciuscià / Shoeshine* (1946) opened in 1947, I went to see it alone
after one of those terrible lovers' quarrels that leave one in a state of
incomprehensible despair. I came out of the theater, tears streaming,
and overheard the petulant voice of a college girl complaining to her
boyfriend, 'Well I don't see what was so special about that movie.' I
walked up the street, crying blindly, no longer certain whether my
tears were for the tragedy on the screen, the hopelessness I felt for
myself, or the alienation I felt from those who could not experience the
radiance of *Shoeshine*. For if people cannot feel *Shoeshine*, what can they
feel? My identification with those two lost boys had become so strong
that I did not feel simply a mixture of pity and disgust toward this dis-
satisfied customer but an intensified hopelessness about everything ...
Later I learned that the man with whom I had quarrelled had gone the

Pauline Kael, *For Keeps* (New York: Dutton, 1994), 16–17

same night and had also emerged in tears. Yet our tears for each other, and for *Shoeshine*, did not bring us together. Life, as *Shoeshine* demonstrates, is too complex for facile endings.

Shoeshine was not conceived in the patterns of romance or melodrama; it is one of those rare works of art which seem to emerge from the welter of human experience without smoothing away the raw edges, or losing what most movies lose – the sense of confusion and accident in human affairs. James Agee's immediate response to the film was, '*Shoeshine* is about as beautiful, moving, and heartening a film as you are ever likely to see.' A few months later he retracted his evaluation of it as a work of art and wrote that it was not a completed work of art but 'the raw or at best the roughed-out materials of art.' I think he should have trusted his initial response: the greatness of *Shoeshine* is in that feeling we get of human emotions that have not been worked-over and worked-into something (a pattern? a structure?) and cannot really be comprised in such a structure. We receive something more naked, something that pours out of the screen.

Orson Welles paid tribute to this quality of the film when he said in 1960, 'In handling a camera I feel that I have no peer. But what De Sica can do, that I can't do. I ran his *Shoeshine* again recently and the camera disappeared, the screen disappeared; it was just life ...'

When *Shoeshine* came to this country, *Life* magazine wrote, 'New Italian film will shock the world ... will act on u.s. audiences like a punch in the stomach.' But few Americans felt that punch in the stomach. Perhaps like the college girl they need to be hit by an actual fist before they can feel. Or, perhaps, to take a more charitable view of humanity, they feared the pain of the film. Just about everybody has heard of *Shoeshine* – it is one of the greatest and most famous films of all time – but how many people have actually seen it? They didn't even go to see it in Italy. As De Sica has said, '*Shoeshine* was a disaster for the producer. It cost less than a million lire but in Italy few people saw it as it was released at a time when the first American films were reappearing ...' Perhaps in the u.s. people stayed away because it was advertised as a social protest picture – which is a little like advertising *Hamlet* as a political study about a struggle for power.

Shoeshine has a sweetness and a simplicity that suggest greatness of feeling, and this is so rare in film works that to cite a comparison one searches beyond the medium – if Mozart had written an opera set in poverty, it might have had this kind of painful beauty. *Shoeshine*, written by Cesare Zavattini, is a social protest film that rises above its purpose. It is a lyric study of how two boys (Rinaldo Smordoni [Giuseppe] became a baker; Franco Interlenghi [Pasquale] became a film star) betrayed by society betray each other and themselves. The two young shoeshine boys who sustain their friendship and dreams amid the apathy of postwar Rome are destroyed by their own weaknesses and desires when sent to prison for black-marketeering. This tragic study of the corruption of innocence is intense, compassionate, and, above all, humane.

References

Agee, James. *Agee on Film: Reviews and Comments.* Boston: Beacon Press, 1958.

The Art of *Shoeshine*

BERT CARDULLO

In this essay Bert Cardullo surveys the critical response to Shoeshine *and then develops a context for the delinquency of its two protagonists in the social circumstance of orphaned children in post–World War II Italian society. He comments on the effects achieved by shooting the last scene in the studio, but De Sica has his own explanation for its being studio-photographed: he had intended to shoot the scene on location, but the producer refused to wait for good weather (see De Sica, 39–40 above). In his analysis of the last scene Cardullo's description of the boys as 'a once beautiful matched pair' has the effect of turning them into figures more porcelain-like than human, yet De Sica himself has said that he did seek to make the boys aesthetically pleasing (De Sica, 24 above).*

Both Monique Fong (whom Cardullo quotes) and Cardullo use the term small-angle lens, *but there is really no such thing. A* long *lens produces a smaller angle than does a* wide-angle *lens. However, of the two lenses, the wide-angle is more likely to produce a soft image with deep focus. In fact, a careful viewing of* Shoeshine *will reveal many shots of exceptionally large depth-of-field. There are a number of* soft-focus *shots in the film, which are achieved by employing standard soft-focus photography methods – either using an unfocused lens, or placing a piece of sheer silk in front of the lens, or using defracted lights.*

It is tempting to read De Sica's *Sciuscià / Shoeshine* (1946) as an indictment of post–World War II Italian society. Pierre Leprohon writes that

Bert Cardullo, 'The Art of *Shoeshine*,' *New Orleans Review* 11:2 (1984), 74–8. Reprinted in Bert Cardullo, *Indelible Images: New Perspectives on Classic Films* (Lanham, Md.: University Press of America, 1987), 91–101 'the theme of *Sciuscià* is the infinitely tragic clash between childhood innocence and adult injustice' (Leprohon, 101). Roy Armes states that

> The blame in the film rests squarely on the shoulders of the adults whose actions are indeed often mean and spiteful. Giuseppe's brother callously involves [the boys] in crime, while the police use underhand methods to make Pasquale confess [the brother's name] by pretending to beat Giuseppe (we see what is really happening in the next room: a policeman is beating a sack while a boy shrieks convincingly). The lawyers are cheaply opportunistic, suggesting that Giuseppe put all the blame on his friend, and the prison officials act foolishly and split up the pair (so that Giuseppe is left a prey to bad influences) and then punish Pasquale for fighting a bully.   (Armes, 148)

Peter Bondanella echoes Leprohon and Armes when he says that in *Shoeshine* 'De Sica dramatizes the tragedy of childish innocence corrupted by the adult world ... [Pasquale and Giuseppe's] friendship is gradually destroyed by the social injustice usually associated with the adult world and authority figures' (Bondanella, 53). Both Bondanella and Leprohon describe a 'tragic' conflict between childhood innocence and adult injustice, but by pitting victims against villains in this way, they are really suggesting that the film is a melodrama.

Shoeshine, however, is much more than the story of two boys whose friendship is destroyed at the hands of a villainous and insensate social system. Society may be ultimately responsible for the death of Giuseppe and the destruction of his and Pasquale's friendship, but De Sica does not portray it as villainous, as consciously or indifferently evil and exploitative. As Monique Fong has written,

> *Shoeshine* is neither an accusation nor a propaganda work ... Great skill is shown in putting the single moral-bearing sentence of the story – 'If these children have become what they are, it is because we have failed to keep them what they are supposed to be' – into the mouth of the corrupt lawyer, a man to whom lying is a profession and whom we saw, just a moment earlier, falsely accusing Pasquale in order to save his own client.   (Fong, 17–18)

Italian society is as much a victim as Giuseppe and Pasquale in *Shoeshine*, and this is perhaps what James Agee had in mind when he wrote that *Shoeshine* 'is ... the rarest thing in contemporary art – a true tragedy. This tragedy is cross-lighted by pathos, by the youthfulness and innocence of the heroes, ... but it is stern, unmistakable tragedy as well' (Agee, 279). The real tragic conflict is not between the two boys and society: it is to be found in a society divided against itself; the tragedy of post–World War II Italian society is reflected in the pathetic story of Giuseppe and Pasquale. We are not meant to focus on the misfortune of the boys apart from the world in which they live; the point of the film is that their misfortune derives directly from this world. De Sica is interested as much in having us examine and question (not blame) the society that destroyed the boys' friendship as in having us pity Giuseppe and Pasquale. He is thus a typical neorealist filmmaker, according to Roy Armes:

> Deep concern with humanity is common to ... all [neorealist filmmakers] but there is no attempt to probe beneath the surface into the mind of the individual, so that concepts like *Angst* or absurdity have no place in neo-realist art, and alienation is defined purely in social terms. In place of the traditional cinematic concern with the complexities of the individual psyche comes a desire to probe the basically human, to undertake an investigation into man within his social and economic context.   (Armes, 186)

No critics to my knowledge have investigated the tragic role that society plays in *Shoeshine*; I would like to do so in the following pages.

Italy was of course in a state of political and economic turmoil after World War II. Many of its inhabitants, especially those in large cities like Rome, where *Shoeshine* takes place, were finding it difficult to survive, since there was a shortage of food and clothing. A black market arose, trading in goods stolen or bought from the American occupation forces. Giuseppe and Pasquale's problems begin when they agree to sell stolen American army blankets to a fortuneteller, as part of a plan by Giuseppe's brother and his gang to rob the fortuneteller's apartment. The boys know nothing of the planned robbery. They use the 3,000 lire that they are paid for the blankets to buy a horse; soon afterwards they are arrested.

Roy Armes says that 'Giuseppe's brother callously involves [the boys] in crime' (Armes, 148). This statement fails to take into account the environment that produces the crime. Giuseppe's brother may be a thief, but he is one in a society where there is little or no work: he must survive, so he steals. He involves his brother in his crime and pays him well. Giuseppe's brother is callous only when seen from the point of view of someone who has never been in his situation; *he* thinks that he is doing his younger brother a favor. Petty crime is a way of life for them both, and the older brother's justification for robbing a fortune-teller is probably that he is robbing the equivalent of a thief: a woman who steals people's money legally by telling their fortunes. Giuseppe's brother is not a villain. Giuseppe turns on Pasquale when his friend names the brother as one of the thieves to prison officials; his loyalty to his brother – to the person who tried to do him a favor, not to a villain who callously involved him in a crime – leads eventually to his death. Ironically, in attempting to help Giuseppe to survive, the brother has helped to get him killed, and has gone to jail himself. Although Giuseppe's brother is not a major character in *Shoeshine*, he is part of the society whose tragedy De Sica is depicting.

Although it is true, as Roy Armes writes, that 'the police use under-hand methods to make Pasquale confess by pretending to beat Giuseppe,' it is equally true that they use such methods because they want to capture the gang that robbed the fortuneteller's apartment (Armes, 148). Like Giuseppe's brother, the police are not villains. They want to stop the black-marketeering that is threatening an already unstable economy, and they use whatever means they can to do so. The police do not, in Armes's words, 'act foolishly and split up [Giuseppe and Pasquale]' (Armes, 148); the pair is split up by chance in the assigning of groups of boys to cells. The prison in which the police house the boys is not by design 'cruel, crowded, wretched, and dirty,' as Monique Fong believes (Fong, 15). It is crowded because many of the boys of Rome have turned to petty crime in order to survive; wretched and dirty because it is so crowded and because adequate funds do not exist to provide for the boys; and cruel because the prison staff is small and overworked, and therefore prone to solve problems by force instead of by disputation. The prison was not even built as one: it was formerly a convent and has been taken over, presumably because of a shortage of space in other prisons.

The deception that the police work on Pasquale is not without its consequences: he and Giuseppe themselves learn deception. In revenge for Pasquale's betrayal of his brother, Giuseppe, along with several other boys, plants a file in his cell; it is found, and Pasquale is severely whipped by the guards. Later in court, Giuseppe is forced by his lawyer to put all the blame for the fortuneteller incident on the older, supposedly craftier Pasquale. (Armes calls the lawyer 'cheaply opportunistic' [Armes,148]; he is not: he is unscrupulous in the defense of his client, like many lawyers.) Pasquale, in revenge for Giuseppe's rejection of him and escape from jail with his new friend Arcangeli, tells the police where to find the two. Giuseppe plans to sell the horse that he and Pasquale had bought and to live off the money with Arcangeli. The police find them at the stable, Arcangeli flees, and Giuseppe is killed in a fall from a bridge. He slips trying to avoid the angry Pasquale, who is poised to strike him.

Tragically, the prison officials, in 'protecting' society from Giuseppe and Pasquale, have brutalized the boys, have robbed them of the very emotion and the very virtue necessary for the survival of humane society: love and trust. Society, in the name of law and order, has destroyed what it should promote: bonding, male and female. Giuseppe is torn not only from Pasquale when he goes to jail, but also from the mysterious little girl Nana, who had been following him through the streets of Rome and is inconsolable in his absence. Once the boys are placed in separate cells, Pasquale can give his love and trust only to the tubercular Raffaele, who himself is ostracized by the other prisoners and who is trampled to death during a fire; and Giuseppe can give his love and trust only to the scoundrel Arcangeli, who leaves him on the bridge at the end the moment he sees Pasquale.

Shoeshine does not simply portray brutality against children, for which society will have to pay no particular price and for which it is simply 'evil.' The film portrays society's brutality against *itself*, in the person of its future: its children. What makes *Shoeshine* so poignant is that we see more than the love between Giuseppe and Pasquale destroyed: we see a love destroyed that could only have grown and spread to their other relationships as they grew older; a love that meant to solidify itself through the purchase of the horse and take flight, to announce itself triumphantly throughout Rome and its environs.

The very title of this film is a clue to its intentions. *Shoeshine* is the pathetic story of Giuseppe and Pasquale, but, as I have been maintaining, that is not all. The tragedy of post–World War II Italy is *reflected* in their pathetic story. Even as the American GIs in the film see the image of their own security and prosperity in their shined shoes, so too does Italian society find the image of its own disarray and poverty in the story of these beautifully paired boys. *Shoeshine* is an illumination of reality, a 'shining' of reality's 'shoes,' if you will, of the basic problems facing a defeated nation in the wake of war: for the ruled, how to survive amidst rampant poverty at the same time one does not break the law; for the rulers, how to enforce the law without sacrificing one's own humanity or that of the lawbreakers.

Early in the film we see the shoeshine boys at work, kneeling at the feet of the GIS, who barely take notice of them except to pay. At the end we look over the shoulder of the prison guard at the screaming Pasquale in the river bed: he is on his knees, next to the dead Giuseppe. De Sica holds this shot for a long time; it is the final one. Pasquale and Giuseppe are still the shoeshine boys, and down at them, as if they were shining his shoes, looks the prison guard, a representative of society. He is confronted with the offspring of war-torn Italy, of his own work: a once beautifully matched pair, now driven apart; the kind of pair without which Italy will not be able to move forward.

Monique Fong remarks on the cinematography of *Shoeshine*:

> It would seem that [the cinematography] might best have been painstakingly realistic, with sharp outline and great depth of field. But on the contrary, the use of a small-angle lens gives soft effects that help to retain the poetic character of the picture and, by contrast, enhance the realistic performances of the actors.   (Fong, 25)

Just as the title itself, *Sciuscià*, corrupts or 'blurs' the Italian word for shoeshine, the 'soft effects' of the cinematography blur reality slightly, especially in the last scene on the bridge, where mist also obscures the image (Fong, 15). Fong thinks that this technique, in addition to giving the film a general poetic character, 'surrounds the adventure with a halo, supplying a new element to serve the basic idea of the picture – the presentation of a realistic story seen through the eyes of children' (Fong, 25). I would alter this idea and take it one step further to say that the 'soft effects' suggest that the story is seen not only through the eyes of children, but also through those of the American occupation troops, the Italian government, the prison officials, and De Sica himself – eyes that, like those of children, do not comprehend fully what they see, do not have sufficient knowledge.[1]

The American GI who looks into his shined boots sees the image of his own victory and prosperity, but his image is tainted by the Italy that surrounds him – one that he has helped to destroy and whose rebuilding it is now his responsibility to oversee. The prison guard at the end of the film looks down on Pasquale and Giuseppe and may feel sorry for them, but how aware is he of society's, of his own, responsibility for their misfortune? De Sica directed the film, but he does not propose any solutions to the social problem he presents. There are no clear villains, no easy answers, so De Sica softens the 'blow' of what we see at the same time that he discourages us from seeking answers to all our questions on the screen. We are in a position to contemplate this social tragedy far better than any character in the film; the audience *infers* the tragedy, while the group protagonist, society, plays it out. We are thus able to consider solutions to the problems that De Sica poses, or to consider the idea of abolishing war altogether. We are the ultimate recipients of De Sica's *Shoeshine*.

Author's Note

1 When writing about neorealism, critics most often follow André Bazin's lead and emphasize its use of nonprofessional actors, the documentary quality of its photography, its social content, or its political commitment. Bazin went so far as to call neorealism a cinema of 'fact' and 'reconstituted reportage' that rejected both traditional dramatic and cinematic conventions (André Bazin, *What Is Cinema?* trans. Hugh Gray [Berkeley: University of California Press, 1971], II: 60, 77, 78, and *passim* [the first seven chapters – over half the book – treat neorealism]). However, as Peter Bondanella points out,

> Certainly the cinema neorealists turned to the pressing problems of the time – the war, the Resistance and Partisan struggle, unemployment, poverty, social injustice, and the like – but there was never a programmatic approach to these questions or any preconceived method of rendering them on celluloid ... In short, neorealism was not a 'movement' in the strictest sense of the term. The controlling fiction of neorealist films ... was that they dealt with actual problems, that they employed contemporary stories, and that they focused on believable characters taken most frequently from Italian daily life. But the greatest neorealist directors never forgot that the world they projected upon the silver screen was one produced by cinematic conventions rather than an ontological experience ... Thus, any discussion of Italian neorealism must be broad enough to encompass a wide diversity of cinematic styles, themes, and attitudes ... Directors we label today as neorealists were ... all united only by the common aspiration to view Italy without preconceptions and to develop a more honest, ethical, but no less poetic language. (Bondanella, 34–5)

De Sica himself stated that his work reflected 'reality transposed into the realm of poetry' (*Miracle in Milan* [Baltimore: Penguin, 1969], 4). And the last scene on the bridge in *Shoeshine* is an excellent example of this poetry: it was shot inside a studio, and relies for its meaning and effect in large part on the manner in which it is filmed (a manner more easily controlled indoors than on location). Bondanella notes that the cinematography of the last scene continues the sense of confinement witnessed in 'a number of shots through cell windows [that] place [Pasquale and Giuseppe] in a tight, claustrophobic atmosphere and restrict their movement' (54). The boys are trapped in the foreground in the final scene on the bridge, since De Sica's small-angle lens does not photograph the image in deep focus in addition to not capturing it in sharp outline.

References

Agee, James. *Agee on Film: Reviews and Comments*. Boston: Beacon Press, 1958.

Armes, Roy. *Patterns of Realism: A Study of Italian Neo-Realist Cinema*. New York: A.S. Barnes, 1971.

Bondanella, Peter. *Italian Cinema: From Neorealism to the Present*. New York: Frederick Ungar, 1983.

Fong, Monique. '*Shoeshine*: A Student Film Analysis.' *Hollywood Quarterly* 4:1 (Fall 1949), 14–27. [EDITORS' NOTE: This journal was the predecesor of *Film Quarterly*.]

Leprohon, Pierre. *The Italian Cinema*. Translated by Roger Greaves and Oliver Stallybrass. New York: Praeger, 1972.

Holding Hands with a Bicycle Thief

MARK WEST

Mark West's original essay delineates the complicated manner in which De Sica's film Bicycle Thieves *on the one hand draws its audience into an empathic connection with Ricci, the victimized father, while on the other hand holds that same audience at a distance from this monumentally fault-burdened protagonist. En route, West suggestively draws our attention to several submerged metaphors in the film which lend the story a significant historical resonance and urgency.*

> A wheel is the sublime paradox;
> one part of it is always going forward
> and the other part always going back.
>
> G.K. CHESTERTON

Ladri di biciclette / Bicycle Thieves (1948) is born in a dark pool of sound, a brief musical introduction that begins with a simple footfall figure, a phantom on a solitary flute, which is then answered by a softly soaring variation in dry luminous brass: a surprise of sound that calls up a world of forms and movement and feelings, sounding the face of an empty black screen. These two musical strands step forward in turn and then transpire into a magnificent tutti passage in the strings: a tough heroic air that turns the exhilarating sadness of the first two motifs into a transcendental wheel of suffering, and thus prefigures, with a kind of mineral clarity, the entire emotional movement of the film.

The deeply affecting sound of these three variations on a three-note descending motif opens out from the darkness like an invisible character, moving and mounting a set of steps unnoticed by a troupe of men;

and then, as if the music were being conducted back down the steps by an official's waving hands, it begins to fade, quenched over by a rising human yammer, and soon falls silent at the official's feet as he shouts the name 'Ricci.' These stepping themes reappear throughout the film operatically, like shadow characters in a Greek chorus. They take our hand and seem to walk us out to an old stage where human desire and enchantment are felt to shy away in a new joyless light, an inhospitable cityscape that resembles the deep-focus canvases of Giorgio de Chirico, but for the faint vibration of fantastic blood, of Rossini and Verdi and Puccini.

The first image that we see in *Bicycle Thieves* is a near-empty bus. It sweeps dryly down a road and across the brightening screen, turns round in a square, and stops near a group of modern buildings. Bright bands of film credits cover the screen like a succession of commercial advertisements, obscuring the movements of an excited group of men who have been waiting near the bus stop. Leaning forward in my chair, I feel a slight trepidation that I am falling behind the unfolding of the film, even though it is scarcely in stride; as if I were watching an old newsreel in which the important historic events must be discovered side by side with the quotidian; in which there is no apparent emphasis or direction to lead the eye to what is important. The men disregard the bus when it stops, but pursue, with mounting anticipation, one of the passengers, a well-dressed official who leads them up a set of steps and into one of the buildings, only to come back out and down again immediately. He has left his hat indoors and now holds some folded papers. He calls down the steps 'Ricci ... Ricci ...,' and then with some irritation, 'Is Ricci here?' But there is no reply until a man at the bottom of the steps breaks away and runs across the square to fetch Ricci, who is reclining in a daydream at the foot of a small public fountain, paddling his hand in a broken stream of spilled water. It is the strangest image in the film, and one that may easily escape our attention. It is an incongruous and playfully absurd activity for a grown man who is supposed to be looking for work and competing for scarce jobs with an eager crowd of unemployed men; but as we see in the opening sequences of *Bicycle Thieves*, Antonio Ricci is frankly apart from others, distant and unconnected to ordinary human striving; though not quite aloof, he is distracted and vulnerable, self-absorbed, somehow brittle, and remote from the world. But suddenly wakened to the sound of his name being called, Antonio lifts his head from its heavy reflection on the face of the pool, and is suddenly up and on his way, freeing himself from the deeps, and, with damp patting palms, a dust as fine as pollen.

This opening sequence sets out the film's intrinsic pattern of pursuit, in a context of institutionalized dependency, and the resulting cycle of pride and humiliation that moves the story along. The unemployed men trail behind the official like a band of obedient children. They compete roughly against each other for jobs and are degraded by the process whether or not they succeed. The society in which they live is a highly bureaucratic world. Queues of desperate and tired people are depicted in a municipal hock shop, a police station, a church, and a seer's parlour. And echoing above all the clamour is the government official's impossible promise to 'try to take care of everyone,' as Flaubert described it, by means of a new bureaucratic order, staffed by a well-meaning 'priestly tyranny' (Flaubert, 20). De Sica's view of institutions anticipates and shares comic similarities with some of Buñuel's spoofs on city life, especially those involving police stations, where the type of bitter comedy that is associated with the early stages of scrambling alienation can also be traced in later, more dehumanized films such as *Alphaville* (1965).

In contrast to this modern collective we have Ricci, who is separate from his community. We may find Antonio's childlike dreaminess rather attractive at first, but his helplessness and deceptions soon become loathsome. It is convenient to disregard that Ricci succeeds in obtaining a job only after telling a lie about the bicycle, thereby founding his own good fortune on the deception of his employer, as well as all the other better-qualified men. So why do we care for him? He will soon do everything a film character need do to dispel our affection, such as bully his wife and child, and persecute an old man and a boy thief, seemingly out of sheer helplessness, yet we are ever-tempted to make excuses for him, excited as he is by the relentless and nerve-breaking pressure of poverty. Indeed, a conviction grows in us during the film that Antonio acts against his own knowledge of right and wrong, against his own inherent goodness, and does so out of an admirable meekness or lack of assurance, an uncertainty and vulnerability, and in circumstances of such peculiar provocation that we become sympathetic and protective, despite his deplorable failings. Our strong feeling of empathy for him turns over and over in the film together with revulsion at his mistreatment of others; and we may come to feel in ourselves an unpleasant tension of inner division disrupt the balance of our judgment of his behaviour, while mirroring Antonio's own painful movement between extremes. In addition to our bond of sympathy and self-division, our affection for Antonio may also stem from the enchantment of sublime poetry, of a human hand at play, dreaming back and forth in public water, and lifting bright innocent music into a dry hot place.

Maria Ricci, like her husband Antonio, is also first seen at a public fountain, though, unlike Antonio, she is working among other women in a small communal area surrounded by barbed wire that recalls images of the recent war. After Antonio tells Maria that he needs a bicycle in order to qualify for the job he has already accepted, he hurries away in premature defeat and forgets to help her until she hesitates on a stone incline, awkwardly trying to balance two heavy pails of water. This sequence illustrates how Antonio's self-absorption is tied to his helpless dependency, and his charming boyishness. The image of the two pails held in skilful balance by Maria harmonically echoes the symmetrical circles of the bicycle itself and provides a contrast with the pail of water that Antonio clumsily handles later during his own brief spell of work. The image of Maria *working* with water also rubs against the image of Antonio *playing* with water, and evokes a suggestion of the sea echoing in the pails and within the banks of her own name, Maria (*mare* 'sea'). In telling Maria about his new job Antonio succintly summarizes the results of his deceptions, complaining that 'I've got a job, but I can't take it.' Yet he has already accepted the official's offer on the strength of his false assurance that he owns a bicycle. Antonio's temper soon bursts at the foot of their apartment staircase, and he howls melodramatically, 'Oh, why was I ever born?' Maria, however, faces up to the problem with a nicely regulated fury; she pulls Antonio and the sheets from the bed with determination and a grand flourish of hidden resourcefulness as she decides to sacrifice the linen, part of her dowry, to get their bicycle out of hock. At the municipal pawnshop she and Antonio negotiate very gamely with a compassionate official and obtain a little more money than was originally offered, but like Antonio earlier, Maria lies about the sheets, saying 'they are linen' before correcting herself, 'linen and cotton.' During this sequence it becomes evident – as we see another official climb like a tightrope artist in a circus, hoisting the Riccis' bag of hocked sheets to the top of an extremely high set of shelves, surrounded by countless other packages – that the whole country seems to have hocked great masses of household goods. The Ricci family's two-year spell without a paying job appears to be a widespread condition. Italy's high level of unemployment gives a special significance to the prospect of financial security after such a long time, but it must also be included in our estimate of what the consequences of continued unemployment would be for the Ricci family. Looking in from a vantage point of relative comfort today, the Ricci household appears to have managed reasonably well for two years with Maria working in the home, Antonio out of work, and Bruno employed pumping gas; and though they suffer hardships, it seems a little melodramatic of Antonio to behave as if they were all about to starve to death, an outcome the film shows to be absurd. If we compare the living standards at the boy thief's dwelling place, a filthy, congested one-room apartment that sleeps four next to the stove, we can see perhaps that the Riccis are considerably better off and more secure than Antonio imagines. In some respects we may begin to feel that the new job is somehow too important, or important to Antonio for all the wrong reasons. Accordingly, the theft of his bicycle introduces an important dramatic catalyst which serves to dissolve Antonio's fantasies of self-worth and contaminate him with a killing sense of failure and life's injustice. From his initial position of doomed gaiety, Antonio seems to fall into a kind of blind trance, and like a figure in Kafka, he becomes obsessed with the pursuit of things that are lost and unobtainable. I am attempting to convey here my own uncertain view that the inflated importance of regaining the bicycle is a kind of inner reflection, projected from the deeps of Antonio's psyche, of an indeterminable fragment splintered off from the rest of his being, and striving to become conscious. In this sense the bicycle becomes *everything* to Antonio, though it is *nothing* in itself.

The third member of the Ricci family whom we now meet is Bruno, Antonio and Maria's five-year-old son. We discover him early in the morning working in the darkness of his bedroom, like a dream. Bruno's hands reach up high above his head and spin the front wheel of his father's bicycle, polishing the rim as it turns in the shadows; and with his circling rag he seems to dispel the very darkness that surrounds him. Then Antonio enters Bruno's bedroom, letting in light from the next room. We can see Bruno's beautiful head more clearly now, held among the lovely shadows like a floating crescent of light that illuminates the morning gloom, framed in the circle of a turning wheel and scintillating there at the centre of the radiating spokes, like a sublime and sacred image. Bruno has already dressed himself in the dark and has almost finished cleaning and inspecting his father's bicycle, long before Antonio has even finished dressing. Bruno knows the minute particularities of the bicycle and he cares for it just as a father might care for his son, insisting on its protection and well-being above everything else. He responds to the bicycle with that special fascination for the logic and structure of machines that is divinely childlike. The bicycle has a Fides frame, apparently from the Latin *fides* ('trust,' 'confidence,' 'reliance,' 'credence,' 'belief,' 'faith'); and we notice how this important initial image of the bicycle, suspended as it is from the apartment ceiling and floating like a set of balances in the beautiful morning light, conveys the way in which the frame holds all the other parts and forces of the bicycle in harmony; how it joins the two wheels that always work in concert with each other, like father and son, each acting congruently with the other: now a generative driving force, and now a steering and directing intelligence. After the bicycle is stolen, we begin to realize that Antonio will never find it again, though he may almost find its frame, and that the real crime, is not that it is stolen, for there is no deep violence in this, but that the minute particularities of its unity and history, so beloved by Bruno, are permanently destroyed when the thieves disassemble it and then graft these parts to other stolen bicycles.

When Antonio comes into Bruno's room, Bruno scolds his father for not complaining to the municipal official at the hock shop who dented one of the pedals while it was in his care. Antonio reacts by telling Bruno to 'keep quiet.' He speaks softly to Bruno, and he laughs lightly at Bruno's seriousness in a gentle attempt to cool Bruno off while not disturbing his sleeping baby brother. But despite the understanding that Antonio shows for Bruno in this exchange he does not seem to register Bruno's deep concern for the bicycle, for right and wrong, and with justice. Bruno openly criticizes his father's obliviousness, but he does not become aggressively intolerant of these typical evasions; and if we sense that these disagreements have become routine between father and son, the film also shows us some of the ways that a child may be father to the man. It is one of the most remarkable things in *Bicycle Thieves*, the way that Bruno continues to express love and affection for his father even though Antonio seldom looks out for Bruno, once the chase has begun, and shows little natural affection except when he is moved by guilt, self-interest, or the demands of an unavoidable responsibility.

In the previous scene Signora Santona, the local seer, implored the heavens to 'give me the light, my Lord ...' This prayer seems to be answered when Bruno opens his bedroom window and lets in a stream of morning light that reveals his baby brother folded away out of sight. Later, as he is about to leave the apartment with his father, Bruno characteristically remembers to close the bedroom shutters out of consideration for his brother's well-being. There are many such occasions in the film where Bruno covers for his father's irresponsibility. The pressure of these inversions accumulates imperceptibly as Bruno's selfless concern for his father seems to be trying in some way to redeem or compensate for Antonio's egotistical despair. The stereotypes of father and son are always in motion, exchanging places and turning into each other. Bruno's innocent love for his father seems to make Antonio more aware of his own childish helplessness, just as Antonio's despair seems to reach out to Bruno and deepen his understanding and maturity, like Blake's contrary states of the soul, innocence and experience. Later in the film the crazy chase after the old man seems to echo this theme once again, this time in a distorted variation on the tradition of respect that is owed to one's elders. Here, anger and violence move up freely from Bruno and Antonio in a disagreeable spectacle of righteous disregard for justice until the old man, who may or may not be involved in the bicycle theft, demands a little 'respect.' Antonio and Bruno are becoming vigilantes, attempting to obtain justice for themselves through force alone, and it is tragic and repugnant to witness how their futile pursuit of a thief results only in further crime and self-abasement.

The film works like a fable and shows how dwelling too much on the pursuit of what has been lost is more likely to foster a cycle of further and more serious losses than restore happiness. This theme is very pronounced at the scene of the near-drowning of a child at the bridge. Antonio is incapable of telling his son about the intense terror that he felt at the possibility of Bruno's accidental death, and neither can he hold on to his momentary sense of responsibility towards his son. There are many occasions for death, and near-accidents are so frequent in the course of the film that we soon come to feel that Bruno has been mortally doomed by his father's selfishness and neglect, though it likely will not be a death by water, but, rather, a grizzly collision with one of the film's numerous wheels. And although Antonio has threatened earlier to throw himself in the river out of despair at the possibility of losing his job, the words are all bluff and exaggeration, as we see at the bridge where he avoids all contact with the river, not even lifting a finger to save the drowning boy whom he fears is his son. Indeed, there is something egregious and profoundly ignoble in the way that

Antonio stands back from the crisis, merely sweating and making faces, while others nearby give what help they can. Then, satisfied that the victim is not Bruno, Antonio flees from the scene as the slippery flesh of the nearly drowned boy is placed in the dust.

Much of the meaning in *Bicycle Thieves* unfolds and builds like music in the space between Bruno's open face, as it is so often fixed on his father, and Antonio's closed face, a face shut down in defeat or illuminated with fantasy, but fixed, for all his self-absorption with loss and gain, on the world outside, an oblivious city that is being choked with the poster images of fake happiness, and with a peculiar serpentine stream of bicycles that constantly weaves through the streets and passageways. Bruno is always set to look *at* things with large deep watery eyes that give everything back. He reaches out to things while Antonio's narrow eyes seem always to take things into themselves, grasping, forever looking *for* things. The film shows how Antonio first loses his marvellous, fragile, human face, and how Bruno gives a variation of it back to him; how Antonio's face is slowly overtaken by the hard mechanical mask of Fascism, full of damaged pride and a desire for authority over others, and how it is finally reclaimed into a more resilient, softer humanity, through collapse and humility, through tears and his gradual transformation into a compulsive thief. *Bicycle Thieves* seems to show that a one-sided preoccupation with redressing loss only results in greater loss, and that loss itself is the greatest and most difficult truth to incorporate into living.

To understand the dangerous instability of Antonio's character we must consider the self-perpetuating cycle of his passivity and aggression. He is intimidated by officials of all kinds, typically leaving Maria to carry out most of the negotiations with officials and clerks; and he is subservient towards his new supervisor at the Poster Office, who, predictably, treats him with official disdain. Antonio hopes to succeed in his new position by adopting a good-natured servility which he mistakenly thinks will be appreciated by those in power. But this submissive foil also calls up in him an inflated complementary feeling of pride that leads to an intolerant aggressiveness; and so, Antonio tends to become more violent and desperate as his wishes are repeatedly thwarted. We have probably all noticed that Antonio is rather too delighted to be wearing a uniform and cap, and how odd it is that Maria accompanies him on his first visit to work and waits for him outside in the street, rather like a mother reassuring an insecure child on the first day of school. On their trip home from Antonio's place of work Maria asks to stop briefly to visit a 'working woman.' Now that it is Antonio's turn to wait for Maria while she visits with Santona, we learn that he is prone to meddling and making officious pronouncements. First he intrudes an uninvited opinion with breezy authority concerning a game being disputed by some young children playing in the street. Next, his curiosity is aroused when a few women arrive and ask him if Santona, 'the one who sees,' lives in the house. Then, having waited only a few moments, Antonio abandons his bicycle to the care of children he does not know, and intrudes on Maria's privacy. As soon as he discovers that she is giving money to a seer, he hustles her out of the apartment, pushing her down the hall ignominiously while criticizing her for being a 'silly fool' and wasting money on 'superstition.' If Antonio does exhibit characteristics of Fascism during his steady decline in the film, it is worth noting that he is also the quintessential embodiment of the very qualities that Fascism most despises. Antonio appears to be threatened by Maria's visit to Santona, and he insists to Maria rather absurdly that *he* found the job, after all, and not Santona. It is a scene that provides another dimension to his catalogue of failings, in the form of a disturbing intolerance concerning the irrational, intuitive side of Maria's character, and it appears to stem from Antonio's self-deluding wounded pride and one-sidedness. It is as if Antonio were crying out to the Fates to turn his wheel, which in the meantime he has charged to the safety of an unknown group of children.

If we examine Antonio's job in the context of postwar Italy, a number of interesting themes immediately present themselves. On the surface, his employment appears to consist of a simple process whereby the traditional images of Italy are to be replaced by a cast of insurgent trolls, transported directly from the victor's stable in Hollywood. Looked at in simplified political terms, Antonio is employed in a national switch from the macho images of power and force of will, typical of Fascist Italy, to an intoxicating siren image of romantic allure, seduction, and submission, characteristic of democratic America. The poster with which Antonio begins his training is a still photograph of Rita Hayworth taken from the 1946 movie *Gilda*. It is a profound choice on the part of De Sica, for it combines everything that is cheap and trashy in Hollywood's depiction of erotic life, with intimations from classical mythology of the most beautiful and profound mysteries. In every respect it is an exquisite image for Antonio to be fumbling with as his bicycle is stolen by a young boy wearing a German cap. The configuration of the coiled torso and head of Gilda broadly resembles such well-known images of transformation as Gianlorenzo Bernini's *Apollo and Daphne* and perhaps even the more famous *Venus de Milo*. And these similarities also serve to conflate modern and classical ideals of female beauty, in particular, the classical ideal of poetic balance between body and soul, a beautiful, tragic vision of life, and its echo in the modern ideal of beauty as depicted in *Gilda*, primarily sexual, and with a pronounced pornographic objective of arousing a strong desire for violent possession. Part of Gilda's strange allure is probably the result of Rita Hayworth's curiously androgynous, muscular frame and style of dancing, combined with her sultry 'tough-guy' talk and wild female energy of transformation; but her deeper attraction, in the light of her captivity by two immoral men who nevertheless expect an ideal purity from women, is almost certainly her defiant quest for freedom.

This new imported imagery is also indicative of the new way of living that has been brought into being by the demands of a changed political and economic reality. This includes a wider network of commercial advertisements intended to stimulate desire and discontent, and to ensure that happiness and fulfilment are always available on the next horizon. But these new images carry their own punishments, and like Antonio we may be most vulnerable to ruin when we are closest to success. For in this new world we are inclined to spend too much time in pursuit of an idealized future, a realm of possibility, an ugly world of excited appetites forever frustrated and denied their fulfillment. And in time we may become preoccupied with unattainable ends and lose all enjoyment of our daily means.

Antonio's bicycle is valuable to him only because it promises to replace his feelings of despair and futility with a sense of purpose and meaning; for Bruno, however, the bicycle is an occasion for a delightful intimacy with the physical world, and an end in itself. Antonio appears to suffer from a kind of nightmare displacement with respect to his pursuit of his bicycle, for it comes to mean more to him than the safety of his own son. The restaurant scene is a particularly good example of how a commercial world of appetite and consumption actually fosters unhappiness. In this scene Antonio treats Bruno to a special lunch in an attempt to buy back his son's friendship after Bruno, echoing his father's own way of speaking to people, had blamed his father for letting the old man escape from the church, and was slapped hard on the face by Antonio. While

Antonio's manipulative treat is by no means admirable in itself, it becomes, in the absence of an apology, plainly despicable when Antonio cynically tries to trick Bruno into drinking wine so that he may use this transgression later to blackmail Bruno into not telling Maria that Antonio had struck him on the face. Even as their meal is served, we see how Antonio's envy steals away his present pleasure as he becomes preoccupied with the splendid table occupied by a wealthy family across the room. Antonio's strong hands now become grotesquely genteel and tentative in this elevated setting, moving above his mozzarella like two polite spiders until he can stand it no longer and pushes his food away in habitual defeat and disappointment, preferring now to calculate his earnings that might-have-been only if. Antonio's inability to enjoy present pleasures is contrasted here with Bruno's great delight in his food. Like his father, Bruno is not sure how to eat his food in a fancy restaurant, and so he looks around to see how others are doing it; but he persists in his own charming way, as usual, genuinely connected to the things around him, as here in a comic tug-of-war with the elastic mozzarella, his pleasure as bright as ever. Antonio, however, interrupts Bruno and gives him the job of completing his calculations, bewildered as usual by his own responsibilities. True, Antonio has other problems in mind in addition to estimating his buying power, and we must pity the way that he loses the simple pleasure of eating the food that he cannot easily afford, paralysed, it would seem, by an imaginary world of inflated payslips and extravagant menus, and spiced by his feelings of shame and bitter disappointment over losing his bicycle. And then, with his income finally calculated by Bruno, Antonio becomes so dejected that he can only muster a short sour breath in hollow homage to a banal piece of commercial brainwashing, concluding his meal, without irony, by sighing, 'What more could you want?' But despite Antonio's persistent egotism, De Sica forces us to struggle between our divided views of Antonio; while we hope that he will find his bicycle without further suffering, on the other hand we also feel that he must come to his senses, wake up and accept the injustice of the world, and value his present life despite everything.

It appears to be the self-divided, two-piece sectional poster of Rita Hayworth, then, that creates the setting for the catastrophic rupture in Antonio's life. As I have already suggested, these posters were deliberately designed to bully the public into a state of continuous desire by exciting *envy*, as the root meaning suggests, through 'vision' and 'the eye.' The poster image of Hayworth appears to offer and withdraw, simultaneously, the possibility of physical touch. Her right arm is raised above her head with the hand folded out of view behind her back, while her left arm is shaped in a v with her hand in view. The image discourages the mutuality of touch while exciting the detached examination of the roving eye is to be preferred. Hayworth was of course a notorious screen siren; even her last name presses this erotic point, joining the playful connotations of fertility and freedom implicit in 'hay' with a more dubious rate of exchange suggested by the notion of 'worth.' Playing the role of Gilda, Hayworth's erotic power seems to combine brilliantly the suggestion of dynamic opposites – 'gild,' from Old English *gyldan*, and 'geld,' from Old Norse *gilda* – thus giving the poster an additional circle of sexual turbulence, while forming a partnership with the underworld power of the bicycle thieves, who in turn make use of her agency of fascination in order to cover their crime of theft. But it is later in the film, during Antonio's humiliating pursuit of the old man, that another mythological aspect of the poster is revealed. The old man carries two cans labelled 'Circe.' These two cans, which originally contained the temptation of red fruits, now release into the heat of the film a faint scent that leads us to consider the poster image of Gilda as an incarnation of the mythological figure of Circe. The cans also connect us again to the sea by way of Maria and her two pails of water, and also to Ulysses' famous comrades of decline, again by way of the sea and Antonio's naval-looking hat that needs to have the band tightened and sewn (in order to restrain his tendency to inflation?). The negative aspects of the poster image of Gilda appear to oversee the theft of Antonio's bicycle, and more importantly, the broader formula of theft that relies on 'envy,' the insatiable human characteristic, aroused here by the qualities of a

Homeric 'witch' able to transform men into sacrificial swine: a mythic picture of the transition from human to porcine sacrifices during the Hellenic period. Circe's isle of Aeaea was a funerary shrine. Its name meant 'Wailing.' Circe herself was the death-bird *Kirkos*, falcon. From the same root came the Latin *circus*, originally an enclosure for funerary games.

As the circle, or *cirque*, Circe was identical with Omphale of Lydia with her cosmic spinning wheel: a fate-spinner, weaver of the destinies of men. Homer called her Circe of the Braided Tresses, hinting that, like Oriental

goddesses, she manipulated forces of creation and destruction by the knots
and braids in her hair. She ruled all the stars that determined men's fates.
Pliny said Circe was a goddess who 'commanded all the lights of heaven.'
(Walker, 168–9)

The poster image of Gilda is a still photograph taken from the fabu-
lous sequence near the end of the film in which Gilda dresses herself in
the darkness of her past and then invites the audience to step down
into a sty of its own lust and help her to take the dark clothes off. In
this strange Bacchanalian rite Gilda deliberately transforms herself
until she becomes identical with her lover's jealous distortions of her
real character, and in a startling paradox he becomes ashamed of *himself*. The dance begins as a deliberate sacrificial offering to the erotic
appetites of the male audience in the gambling club, but it precipitates
a sudden awareness of mutual 'guilt' that harmonizes with the music
of the film's title, *Gilda*, and calls up in the hearts of the two men who
are both in love with her a mock-profound sense of decency and forgiveness. This violent force of transformation and subsequent liberation is made possible by a kind of public confession or acting out by
Gilda of her *guilt*, and it foreshadows Antonio's own enactment of
guilt, that I consider to be so important for a proper understanding of
the dark inner music and obsessional structure of *Bicycle Thieves*.

One wonders, incidentally, whether many Italians were aware in
1946 of the grizzly humour that was expressed in painting Hollywood
'bombshells,' such as Rita Hayworth, on the noses of Allied bombers
during World War II, invoking among ghouls and swine the morbid
hilarity of an obscene pun.

During the training session in which Antonio learns how to mount
the *Gilda* posters correctly, his instructor kicks out of the way a couple
of children who are making music and begging for money in the
streets. Before they disappear it may strike us that their childish music
and distractions were an important kind of warning, intended to wake
the men and distract them from their ignoble work. These children
recall the odd file of children at the beginning of the movie, marching
behind a Pied Piper figure who is carrying a shepherd's crook and
leading them breezily up a stone face in the opposite direction to Maria
and Antonio, with their pails of water.

As Antonio awkwardly assembles the two sections of the Hayworth
poster, her image seems to decay and then coalesce by turns, like an

apparition, or ripples moving across the surface of a pool. This moment is like an invocation of morbid enchantment, and Antonio's watery brushwork seems, by way of a mysterious magic, to release or in some way give birth to an evil double of himself, taking the form of a young thief with a baby face and a German cap. Gilda's face becomes grotesquely wrinkled by the water and glue intended to fix it before the public eye, and while Antonio blindly continues to pat over the gargoyle face, straining to remove the action of too much water, the band of thieves weaves around him, working elegantly and in close concert, and then suddenly the boy steals Antonio's bicycle. Each thief plays a small part in a larger program of transformation which includes disassembling the stolen bicycles and combining the alien parts into new configurations. This procedure of reversing the bicycles' history of production echoes the theme of inversion that is central to the movie, and the mixing together of disparate parts also suggests a number of mythological cycles, including Circe and Orpheus. Working together in this pseudo-industrial style the bicycle thieves act less like criminals and more like members of a community of like-minded industrial workers. In any case it is made quite clear that the community of thieves sticks together and exhibits greater loyalty than the better-off communities that we observed earlier during the boisterous competition for work.

The theft of Antonio's bicycle creates a sudden dizzying loss of purpose. As he makes his way home after his disastrous initiation into the world of work, Antonio immediately begins to transgress minor social norms; for example, he jumps a bus queue. This rather insignificant example of Antonio's repeated incivility and selfishness is nevertheless a sign of his own overriding sense of special status and his disregard for other people who quite clearly have their own struggles to bear. But like many other social exchanges that occur during Antonio's long pursuit of the boy thief, De Sica uses this moment to test Antonio's reactions under strain. When Antonio finally meets up with Bruno, he lies once again, saying that the bicycle is broken. But this evasion is nothing compared to the irresponsible way he then pushes Bruno into their apartment and flees from Maria before she has had time to ask him what has happened. Instead of sitting down with his family and talking things over, Antonio seeks help from Biacco, an old friend who is found rehearsing a comic theatre piece for the music hall, in noisy competition with a fevered political meeting warming up in the same area: 'play' and 'work' entwined in conflict once again. By this point Antonio is already in deep despair, and his grip on himself is beginning to soften like a slow tire leak. He is losing his faint contact with the world around him, most dangerously so with Bruno. It is quite probable that Maria would have been able to solve the problem of replacing the stolen bicycle if Antonio had confided in her, and she would surely have rejected the insane risk and futility of pursuing professional thieves. There are numerous reasons why Antonio prefers to seek the help of his male friends, however ridiculous or ineffective they may be, for it appears that when Antonio lost his bicycle, he also lost face, lost his pride, his place in the world and his family, and we never see Maria again.

During Antonio's long pursuit of the thief we are exposed to a larger community shaped by social injustice, poverty, and crime. The chase scene takes us through a curious church from which the religious images have been removed to a storage room, and, apparently turning over a new social leaf, has become a barbershop and soup kitchen, a layover for the poor, seeming to care more for the brass tacks of this world than the more traditional spiritual preoccupations with the world to come. Indeed, it appears that this particular church has turned itself into a place where wealthy patrons and privileged providers may prance in the company of suffering and sorrows which they themselves may be partly responsible for, directly or indirectly, because of their social positions, wealth, and power. The activities in the church seem to call out for comparison with Santona's parlour where her patrons are depicted as if in church, surrounded by religious images, ritual, and pronouncements. Santona lives at Via Paglia, near the boy thief, and despite the associations that can be derived from the root meaning of *paglia*, 'straw' things, or false things, Santona nevertheless manages to minister to the spiritual needs of her patrons, nicely complementing the sexual imagery provided earlier by Hay(worth). She dispenses advice on the basis of what is self-evident, often in the form of undiluted insult, as in the case of the young man whose female partner wishes to leave him. Santona tells him 'you are ugly,' and explains that he should 'sow his seed in another field.' She speaks metaphorically but nobody ever seems to understand her agricultural imagery. And yet, in defiance of our likely prejudice in the matter of her credibility, Santona, whose name is a kind of musical sonata, seems to get things right, and her advice, though simple and cynical, may well be worth the currency of the day.

The next community that we observe is a group of prostitutes taking their breakfast. After a chase around the brothel, which briefly involves Bruno, Antonio pursues the boy thief to his sordid dwelling. It is here, in this new community, that any privileged ideals concerning the clear separation between good and evil, and the causes of each, must take due consideration of the self-evident cycle of poverty and crime. In the sublimely inspired climax to the street fight between Antonio and the boy thief, De Sica illuminates this cyclical pattern by brilliantly showing how the boy who 'snatched' Antonio's bicycle is now suddenly 'seized' again by his own birthright, his epilepsy (Greek *epilēpsia* from *epilambanein* 'to seize'), in a pathetic and fatalistic echo of the root meaning of the name for the disease and the unforgiving net of his social circumstances. In an unexpected conclusion to this terrible scene, and providing an elegant variation on the theme of pails and water, the dusty, humiliating violence of the aptly named Via Panico is snuffed by yet another pail of water, this one tossed at Antonio by an evil clown in a high window, just to 'cool him off.'

The poetry in *Bicycle Thieves* is simply enchanting, and the cinematic technique is profoundly artful. I had read about neorealism and discussed with colleagues the many theories that have grown up around this film and others from the same period; now I wonder if early neorealism was, just as Bazin suggested (Bazin, 47–60), more than anything else, simply an aesthetic and moral rationalization of Italy's grotesque wartime aggrandizement through the spectacle of Fascist ideology, dressed up in a dogma that was absurdly distorted by masculine preoccupations with will and power, with symmetry and force, with technology, and above all, with order and certainty. The whole problem with Fascism, as Jacob Bronowski has argued so movingly, was the arrogance and inhumanity of its dogma. The tragic paradox in this political and cultural philosophy was that the Fascists were absolutely certain about extremely complex human matters at exactly the same time that the most brilliant scientists of the day were saying what art has always known, that knowledge is cumulative, stroke on stroke, and is never complete:

We are aware that ... pictures do not so much fix the face as explore it; that the artist is tracing the detail almost as if by touch; and that each line that is added strengthens the picture but never makes it final. We accept that as the method of the artist.

But what physics has now done is to show that that is the only method to knowledge. There is no absolute knowledge. And those who claim it, whether they are scientists or dogmatists, open the door to tragedy. All information is imperfect. We have to treat it with humility. That is the human condition; and that is what quantum physics says. I mean that literally.   (Bronowski, 353)

Our concepts of reality must be tempered and conditional, since in Bronowski's view 'human knowledge is personal and responsible, an unending adventure at the edge of uncertainty' (Bronowski, 367). The philosopher of science Karl R. Popper argued this same view throughout his career, insisting again and again that objective facts do not exist and that '*all* our knowledge grows *only* through the correcting of our mistakes' (Popper, ix). If these views are correct, then the growth and safety of civilization will depend on humility and the ability to acknowledge error.

The directness and special poignancy of neorealism unfold from the convolutions of a delightful paradox. When the neorealist method succeeds best, it is a style that reveals the plainest truths, as well as the deepest mysteries of reality and experience, *as if* unadorned and untransmuted by mind. But unstructured, shapeless films such as these, if they exist at all, would be comparatively meaningless in themselves. It may be an inevitable, though perhaps inadvertent, achievement of the neorealist film-making that it teaches us that reality, and nothing but reality, as the phrase goes, is just not enough. These passing simplifications may shelter some broader implications for certain aspects of traditional neorealist theory.

One of the most systematic and deeply affecting cinematic techniques used in *Bicycle Thieves* is the relentless pursuit of Antonio by the camera's persistent eye, a chase that mirrors Antonio's own search for his bicycle. Antonio's gradual accumulation of humiliation becomes almost unbearable even before his final metamorphosis into the thief that he has been chasing all along. The camera never seems to hesitate to show us all of Antonio's human frailty and pain, and this method of exposure amounts to a form of artistic persecution in itself. Antonio's search for his lost bicycle seems to point to some kind of truth about our destructive habit of trying to put everything right, an insistence on order and justice that can become a form of self-righteous madness. This frantic search for a stolen bicycle also parallels the director's implicit search for truth, and his choice of neorealism as the method to achieve this objective. In De Sica's own definition of neorealism, he concedes truth to the art of poetry, mystery, and uncertainty:

> Most films today are made in a realistic style, but they are actually opposed to neorealism, to that revolution in cinematic language which we started and which they think to follow. Because neorealism is not shooting films in authentic locales; it is not reality. It is reality filtered through poetry, reality transfigured. It is not Zola, not naturalism, verism, things which are ugly. (De Sica, 31 above)

So let us continue to delight in the poetry, in the infinitely pleasing details of *Bicycle Thieves*, such as the clown-figure, Biacco, who collects garbage and directs music-hall sketches, whose very name seems to enfold the ghost of a *bicicletta*, and who tells us a kind of secret to ponder, that the stolen bicycle is prob-ably at Piazza Vittorio. And the lovely way that Santona's address at Via Paglia connects her to Rita Hayworth and the poster from *Gilda*. But the crowning image of poetry and transfiguration in the film must surely be the way that the movie poster becomes a kind of hub that harmonizes the two wheels of the film camera (or projector), connected as they are by a clicking ladder of film, with the two clicking wheels of Antonio's bicycle, connected as they too are by the film-frames of his ladder.

And for all its deceptive simplicity, *Bicycle Thieves* keeps asking a rather daunting question: what exactly is Antonio really looking for? Signora Santona has an answer, and it is a pretty one: 'I can only tell you what I can see ... Listen ... either you will find it immediately or you will never find it.'

The Wheel humbles itself
To be exalted ...   CHESTERTON

Antonio finally accepts that his bicycle is truly lost forever only after he has caught up with the boy thief. But even this realization does not free him from his obsessive mission. The finale of the film opens with Antonio in a state of intense anxiety and closes with tremendous physical violence. He stands at a crossroad bewildered by a dilemma. Before him is a soccer stadium from which a succession of collective cheers forms a monstrous swell of exuberant barbarous sound, like a sea of approbation smoking above a vanquished enemy. Antonio then switches his nervous gaze from the stadium to a mass of bicycles parked nearby in a long serpentine band. Then he looks across the street and we see, in effect, a mysterious double of Ricci himself, in the form of a solitary bicycle leaning against a wall. The atmosphere of this sequence darkens as a strange new tension is created by the contrast between the ecstasy of the noisy fans, separated from their bicycles, and Antonio's avid gaze. The setting of the soccer game may seem at first to be entirely alien to the rest of the film, but it actually provides a kind of musical field of reference in which two important metamorphoses take place. First, the wavelike cheering of the soccer fans suddenly modulates from an ugly inhuman sound, while the game is in play, into the final, sublimely beautiful sound at the end of the film, immediately before the music of the closing credits, as the soccer fans make their way home on foot: the sound of individual voices rising and falling within a large frame of street sounds, no longer the collective noise of uniformity, but a liberated sound of lovely, crackling, *delicate*, individual voices, full of life and beauty, and mounting like a musical vapour, gently fading up in the dusty evening light. The second transformation takes the restrictions that the game of soccer imposes on the players' use of their hands, and answers these with the closing image of the film: Antonio and Bruno walking hand in hand, dissolving into darkness.

When a file of racing bicycles speeds past Antonio, sounding like the clicking rattle of a serpent, he makes up his mind to steal the solitary bicycle; a crime like most crimes, stemming from a prior injustice. Antonio instructs Bruno, 'his conscience,' to go home, and unaware that Bruno has missed the bus, Antonio walks into a lonely de Chirico-like space and seems to turn into a cold distant shadow. It is here that one may feel drawn almost irresistibly into full sympathy with Antonio's fall, like Narcissus, into an image of himself, for:

one *almost* participates in the crime, and the trivial details become obsessively important. It has besides a secondary impact, by which, as one feels it, one discovers that one has been permanently involved in the nature of the crime: one has somehow contributed to the clarification of the true residual nature of crime in general through having contributed to the enactment of this crime in particular. It is the feeling of this impact that leads us to say our powers of attention have been exhausted. But there is a third and gradual impact, which comes not only at the end but almost from the beginning to the end, creating in us new and inexhaustible powers of attention. This is the impact of what Dostoevski meant by punishment. The three impacts are united by the art of the novelist, and they are felt simultaneously. It is only that we are not aware at the time of the triple significance, and must, when it does transpire, rebuild it analytically. Thus we may come to estimate what it is that we know, what it is that has been clarified in the history of Raskolnikov which we had known all along in ourselves without being aware of it: we estimate our own guilt.   (Blackmur, 311)

Now, having come to the end of his chase, Antonio rides a stolen bicycle away from Bruno and into the centre of the film's final circle of catastrophe. He is chased by a number of soccer fans and soon brought to ground while Bruno watches helplessly from a distance. A trolley bus passes close by, briefly interrupting the men in their wild attack on Antonio. They push him forward, striking him and casting mockery and scorn on him like mad foam through their bared teeth. In this pandemonium Bruno calls out to his father, 'Papa,' 'Papa,' but the wrathful chorus of men hears no distraction and continues to drown Antonio in a wicked wreath of insult: 'thief,' 'swine,' 'criminal,' 'bastard,' 'faceless scoundrel,' 'bugger,' and 'crook.' Terrified and sobbing, Bruno reaches up into the mob in an attempt to catch hold of his father, as if to keep Antonio from sinking forever under the weight of their balling fury. Once again, it is the contrapuntal music that sounds between Antonio's stone-still face, now showing immense new dignity as he is whipped by the tongue of the mob, and Bruno's boiling face, as he mops his bewildered eyes with a circling rag and cries out to his father, that is so deeply affecting and profound. Antonio faces the shattering violence of the mob with a terrible stillness, a heroic defiance that recalls the general composition and sublime dignity that rests on the face of Christ as depicted in the later version of Titian's *Christ Crowned with Thorns* (Munich). During this transfiguration it is as if Antonio's progressive decline into authoritarian, fascistic behaviour, finally *turns*, and begins to redeem itself as a faint echo of Bruno's face as we first saw him at the centre of the bicycle wheel. The meaning of Bruno's face, next to the wheel, and surrounded by darkness, is now more clear: for together, the face and the wheel suggest how human frailty and failing may be integrated and transmuted into a transcendent new form of resilient wholeness, like the delicate radiance of slender individual spokes bound to a central hub, which, after all, is the exact opposite of the reiterative image suggested by the root meaning of *Fascism*, Latin *fasces* 'authoritative rods tied together by a band or cord.'

The owner of the bicycle slaps Antonio's face hard, jarring him into a new kind of wakefulness, and then De Sica sets Antonio free. The owner looks down into Bruno's face, and then up at Antonio; he sees the child's fear and the violence of his confusion, and then sees everything that passes between father and son; he answers the tears on Bruno's face with an act of forgiveness that is one of the finest moments in all of cinema.

Antonio then walks slowly into a large meandering crowd, and it is strange and wonderful how the people all around him are so alive to themselves and yet completely oblivious to him. This sense of anonymity and the strange consolation in the distracted eye of the world, together with the excruciating shame that is choking Antonio, draw us to the centre of his isolation just as we realize he is about to leave us.

The closing sequence sweeps us along with the shadows of Antonio and Bruno as they slowly disappear into the dark texture of the film, creating the impression that they are coursing down into a funnel of spiralling sound, helplessly. The appearance of the city is now softened by a sudden switch to a shallow camera focus that establishes balance and harmony across the frame. This change in photographic method replaces the technique used earlier in the film, predominantly one of deep focus which created a de Chirico landscape in which people were isolated and dominated by the authority of urban structures filled with a stillness and emptiness, resulting from this technique's absolute separation of light and shadow. As Bruno hands his father's hat back to him in a humble gesture of respect, the movement of Bruno's hand seems to call back magically the transcendent sound of the film's opening phantom tutti; and as the music sweeps off the tips of Bruno's fingers, we notice that this new variation has shed the melancholy of its previous descending pattern. It sounds like a mysterious herald now, singing like foam upon a seashore, salted with a luminous shower of crackling human voices as it falls back into the face of darkness.

Each stop during Antonio's pursuit of the thief has felt like a station of the cross. The last sequences in the film release Antonio from his spinning field of obsession, through shame and suffering.

And now a blessed fairy tale begins. A bus bleats mechanically over a ravelling crowd, then bumps Antonio's senseless shoulder. Slowly now, Antonio and Bruno are being absorbed by a strolling mass, soccer fans that hold together, in the poetry of play, the turning wheels of triumph and defeat. We feel the camera's persistent pursuit, as if it were still obsessed with an insatiable envy of reality itself. But suddenly the camera halts, falls behind, and begins to *listen,* as Antonio and Bruno slowly disappear into the soft, gently flowing stream of passers-by; and as the screen begins to turn pale and then darkens, we may imagine the force of faith on the face of a child; we may try to breathe over our own bursting tears, as Bruno takes his father's hand and then stumbles; and as the hard face breaks, we may feel dizzy to witness the most exalted human act, holy above all others: the way that we fall, as we reach up; the way that we touch, as we fill with shame; and the way that we love, face to face, held tight as now, by the new-found frame of their hands.

When Bruno sees himself reflected back in his father's tears, and feels the strength of his father's trust; when he takes hold of his father and stumbles, the camera too is now confident in belief and lets them dissolve, like all sound, forever echoing a return to silence. Antonio's high-held head floats first above the crowd, then sinks slowly into its softly flowing folds as the city comes up in gentle focus, balancing the landscape and its people.

And now *we* reach into darkness. We can almost touch the two figures before they disappear. We see into the shadowing gloom with their own watery eyes, and as this miracle of transfiguration enfolds us in its special creed of enchantment, we hear and see now that the clicking swarms of bicycles have all but vanished.

References

Bazin, André. 'Bicycle Thief.' In *What Is Cinema?* Volume 2. Translated by Hugh Gray. Berkeley: University of California Press, 1967.

Blackmur, R.P. *Selected Essays of R.P. Blackmur.* New York: Ecco Press, 1986.

Bronowski, Jacob. *The Ascent of Man.* Boston: Little, Brown, 1973.

Chesterton, G.K. *Alarms and Discursions.* London: Methuen, 1927. The quoted lines are found on pp. 184 and 185.

Flaubert, Gustave. 'Two Letters from Gustave Flaubert to Louise Colet, Newly Translated by Geoffrey Wall.' *London Review of Books* 17:12 (22 June 1995), 20.

Popper, Karl. *Conjectures and Refutations: The Growth of Scientific Knowledge.* New York: Basic Books, 1965.

Samuels, Charles. *Encountering Directors.* New York: Putnam's, 1972.

Walker, Barbara. *The Woman's Encyclopedia of Myths and Secrets.* San Francisco: Harper & Row, 1983.

Zavattini, Cesare, and Vittorio De Sica. *Bicycle Thieves: A Film by Vittorio De Sica.* London: Lorimer, 1968.

Bicycle Thieves: A Re-reading

FRANK P. TOMASULO

In this 1982 essay Frank P. Tomasulo argues that Bicycle Thieves, *no less than a Hollywood film, sutures its viewers into an ideological mind-screen of received wisdom. The film attempts to wash its hands (and all of Italy's) of any guilt of fascism by deflecting crypto-fascist dimensions of Italian life onto German culture. Tomasulo discusses the way in which the latent conservatism of the film is revealed in the structure of the Ricci family with its unquestioned patriarchal form and unreflective honouring of authority, and points out how Ricci's internalization of patriarchal values affects his relationship with his wife and son.*

> We need to interpret interpretations more than to interpret things.
>
> MICHEL DE MONTAIGNE

Criticism is not an innocent discipline and never has been. The overdetermination of aesthetic functions and values in bourgeois criticism has ideological effects. The task, then, is to show the text as it cannot know itself, to reveal the conditions of its making which are inscribed in its structuration but which are effaced by that very structuration. Though Italian neorealist cinema has been called 'a revolutionary cinema in a non-revolutionary society' (Houston, 29), a re-reading might see those political adjectives reversed. *Ladri di biciclette / Bicycle Thieves* (1948), in particular posits a series of displacements and substitutions, metony-

From '*Bicycle Thieves*: A Re-reading,' by Frank P. Tomasulo, from *Cinema Journal* 21:2 (Spring 1982), 2–13. By permission of the author and the University of Texas Press

mies and metaphors, within a process of signification which orders them into a particular type of discourse.

> Adam Smith's contradictions are of significance because they contain problems which it is true he does not resolve, but which he reveals by contradicting himself.
>
> KARL MARX, *Theories of Surplus Values*

There is an ostensibly innocuous scene in *Bicycle Thieves* which can be seen as emblematic of a dichotomy at work in the text itself. As Antonio Ricci discusses his plight with his friend Biacco, producer of the variety show rehearsing in a basement, a group of Communist Party members infiltrate the space of the rehearsal hall, creating a disturbance. One of the singers (the one who had trouble getting the right pitch on '*Gente*' [people]) moves forward and says: 'Either we rehearse or we have a meeting!' This scene can be read as privileged in articulating a contradiction between art and politics which is a major antinomy of the film. Further, the song's lyrics actually deal with oppression, but the debate over pitch displaces the political content onto aesthetic form.

The text provides us with certain socially determined representations of postwar Italy (unemployment, alienation, housing conditions, the Church, etc.), but they are divorced from any real conditions to which these representations might refer through the workings of ideology. Elements of the historically 'real' do enter the text, but they are displaced and become, as ideology, present as determined and distorted by their very absences. *Bicycle Thieves*, therefore, has a peculiarly overdetermined relation to historical reality. Rather than making direct homological comparisons between real Italy circa 1948 and the Italy of *Bicycle Thieves*, it is important to note that the latter's imaginary Italy is the product of a representational process which signifies not so much 'postwar Italy' as certain of postwar Italy's ways of signifying itself. In *Bicycle Thieves* (and in much of the neorealist canon), ideology presents itself to the text as 'Life,' rather than as a system of concepts. It is the nature of this ideology, as well as the aesthetic modes of articulation of that ideology, which is at stake.

Are the contradictions of the text the same as the real social/historical contradictions, in some sort of mirror relationship? No, since it is precisely ideology's function to efface contradictions. The contradictions exist only between ideology and what it masks: history itself.

Textual dissonances, then, are the effect of the film's production of ideology.

The eclecticism of Italy's 1948 Constitution is apparent; it is a mélange of Catholic social doctrine, Marxism, and welfare state liberalism. It posits 'a democratic Republic founded on labor' with 'inalienable duties of political, economic, and social solidarity.' Article Four guarantees full employment (in the year of Italy's highest level of *un*employment – estimated at 24 percent) and regulates child labor. In addition, the Constitution pledges 'the material and spiritual progress of society,' a phraseology obviously hammered out between competing forces.

The Christian Democrat victory in 1948 (gain of four-and-one-half million votes over 1946) over the Popular Front (loss of one million votes) has been attributed in part to the influx of American Marshall Plan aid and the threat of its withdrawal in the event of a Communist-Socialist election victory. In addition, between 1946 and 1947, UNRRA-CASAS funds were used to build modern, though cramped, housing units (of the type seen in *Bicycle Thieves*). This measure – along with increased social assistance programs, pensions, and family allowances – helped to stem the tide of social unrest brought about by the revocation of the ban on job dismissals in July 1947. Mario Cannella's implicit and explicit critiques of the P.C.I. (Partito Communista Italiano) in this period (Cannella, 5–50) center upon the collaboration in the economic reconstruction of Italy. The P.C.I. did not, for instance, demand a redistribution of wealth, nationalization of industry, or institution of a welfare state; neither did the films of that period.

There are unquestionable links between neorealism and its social/ historical moment, yet the films – including *Bicycle Thieves* – seem unable to deal with the real forces at work within the society, so displace them and attempt to close the discourse around these displacements. As in Adam Smith, the contradictions show but are not resolved within the text, so no perspective for struggle is offered. *Bicycle Thieves* offers several (inadequate) solutions to the problems raised. A social democratic resolution is proffered, whereby the revelation of injustice will lead to its eradication. Another is the universalization of the problem to a mythic dimension ('the poor are always with us'), undergrounded in the specificity of historical conditions. Love (personal, familial, Christian, *ad infinitum*) can resolve the conflicts ('Love conquers all') and alienation because they are originally posited as interpersonal forces, not part of an interclass struggle. Indeed, though

Bicycle Thieves has been hailed as a progressive film, an outcry of protest, and 'the only valid Communist film of the past decade' (Bazin, 51), there is no class analysis at all; rather, this sort of analysis is displaced to a moralist/idealist (even a Christian) critique of social injustice. At best, therefore, the film is reformist; at worst, it legitimizes the ideology of bourgeois liberalism.

> The true function of the cinema is not to tell fables ... the cinema must tell a reality as if it were a story; there must be no gap between life and what is on the screen.
>
> CESARE ZAVATTINI

Neorealism, as manifested in *Bicycle Thieves*, is not an alternative signifying practice to the Hollywood classical narrative; it is not a new rhetoric. Although it purports to be 'life' – as opposed to dominant cinema's positioning of a spectator – there is a construction of a subject. This may perhaps be the construction of a social subject through an intersubjectivity based on *doxa* ['received opinion,' a term coined by French sociologist Pierre Bourdieu] and parable within an ideological social matrix.

Bazin's claim that *Bicycle Thieves'* narrative events are ateleological ('No one seems to have arranged them in order on a dramatic spectrum') needs to be reexamined. The dramatic construction of the film's narrative is modeled on the eleven steps of classical plot development (Freytag's triangle, Scribe's nineteenth-century 'well-made play,' Aristotelian tragedy, etc.). The film's published screenplay notes ten major dissolves, each a rather explicit touchstone for a dramatic increment: 1 / EXPOSITION – sets the time, place, atmosphere, background, and characters; 2 / POINT OF ATTACK – states the problem (Will Antonio Ricci find work?); 3 / COMPLICATION – he needs a bicycle to get the job; 4 / DISCOVERY – introduces new characters (wife, Bruno, boss) and new events (Ricci obtains the needed bicycle and starts work); 5 / REVERSAL – the bike is stolen; 6 / CONFLICT – the search for the bike, culminating in the Pathetic rainstorm; 7 / RISING ACTION – the pursuit of the Old Man; 8 / CRISIS – Ricci finds the thief, foreshadowing the turning point; 9 / CLIMAX – the high point of intensity (enunciated by *champs-contre-champs*[shot/countershot] editing), Ricci steals the other bicycle; 10 / FALLING ACTION – Ricci is released by the mob; and 11 / RESOLUTION – catharsis of tears and father-son understanding.

We know that over six months were spent on the writing of the screenplay. (Bazin: 'Few films have been more carefully put together, more pondered over, more meticulously elaborated – but de Sica gives dramatic necessity the character of something contingent, accidental' [Bazin, 68]). Yet chance – according to Annette Michelson – is the metaphysics of capitalism. What Bazin sees as the contingency of Bruno's pissing against a wall may actually serve comic relief purposes, as well as show the primacy of economic necessity (in the text's discourse – finding the bicycle) over biological necessity (urinating).

Thus, *Bicycle Thieves* evinces a novelistic/dramatic narrative structuration which relies heavily on the creation of a closed system and character individuation through mimetic and perspectival representation of visual space. This is also achieved through a system of organized gazes (shot/countershot, spectator/screen, camera/event). Tragedy is a dramatic construct, but (divorced from Chance) it is also part of the texture of life in real human societies.

Perhaps the major stylistic achievement of neorealism (although pioneered by earlier works) was the exploration of – and into – physical space. *Bicycle Thieves* sets up several spatial dialectics. One major one involves the relationship between a single unit subject to a mass background or real environment in what can only be described as *social shots*. This goes somewhat beyond the dominant cinema's inscription of free-standing individuals apart from their painted-on or rear-projected backgrounds, yet the foreground/background tension of the *mise-en-scène* structures a tension between the individual and his society which is a major mystification and displacement of the real conflicts and antagonisms which constitute the social fabric. Though the film depends on precise, to-the-frame editing of sutured shot/reverse shots to show that there is no camera in front of the scene being filmed, this strategy sets up a protagonist/antagonist dialectic which further displaces the class struggle.

The spatial constriction of interior locations (the Ricci apartment, the pawnshop, work place, police station, basement, church, seeress's flat, thief's place, brothel) – articulated through various compositional masks – sets up a structure of inside and outside which reinforces the individual/collectivity antinomy. Likewise, the closing of doors and shutters can be read in these terms. Window shutters are rudely shut in Ricci's face as he proudly hoists his wife up to see his new locker room; when searching the thief's apartment, a neighbor across the way closes her shutters just as the policeman says 'You're out of luck.' Doors are locked throughout the church as Ricci chases after the Old

Man. Thus, openings are closed on him at sites associated with work, neighbors, and religion. None of these offers any hope for integration of the hero or for a solution to his problem. Thus the film again displaces a basically social struggle onto the level of an inner malaise, a phenomenon frequently observed in films made in repressive cultures (e.g., American films of the 1950s).

A frequently deployed spatial strategy of *Bicycle Thieves* is the pan or dolly shot which initially constricts or flattens space only to open up or stretch the horizon line into deep background space through camera mobility. In a film with many moving camera setups (Steenbeck analysis reveals 250 moving shots), many crucial spatial articulations follow this pattern.

Antonio Ricci is introduced in just such a shot. Initially Ricci is alone sitting in the street; as he moves toward the employment office, the camera pans with him, integrating him into the social group of other unemployed men. Maria is introduced in a group – amid the collectivity of women at the public fountain – fighting over water behind a barbed wire fence. The camera pans with her as she leaves the flatness of the frontal composition and ends up in a medium two-shot with Antonio. This shot, vertically bisected by a pole, places Maria on screen left with a deep-focus background extending into deep space behind her. On screen right, her husband's space is restricted by the background barbed wire. This composition lasts for as long as Ricci's dialogue: 'I feel wretched. There's an opening and I can't fill it.' Then, the camera retraces its initial pan to follow Ricci and his bucket-carrying wife walking into a wider vista (first along a flat, frontally positioned wall, then into the background space of new tenement buildings) with several vanishing points.

This pattern of camera restriction on the individual (foreground/ background, screen right/screen left, top/bottom) leading to a limitless horizon of background space with multiple vanishing points (*à la Veronese*) shows an authorial inscription of open possibilities on the spatial level for the characters which is ultimately frustrated on the narrative plane. These shots (over 30 such compositions dot the film's spatial discourse) may be read – progressively – as 'saying' that Ricci is indeed imprisoned, trapped in a net of selfhood, which he could overcome by making meaningful contact with his environment and other people who populate that background space.

On the other hand, several key scenes show the impossibility of such a resolution. The violations of classical perspective consist of 'aiming' or positioning the lines perpendicular to the plane of the picture at several points (rather than the unitary vanishing point) grouped near each other in a dynamic zone. This tends to open up space. In addition, De Sica composes background buildings in the manner of early Italian landscape painters with *fabbriche* [factories] in the distance, sometimes to the right, sometimes to the left. This contributes to the inscription of a vanishing *area* or *zone*, similar in some ways to a stage backdrop; however, this perspectival articulation does not close the background space; rather, multiple perspective breaks up space. The fissures inherent in such a schema are represented throughout the narratival, characterological, and ideological frameworks.

Bruno is introduced through the spokes of the already overdetermined bicycle as he polishes the frame. When Bruno occupies the frame alone, his space is almost always restricted; when it is not, he is nonetheless restricted by the offscreen space above him (the adult world). The boy's gaze is always directed up at his father (directed up by De Sica's offscreen voice, almost audible in this post-dubbed film).

It is the spatial inscription of the personal versus societal dimension (a displacement of the largely offscreen class struggle) which justifies Ben Lawton's remark that 'neorealism reflected the Italian fascination with the American dream and its glorification of the limitless potential of the individual' (Lawton, 9). It becomes, in a sense, a metonymic displacement of an authentically phenomenological space – a closed space produced from within itself – onto a space organized from the vantage of another, absent site, the site of ideology, the closure of classical (or near-classical) representation. This is not, strictly speaking, a fixed center or locus/site; rather, it is a function. Within the framework (in cinematic terms, the frame-work) of the text, ideology *seems* to determine the historically real, rather than vice versa; but, ultimately, history is the real signifier of cinema, as it is the ultimate signified.

Thus, the overdetermination of the bicycle (as job, home, pride, faith, hope, Italy, physical and social mobility, etc.) and the theft (displacement of the class robbery of capitalism onto a lumpen-proletariat petty crime) allows for a continual succession of disappointments and fissures of our unity as acting subjects, yet the text masks the basis of this subversion in the real historical forces. One arena of that struggle was the polarization between bourgeois forces and the Popular Front circa 1948. Likewise, the thief's German hat (referred to twice in the film) reworks the continual neorealist displacement of blame onto Nazism, rather than homegrown Italian fascism. Even Ricci's theft of a bike at the end is a displaced form of revolt and protest, enunciated in a structured discourse of glance/object/reaction shots (as well as swelling shouts on the soundtrack) between Ricci, the thousands of bikes parked outside the stadium, and the lone bicycle against the wall. This structuration of looks, including p.o.v. shots, sets up a closed suture system similar to Hollywood classical narrative which designates nodal points of (displaced, internalized) conflict: Ricci and the employment bureaucrat, the family and the pawnshop attendant, Ricci and the police inspector, Ricci and the thief, etc.

But Ricci, as a traditional identification figure, is a character whose position of social knowledge is unknown to him. He internalizes the class conflicts of his society, a society whose roots are still in fascist structures. When Ricci tries on his new uniform, Maria says, 'You look like a cop!' Ricci playfully tussles with her over this insult. (The low esteem in which the police are held in Italy is unmatched in the world, except perhaps in Ireland. This predates fascism somewhat, although the fascist laws on public safety [1931] reinforced these feelings.) But he is allied with the privileged class in many ways. On the job, he ignores the begging street urchins. With his own son, he evinces the characterological rigidity and authoritarian ideology of patriarchy which Wilhelm Reich finds at the basis of fascism.

> In the figure of the father the authoritarian state has its representative in every family, so that the family becomes its most important instrument of power ... The structural reproduction of a society's economic system in the psychology of the masses is the basic mechanism in the process of the formation of political ideas.
>
> WILHELM REICH, *The Mass Psychology of Fascism*

Yet Ricci often manifests a childlike helplessness, an inability to gain control of his own life (like Umberto D.). The Oedipal configurations (Bruno/Antonio, Antonio/the State) are marshalled into the service of a patriarchal family structure, made even more evident by the narrative disappearance of the wife/mother after fulfilling her plot function of pawning the family linen. When she is referred to (during the restaurant scene), Maria is reinscribed into the narrative as a censoring agent – 'If your mother only knew ... (I was letting you drink).' She thus becomes a displaced super-ego, especially since Antonio is still trying desperately to deny his own authoritarian tendencies (and resultant guilt). The whole restaurant scene may be viewed in this

light: as Antonio's attempt to 'make up' with Bruno for the unpro-
voked slap (displaced onto Bruno from social/political forces and, in
the film's discourse, from Antonio's own self-doubts) and imagined
guilt (thinking that Bruno was drowned). *Bicycle Thieves'* ultimate dramatic resolution – the father-son handclasp – demonstrates the film's
failure to think beyond the level of the family melodrama. There is
hope in family unity and solidarity, even if one's society and one's
comrades are unresponsive.

Bruno imitates his father on several occasions. He puts his lunch in
the front pocket of his overalls like his father. When they sit on the
curb at the end, their 'body language' (Reichian character armour) is
exactly the same. The Oedipal injunctions – 'You should not *be* the
father / You must be *like* the father' – become a redirection of libidinal
cathexis in the service of ideological interpellation. Bruno is physically
and psychologically dwarfed throughout the film. He is positioned
next to the massive architectural monuments built by Mussolini in his
attempt to recapture the glory that was Rome. Two merchants at the
Florida slap his hands as he searches through bike parts, a pederast
accosts him in the same location, he falls onto a rainy street (unseen by
Antonio), he is almost run over by an automobile (again Antonio is
looking elsewhere), and he even diminishes his own stature by genuflecting and crossing himself in church – rendering homage to the
supreme patriarch, God. A priest even strikes Bruno, an action repeated shortly thereafter by Antonio; the boy is thus struck by two
'fathers' – an ecclesiastical and a biological one. Earlier, Bruno had
been spatially trapped between two fathers: Antonio and the Austrian
monks in the rain scene. The rain here may be a metonymic structure
for the sorrow depicted throughout the film, yet it displaces this psy-
chological/economic misery onto a natural event, thereby naturalizing
and eternalizing suffering, rather than seeing the historical/economic
basis for exploitation. The 'rain,' incidentally, was produced by the
Roman fire brigade (so much for Bazinian phenomenological integrity!). The German accents of the monks are in line with the German
hat of the thief: a displacement of vestiges of Italian fascism onto
Nazism.

Ricci himself incorporates patriarchal suppression in all his dealings
with authority figures, notably the police. He seeks relief and justice
from the police on three separate occasions. The detective in the police
station mechanically files the report ('Nothing, just a bicycle'), more
interested in the *Nucleo Celere* (flying squad) of anti-riot jeeps down

below. Ricci is thrown back on his own individual initiative ('Then it's up to me') in the search and, in the very next scene, he individualistically tries to sneak in line to catch a bus. In a metaphoric/metonymic compositional arrangement, Ricci moves away from the camera, separated from the masses by a fence; the crowd moves toward the camera. This sort of push-and-pull movement (repeated throughout the film) into the depth of illusionist projection of space and out toward the spectator tends to set up and resolve a displaced dialectic between solitude and solidarity. The displacement is in the inscription of collectivity. Whenever a social group is shown (the unemployed at the employment bureau, the women at the fountain, the line at Signora Santona's, the bus line, the peddlers at the Florida, the crowd outside the thief's house, the mob who apprehend Ricci), there is conflict. The Party meeting in the basement intrudes on the rehearsal, but the camera (and Ricci) seek resolution with the artistic. No scenes of an organized coalition of workers are seen; instead, groups are set in opposition to individual fulfillment. Thus, the structural absence of a major segment of the postwar republic betrays an ideological position in terms of the 1948 political climate which substitutes a social democratic model of statism – even though state and church intervention throughout the film are unsatisfactory.

Ricci's second encounter with the police ends unhappily as well. At the Florida, a policeman confirms that the painter did not steal Antonio's bike. Once again, Ricci defers to the police officer. Even upon catching the thief (a miracle which follows hard on the seeress's prediction and the ringing of a church bell), the police cannot help.

The treatment of the Catholic Church in *Bicycle Thieves* is fraught with contradictions. Ostensibly anticlerical, the film also posits a quasi-mystical aura of Christian brotherhood – which cuts across class lines – as a level of discourse, with young Bruno at its moral core. Indeed, the historical critique of clericalism in Italy (especially for its complicity in the rise of fascism, the Lateran Pacts, etc.) has been pursued by both progressive and bourgeois elements. The charity ward scene in *Bicycle Thieves* might actually present a Holy See strategy of feeding the poor to diffuse political unrest. During the 1948 election campaign, the Church actively pursued a policy of 'competition' with the workers' left (and the P.C.I. in particular) through a policy of social and economic reform to advance the *classo subalterne*. Though De Sica/Zavattini may poke gentle fun at this policy ('You can't eat until after Mass'), it is certainly non-threatening despite the over-reaction of *L'Osservatore*

Romano, the Vatican house journal: 'The time has come to sweep the country of the garbage known as realist films.' The weeded church-yard, the Austrian priest, the continual presence of crucifixes and religious icons (even at Signora Santona's), the tracking shots of darkly lit poverty-stricken worshippers in the church (in sharp contrast to the overdressed lady and the elegant young man), and the irony of the *Pietà*-like scene of the thief and his protective mother all seem to point to anticlericalism. But this overdetermination is ultimately undercut by the true Christian underpinnings of the film's ideological compromise. Antonio is hushed in church, but he is also hushed in the Party meeting. Religion seems to get in his way – the icons in the church's anteroom, the genuflecting in mid-chase, etc. – yet the superstition of the seeress ('Even your mother's saints can't help us') and the highly over-determined vespers bell which signals the spotting of the thief (articulated through a complex conflict of p.o.v.s, in tight, oppressive close-ups) reinscribe a deeper level of religiosity in the film's ideology – that of the displacement and suppression of the authoritarian family (the *Holy* Family, and all that suggests), the state, and the church. The regimentation in the church ('Line them up neatly') is no different from the general groupings in the society with remnants and vestiges of lingering fascism (see Freud's essay 'Two Artificial Groups: The Church and the Army').

The film tries desperately to explode the myth of the solidarity of the poor. It is Ricci's fellow poor – the thief himself, the Old Man, his helpless friends, the Party leaders (who only see the large-scale issues), even his son – who betray him constantly. The historical fact of worker solidarity is carefully elided in favor of a populism at best (the rehearsal), an intra-class antagonism (the thief) at worst.

> Representation is not defined directly by imitation: even if one gets rid of notions of the 'real,' of the 'vraisemblable,' of the copy, there will still be representation for so long as a subject casts his gaze toward a horizon on which he cuts out an apex ...
>
> ROLAND BARTHES, 'Diderot, Brecht, Eisenstein'

Every text internalizes its social relations of production; through the conventions established it internalizes the way it will be consumed. *Bicycle Thieves* is the product of a specific, overdetermined conjuncture of elements and formations, and encodes within itself its own ideology of how, by whom, and for whom it was produced. This study has attempted to avoid an 'illustrative' view of the film to study social/historical conditions. Rather, cinema as an institution, neorealism as a (close to classical) rhetoric, and *Bicycle Thieves* in its effectiveness can be seen as belonging to both base and superstructure because they figure in material production, ideological formation, and the nexus between the two. The film has certain elements of intertextuality – Ricci's new job is posting Rita Hayworth advertisements, a boy dressed as Charlie Chaplin (holding hands with a young girl in bridal veil) walks past Antonio, a photo of Gable is seen on the brothel wall, someone says 'The cinema means nothing to me,' etc. – but the linearity of the narrative, use of perspectival vistas, sutured editing, character identification techniques, traditional figurations (dissolves, fades, wipes, etc.), and representational strategies all mark the film in the mode of dominant cinema.

Likewise, *Bicycle Thieves'* relation to the forces of production and the social/historical realities of 1948 Italy marks it as a film of ideological compromise, rather than a film of revolutionary import. Though Zavattini has said: 'The cinema had completely failed in its purpose by choosing the path of Méliès rather than that of Lumière,' he neglects to mention that Lumière was a chronicler of bourgeois society (the parades and dignitaries) and of bourgeois family life (*Baby's Breakfast*) from the point of view of an industrialist basically satisfied with himself and his social matrix. *Bicycle Thieves* also reflects an organizational principle which implicitly accepts bourgeois society, within the framework of the social democrat modification of high capitalism. Its philosophical underpinnings are idealist, individualist, and transcendental, and careful deconstruction of the text elucidates its ideological displacements and structural absences.

References

Bazin, André. *What Is Cinema?* Volume 2. Translated by Hugh Gray. Berkeley: University of California Press, 1972.

Cannella, Mario. 'Ideology and Aesthetic Hypotheses in the Criticism of Neorealism.' *Screen* 14:4 (Winter 1973–4), 5–60.

Houston, Penelope. *The Contemporary Cinema.* Baltimore: Penguin, 1963.

Lawton, Ben. 'Italian Neorealism: A Mirror Construction of Reality.' *Film Criticism*, 3:2 (Winter 1979), 8–23.

Neorealist Aesthetics and the Fantastic: *The Machine to Kill Bad People* and *Miracle in Milan*

PETER BONDANELLA

Peter Bondanella has written extensively on Italian film; among his major works are Italian Cinema: From Neorealism to the Present *and two books on Federico Fellini. This essay, which first appeared in* Film Criticism *in 1979, explores the allegorical dimension of* Miracle in Milan. *Bondanella is interested in the meta-cinematic nature of the relationship of fantasy and reality in* Miracle in Milan *as a trope of the artistic process itself, and he makes a strong case for the compatibility of allegory and neoralism. His argument is reminiscent of Claude Roy's earlier but rather different discussion of the issues of allegory in* Miracle in Milan *in an essay published in* Cahiers du cinéma *in 1951. Roy was one of the first critics to see in* Miracle in Milan *a revision of neorealism. Like Bondanella, he suggests that realism and allegory are not necessarily at odds, but he and Bondanella differ substantially in their attitudes towards the idea of the imagination. For Bondanella the concept of meta-cinema is significant because of his sense that what we call reality is to some degree imagined, a concept that he explores especially in his writings on Fellini.*

We have included in an appendix at the end of this essay a short excerpt from Roy's work (see 179–80 below).

Looking back at the Italian neorealist novel in 1964, Italo Calvino declared that neorealists 'knew all too well that what counted was the music and not the libretto ... there were never more dogged formalists

Peter Bondanella, 'Neorealist Aesthetics and the Fantastic: *The Machine to Kill Bad People* and *Miracle in Milan*,' *Film Criticism* 3:2 (Winter 1979), 24–9. Revised and reprinted in Bondanella, *Italian Cinema: From Neorealism to the Present* (New York: Continuum, 1991), 91–5 than we; and never were lyric poets as effusive as those objective reporters we were supposed to be' (Calvino, vii). However, traditional approaches to Italian neorealist cinema (as opposed to fiction) have usually accepted the premise that these films constitute a cinema of 'fact' or 'reconstituted reportage.' Neorealist aesthetics are, therefore, explained in terms of social themes, the use of nonprofessional actors, on-location shooting, documentary effects, the rejection of theatrical or cinematic conventions, and a respect for the ontological wholeness of time. This view ignores Calvino's warning and overlooks the fact that major works of Italian literary neorealism treat mythical or symbolic realities (not primarily social ones), employ unreliable or subjective narrators, and embrace a clearly anti-naturalistic narrative stance, breaking the rules of literary realism established by James, Zola, or Verga.[1] If the term 'neorealism' is to retain any special significance, it should refer to the similarities between literary and cinematic works typical of a fixed historical moment and a specific artistic style. As I have argued elsewhere, a careful analysis of major neorealist films reveals their consistent focus not only upon social reality but also upon the dialectic of reality and appearance, usually the appearance or illusion of reality produced by artistic means (Bondanella, 220–39).

If we approach post-war Italian cinema from this perspective (one gained, in part, from an assessment of its literary counterpart), we derive certain critical advantages. A wider variety of works can be included within the rubric of neorealism (especially those which do not deal primarily with social problems or which are conceived in a comic vein). Furthermore, we need no longer feel compelled to discuss the so-called 'crisis of neorealism' as if it were an integral aspect of Italian cinematic history: the early works of Federico Fellini or those by Rossellini in the 1950's cannot be said to constitute a 'betrayal' of realist principles, since such principles were never accepted entirely by the directors in question. This 'crisis' can now be more accurately considered as a crisis in the history of neorealist criticism which reflected the views of men such as Guido Aristarco, Andre Bazin, and Cesare Zavattini.[2] Nonetheless, expanding the meaning of the term neorealism leaves an important task unfinished. Works usually overlooked in discussions of neorealism because of their deviation from a purely realist aesthetic must now be reintegrated into a more comprehensive interpretation of this moment in film history. Both self-conscious treatments of the interplay between reality and appearance, Rossellini's *La machina ammazzacattive / The Machine to Kill Bad People* (1948) and De

Sica's *Miracolo a Milano / Miracle in Milan* (1950) illuminate issues crucial to any reconsideration of Italian neorealism.

According to many leftist Italian critics, these two works evince a generally conservative reaction and prove that a political and economic crisis in Italian society was systematically ignored in the cinema on account of political or financial pressure on directors and producers, who displayed a cowardly willingness to make films for escapist entertainment rather than for progressive social change.[3] However, this is an unfounded assessment of these two films, for both Rossellini and De Sica explicitly rejected a strictly realist aesthetic during this period. De Sica remarked that he made *Miracle in Milan* to resolve problems of 'form and style' (De Sica, 13). In 1952, Rossellini defined realism as 'simply the artistic form of truth' (Verdone, 70) and stated that he had made *The Machine to Kill Bad People* in order to shift his work toward the traditional Italian *commedia dell'arte*. He declared that men possessed two opposed tendencies, each of which the cinema must respect: 'quella della concretezza e quella della fantasia. Oggi si tende brutalmente a sopprimere la seconda ... Dimenticando la seconda tendenza, dicevo, quella della fantasia, si tende a uccidere in noi ogni sentimento di umanita, a creare l'uomo robot: il quale deve pensare in un solo modo, e tendere al concreto' ['that of concreteness and that of imagination. Today we tend to brutally suppress the second one ... By forgetting the imaginative tendency, as I was saying, we tend to kill in ourselves every feeling of humanity and to create the robot-man who thinks in only one way and tends toward the concrete'] (Rondolino, 5).

Despite the marked differences between the earlier works of Rossellini and De Sica, *The Machine to Kill Bad People* and *Miracle in Milan* share a remarkable number of stylistic and thematic similarities. Both employ frequent comic gags that betray obvious debts to silent film comedy (Chaplin and René Clair) or to traditional Italian comic theatre (Rossellini's subject was suggested by Eduardo De Filippo); Rossellini's work even opens with a traditional prologue in verse and a stage full of characters set up by the hand of a puppeteer or *capocomico*, and it closes with a rhymed epilogue and a moral. Because of this link to similar dramatic and cinematographic conventions, both films reveal a similar approach to characterization. Neither director is principally preoccupied with the subtle psychological nuances he achieved in such works as *Germania, anno zero / Germany Year Zero* (1947), *Bicycle Thieves*, or *Umberto D.* (1951). Instead, characters are almost without exception motivated by a single force – greed and self-interest on the one hand, or pure goodness on the other – and their actions identify them as traditional comic types. The storyline of each film is equally simple and represents what may best be described as an allegory or a fable involving the relationship of the rich to the poor, the evil to the good. Although Rossellini's film is perhaps simpler from a technical point of view because it contains fewer special photographic effects while De Sica's exploits surrealist comic effects in the manner of René Clair, it is also more richly plotted, with sub-plots parodying both the story of Romeo and Juliet and Rossellini's own film *Paisan* (in particular the story of the arrival of the Americans in Italy). While the thematic content continues what is usually considered a typical neorealist preoccupation with social justice and socio-economic problems in post-war Italy, it is precisely their attention to style which makes these works significant. In Rossellini, there is an extended treatment of the very nature of photography, while in De Sica the conventions usually associated with neorealism are brought into question. In so doing, each director provides the viewer with a clearer idea of the limits of neorealism in his works.

With *The Machine to Kill People*, Rossellini presents an extended meditation, albeit in a comic vein, on the relationship between photography or artistic reality and the equally noble reality of ethics and moral conduct. A demon grants to Celestino Esposito, a professional photographer, the miraculous power of causing evildoers to disappear from the face of the earth by means of his camera (*la macchina* of the original Italian title). A good man consumed by moral indignation, Celestino takes his weapon and turns upon those in his village who exploit the poor and act only out of self-interest. Soon, several of the town's most illustrious citizens (Donna Amalia, the loan-shark; the mayor; the policeman; the owner of a fleet of fishing boats and trucks) suffer the same comic fate: once Celestino photographs a previous picture of them, they are frozen in that pose and pass to their reward. As the film progresses, Celestino becomes impatient with all the inhabitants of the village. The poor, themselves no better than the rich, have exactly the same greedy motives alluded to in the prologue, where we have already been warned that 'In the end, nice or not / they resemble each other a lot.' Rapidly demoralized by this discovery, Celestino embarks upon a plan to destroy everyone, since all are imperfect, and in the very act of doing so he murders the good town doctor who has been trying to stop him from photographing another picture of the entire village. Driven by remorse, Celestino decides to punish himself with his magic camera but only after he has eliminated the demon who granted him this miraculous power. Before he can succeed, however, the demon reappears, becomes a convert when Celestino makes the sign of the cross, and restores Celestino's victims to life as if nothing had ever happened. A final moral is delivered in the epilogue: 'Do good but don't overdo it! / Avoid evil for your own sake / Don't be hasty in judging others. / Think twice before punishing.'

Rossellini is chiefly concerned with the symbolic importance of the camera and, by extension, the nature of photography itself. In good neorealist fashion and reminiscent of statements made by such important figures as Cesare Zavattini, Celestino views the camera as a means of separating reality from illusion, good from evil, substance from appearance. Photography is, for him, a metaphor for a way of knowing, for a means of apprehending essential moral and ethical facts; it enables him, so he believes, to penetrate the surface of events to the bedrock of reality and to fulfil a god-like role in his small village (not unlike that of a film director on the set). Interestingly enough, Celestino does not perform this miraculous photographic feat with a direct duplication on film of objects in the 'real' world. Instead, he must first take a photograph of another photograph to accomplish this. As any good Platonist knows, he is two steps removed from the world of tangible objects or sensory reality by the time he takes the second picture and is engaged in the essentially self-reflexive act of producing a work of art from another work of art, not from reality itself. While creating an elaborate joke of Celestino's self-delusory activity, Rossellini emphasizes a fundamental characteristic of filmic art. In a comic manner, he tells us emphatically that photography (and by extension, the cinema as a branch of this art form) is incapable of separating good from evil or of readily distinguishing reality from appearance. Celestino takes the demon to be the patron saint of the town, and when he attacks the rich to help the poor, he learns that some of the wealthy are not entirely evil (Donna Amalia's will leaves her money to the three poorest people in the village), and that the poor share the selfish vices of the rich. Nowhere is there any clear distinction between diametrically opposed metaphysical or ethical positions. The camera, viewed as a means of acquiring knowledge of social reality by overly optimistic neorealist theorists, has been reduced to a fallible instrument which reflects not reality but human subjectivity and error.

The main character of De Sica's *Miracle in Milan*, Totò, is as con-

cerned over good and evil as Celestino. Yet, he is infinitely more innocent and naive, without a malicious thought in his heart. A white dove
given to him by his foster mother Lolotta enables him to fulfil the
wishes of every poor person living in the shantytown outside Milan
until it is taken away from him, and he and his friends are forced to
escape their wicked oppressors by flying on broomsticks over the
cathedral of Milan! Here, we are clearly in the realm of fantasy, of the
fairy tale or the fable, in spite of the often-cited remark of the script-
writer, Cesare Zavattini, that 'the true function of the cinema is not to
tell fables' [Zavattini, 53 above]. The film attacks the very definition of
neorealism canonized in the essays of André Bazin. Although the storyline of this fable echoes the social concerns characteristic of neorealist works, De Sica's style departs even more radically than that of
Rossellini in *The Machine to Kill Bad People* from the traditional defini-
tions of neorealism. Chronological time is rejected, as is duration or
ontological wholeness; common-sense logic is abandoned as well, and
the usual cause and effect relationships between objects in the 'real'
world are replaced by absurd, even surreal events (the sunlight shines
in only one spot at a time; angels or magic spirits visit earth; people are
granted any wish they desire). The fantastic is bodied forth by a number of special effects that appear only rarely in neorealist works: people fly over the cathedral of Milan on broomsticks, thanks to process
shots; images are superimposed upon other images; smoke seems to
reverse its course; rapid editing makes it seem that hats chase a character out of sight of the camera's eye.

De Sica goes beyond Rossellini's metaphoric discussion of realism
through the symbolic image of the camera and concentrates upon the
place of the imagination itself (which may, as in *Miracle in Milan*,
employ the camera as a means of expression). The entire film is thus an
extended metaphor, a hymn to the role of illusion and fantasy in art, as
well as in life, and is not merely a frivolous entertainment. De Sica tells
us that the human impulse to creativity in the work of art, like the
broomsticks which carry the poor over the church steeples of Milan, is
capable of transcending social problems but not of resolving them.
Filmic art can only offer the consolation of beauty and the hope that its
images and ideas may move the spectator to social action that will
change the world.

Rossellini's film questions the cognitive potential of the camera and
undermines the belief that good and evil are easily distinguished. De
Sica's work affirms Rossellini's doubts that the poor or downtrodden

of the world are morally superior to the wealthy or their exploiters (indeed, the poor in the shantytown of *Miracle in Milan* aspire only to becoming wealthy themselves and are equally selfish), but it makes an even more positive statement about the place of the imagination (the element of *fantasia* Rossellini mentioned in his remarks concerning *The Machine to Kill Bad People*) in both filmic art and life. While Rossellini limits the power of the camera to discover reality, De Sica demonstrates that the camera can uncover new dimensions of experience through the poetry of the creative fantasy. Seen from this perspective, each work reveals itself to be not merely a comic fable about the rich and the poor, but also a significant treatment of the relationship between reality and illusion. The distance traveled by Rossellini or De Sica since *Paisan* or *Shoeshine* is not as far as most believe and is more a change of degree than of kind. *The Machine to Kill Bad People* and *Miracle in Milan* clearly mark the outer boundaries of the Italian neorealist movement since they push the dialectic of realism and illusion almost to the breaking point.

Notes

1 These general remarks apply to such neorealist masterpieces as Elio Vittorini's *In Sicily* (1941), Carlo Levi's *Christ Stopped at Eboli* (1945), Italo Calvino's *The Path to the Nest of Spiders* (1947), and Cesare Pavese's *The Moon and the Bonfires* (1951). Vasco Pratolini is the only major writer whose works (especially *Metello*, which appeared in 1955) adhere closely to the canons of literary realism. For the most recent survey of the interrelationships between neorealist film and neorealist fiction, including a perceptive critique of traditional approaches to this material, see the entry on 'Neorealism' by Ben Lawton in the *Dictionary of Italian Literature*, ed. Peter and Julia Conaway Bondanella (Westport, Ct.: Greenwood Press, 1979), 353–7.

2 See Guido Aristarco, *Antologia di cinema Nuovo: 1952–58* (Florence: Guaraldi, 1975), esp. 1–151; various essays by Bazin, now available in English in *What Is Cinema? Vol. 2* (Berkeley: University of California Press, 1971); a brief exchange of positions between Aristarco and Fellini in *Federico Fellini: Essays in Criticism*, 60–9; and Cesare Zavattini, 'Some Ideas on the Cinema,' in MacCann, 216–28.

3 For a recent expression of this widely held opinion in Italy (with particular reference to *Miracle in Milan*), see Alfonso Canziani and Cristina Bragaglia, *La stagione neorealista* (Bologna: CLUEB, 1976), 95–9.

References

Bondanella, Peter. 'Early Fellini: *Variety Lights, The White Sheik, I Vitelloni.*' In *Federico Fellini: Essays in Criticism.* Edited by Peter Bondanella. New York: Oxford University Press, 1978.

Calvino, Italo. *The Path to the Nest of Spiders.* New York: Ecco Press, 1976.

De Sica, Vittorio. *Miracle in Milan.* New York: Orion Press, 1968.

MacCann, Richard Dyer, ed. *Film: A Montage of Theories.* New York: Dutton, 1966.

Rondolino, Gianni. *Roberto Rossellini.* Florence: La Nuova Italia, 1974.

Verdone, Mario. 'A Discussion of Neorealism.' *Screen* 14:4 (1973–4), 69–77.

Appendix: Reflections on *Miracle in Milan*

CLAUDE ROY

Miracle in Milan (like *Passport to Pimlico*) is a film which breaks this habit of snoozing in front of the screen, which was the case with so-called pure realism. The viewer of *Bicycle Thieves* was asked to go out on the street, into the restaurant, and into the home. The viewer of *Miracle in Milan* is asked to play the game. And the game consists not only of describing images as they appear, but of naming things as they are. The *game* is about pouring forth the *most* reality possible by contrasting images of what is *least* likely. There is no likelihood that a magic dove should give such powers to Totò; there is no likelihood that the poor people of Milan fly on broomsticks; there is no likelihood that businessmen talk like the characters of Granville and that their discussions be transformed into dogs' barking and wolves' howling. But ... it is very plausible that the poor people would be chased out by the rich; that the *trusts* might not be at all concerned with the happiness of the people they are exploiting; that the Mobic (who in the film have become the Moppi) are, in reality, absolutely identical to the ones Zavattini describes in chapter 3 of his novel and in the film. There is no

From Claude Roy, 'Reflexions sur (et à propos de) *Miracle à Milan,*' *Cahiers du cinéma* 7 (December 1951), 29–39. Translated by Jean-Pierre Allard likelihood that the policemen would be struck by paralysis with their truncheons in the air, singing opera songs against their will. But all of Italy has recognized in *Miracle in Milan* the mercenary 'dirty workers,' the 'célèbre' ... The use of allegory in a contemporary setting is not a way to tell more easily things which are in fact difficult to tell. It is, on the contrary, a way to play with the difficulty, because the inquisitive and critical mind of the viewer will be constantly in an awakened and warned state. Allegory is not presented here with the deceptive manners of a good fat girl who knows how to take the famous naturalized slice of life slice by slice. Allegory requires from the viewer that s/he constantly untangle the wisely mixed-up threads of fiction and reality. Allegory is an *enlightener*. There are two essential conditions which make allegory a valid genre. The first one is that truth be its object: truth, and not arbitrary games of the imagination ... The second one is that allegory should not be a cold-blooded monster.

Miracle in Milan: Some Psychoanalytic Notes on a Movie

ALEXANDER GRINSTEIN

Alexander Grinstein's essay provides not a contemporary psychoanalytic perspective on the film Miracle in Milan *but rather an early use of object-relations theory. Developed by a group of British psychoanalysts (Ian Suttie, W.R.D. Fairbairn, and Donald Winnicott) who, like Lacanian psychoanalysts, owe a debt to Melanie Klein, object-relations theory stresses the role of identity rather than sexuality in psychological dynamics. Dr Grinstein's essay complements the discussions of* Miracle in Milan *by Wegner and Bondanella by exploring another possible allegorical dimension of the film. We have excerpted that portion of Grinstein's discussion that bears on the film.*

Recently a new movie by the famous Italian director Vittorio De Sica made its appearance in theaters throughout this country. It won the Grand Prize of the Cannes festival and the Grand Prize of the International Critics in 1951. The New York Film Critics awarded it First Prize as best foreign film for the last year. Unlike his other pictures, such as *Ladri di biciclette / The Bicycle Thief* (1948) or *Sciuscià / Shoeshine* (1946), which express in a profound and deeply moving manner the intensity of human emotions in real life situations, this new picture [*Miracolo a Milano / Miracle in Milan* (1950)] evokes no such stirring experience. It is much more subtle in its appeal, yet delicate and sensitive in its understanding. De Sica, himself, describes the movie as a 'fantasy.' 'It is,' he says, 'a fable suspended half-way between whimsy and reality –

Alexander Grinstein, '*Miracle in Milan*: Some Psychoanalytic Notes on a Movie,' *American Imago* 10:3 (Fall 1953), 229–45 a fable that is intended more for grown-ups than for children, but still nothing but a fable.'

The story and screenplay of the movie are by Cesare Zavattini, based on his novel *Totò Il Buono / Toto, the Good*. He is De Sica's closest collaborator and has also been the author of the script for *Shoeshine* and *The Bicycle Thief*.

...

This film presents two important psychological problems: Wherein does the great appeal of this film lie? What actually constitutes the miracle in the film?

The film is not in any way religious and makes no pretense of being so, although it is my understanding that it has been considered irreligious. Moreover, the film might be said to deal with a clash between communism and capitalism, communism being represented by the little society of poor people, and capitalism by Mobbi and his henchmen. However, this too does not seem to be the main issue of the film. Cortesi writes:

> The suggestion made by some Italian newspapers that *Miracle in Milan* tends to excite social animosities causes De Sica to come as close as he ever does to losing his temper. 'I have no interest in politics,' he replies. 'I am a member of no party, I am not a propagandist of any ideology. *Miracle in Milan* is inspired by nothing but a Christian feeling of human solidarity. In it, I speak the natural language of a man who does not close his eyes to the sufferings of his fellows, the language that Christianity has been speaking for the last twenty centuries.'

De Sica, himself, says:

> Although it has grotesque and fantastic elements, my latest film once again portrays the drama of the poor people who live their isolated lives in the midst of other men. Yet the story is basically a fable. I must confess I was attracted by the idea of being able, in the contemporary idiom and using the most common form of expression, the motion picture, to create another version of the old and romantic story of the rich man and the pauper. It is an uneven battle, but the pauper, with miraculous cleverness and courage, always succeeds in coming out on top in the end. Most often the force that drives and guides him is love and, in the end, it is goodness that is rewarded and evil that is punished. This is the story which men pass on from generation to generation as a lesson to children and a warning to adults.

During the entire film, a certain aura or quality persists which may be best described as definitely *dreamlike*. The rapid shifting of scenes, the magical wish fulfillent of the miracles in which all the wishes of the populace are granted, the ridiculousness of some situations (as, for example, having two angels stopped by a traffic light), the liberal use of symbolism, all give it the character of a dream. This gives us a clue as to the appeal of the film, namely, that just because it is like a dream, anyone can participate in it and weave into it a gratification of his own personal unconscious wishes.

The underlying thesis of the film is that all of one's wishes can be fulfilled, wishes of a conscious nature, or ego wishes, such as reality desires, as well as wishes that are infantile in their origin. It is interesting that it is this very fact of wish fulfillment that is used on the billboards and advertisements of this film. Some examples of this are: 'Your most intimate desires ...'; 'You are in this picture ...'; 'Your most intimate emotions ...'; 'Your most secret desires ...'; 'An uninhibited comedy ...'; 'With all the humanity, passion and power ... De Sica now turns his master's touch to a great human comedy of the "lonely ones" who dare believe that man's deepest longings can come true ...,' etc.

In its structure the film is elaborated according to the typical structure of a daydream. Freud writes:

> The activity of fantasy in the mind is linked up with some current impression, occasioned by some event in the present, which had the power to rouse an intense desire. From here it wanders back to the memory of an early experience, generally belonging to infancy, in which this wish was fulfilled. Then it creates for itself a situation which is to emerge in the future, representing the fulfillment of the wish. This is the daydream or fantasy, which now carries in it traces both of the occasion which engendered it and of some past memory. So, past, present and future are threaded, as it were, on the string of the wish that runs through them all. A very ordinary example may serve to make my statement clearer. Take the case of a poor orphan lad, to whom you have given the address of some employer where he may perhaps get work. On the way there he falls into a daydream suitable to the situation from which it springs. The content of the fantasy will be somewhat as follows: He is taken on and pleases his new employer, makes himself indispensable to the business, is taken into the family of the employer, and marries the charming daughter of the house. Then he comes to conduct the business, first as a partner, and then as successor to his father-in-law. In this way the dreamer regains what he had in his happy childhood, the protect-

ing house, his loving parents, and the first objects of his affection. You will see from such an example how the wish employs some event in the present to plan a future on the pattern of the past.   (Freud, 177–8)

One can readily see how, in the movie, Toto, after leaving the orphanage and not finding anyone who will respond to his friendly 'good morning,' weaves the fantasy (the rest of the movie) where he becomes successful, attains in a thinly modified way his past, but in a new society, and achieves his wish that he is then transported into a land where 'good morning really means good morning.'

The dominating theme about which the entire film revolves, and which seems to me to account for its specific appeal, is the relationship of Toto to his foster mother, whom he actually regards as his mother. Toto, it will be remembered, was abandoned by his 'natural' mother in a cabbage patch. He was abandoned by the Old Lolotta, whom he came to regard as his 'mother,' by her death. Such an interpretation on the part of children to the death of a parent is a familiar one in psychoanalytic work. He is literally abandoned by the orphanage, which turned him out into the world without any manifest provision for his lodging or work, even though he is now a grown man. As a result of these experiences, Toto is motivated by a powerful infantile wish to return to his mother or to establish once more a union with her. It is this longing which is expressed throughout the film, becoming particularly apparent when this wish finally becomes gratified at the time of his actual reunion with her above the cloud of smoke, while he is on the pole. This event must be considered the first of the real 'miracles,' being the first spectacular event in the film where any 'trick photography' is used.

That Toto was very much influenced by the memory of his foster mother is affirmed by many examples in the film. Psychoanalysis teaches us that when object relations fail or are disappointing, identification with the unsatisfactory love object takes place. By means of this mechanism of defense, the individual can retain and preserve the love object within himself without the necessity of giving it up. Such a manifestation may be observed in Toto's character structure. There is a certain femininity about him which is unmistakeable. We get the first indication of this in the incident when Toto gives the tramp his valise after removing from it its contents, including his mother's picture. This action expresses the statement: 'The image of my mother is of paramount importance to me. You may have my valise for I will be as kind and as generous to *you* as my mother was to *me* when I was a child.' The very next morning we see how he plays with and protects a child from the windstorm. His actions are very maternal in nature. More illustrative than these examples is the manner in which he asks children, 'How much is 5 × 5, or 3 × 3?' In this way he clearly acts like his foster mother teaching him the multiplication tables. The situation is carried further by his insistence on actually changing the names of the streets of the little community to examples of multiplication. In this we see the mechanism of his identification with his 'mother' carried to a high degree. Not only is he *like* his mother in this activity, he actually *is* his mother. Even in the task of building the community of dwellings out of the debris of the field, he acts out the behavior of his 'mother' when she built a city out of toys for him on the floor around the river of spilt milk. In his giving the people their wishes, assigning them their dwellings, and later in his granting them their 'wildest desires,' when empowered to do this with the aid of the dove, he acts like the good, kind, indulgent mother. One distinctly has the impression that the mother gratified his own demands a great deal, regardless of how difficult they may have been. She *would have* given him the moon if it were possible.

The theme of Toto's reunion with his dead mother reminds me of a dream which was told to me by a male homosexual patient. He had in reality lost his mother at eight years of age, and his entire life had been influenced by his reaction to her death. In fact, one important determinant of his homosexuality was his identification with his mother. He had never accepted her death, utilizing the mechanism of identification to keep her alive, within himself, so that he would not have to part from her or mourn for her. He persistently avoided this task in his analysis, and finally, for various reasons, interruption of treatment became necessary. The dream in question occurred during the night preceding the second last analytic hour. In the dream he is in a strange, beautiful land, which he somehow thinks must be heaven. There he meets a woman, who looks like a friendly neighbor lady, but he recognizes in the dream that it is really his mother. He is very pleased. In his associations he recognized his wish that the analysis give him back his mother. If it did not, it was of no value to him. At least in heaven he hoped that he would be reunited with her. We discussed the interruption of his analysis and he indicated that he did not want to say 'goodbye.' To avoid this he telephoned me, cancelling his last appointment, rationalizing this on the basis of it being 'unproductive anyway,' and 'I don't think it would be of any use or value.' Thus, in his fantasy life he continued his identification with his mother, avoiding the traumatic separation from her, and maintaining the hope that he would be reunited with her. He did not appear for his meeting with me, as his mother did not appear to him, thus doing actively what he was forced to experience passively at the time of her death. In dealing with this material, we see a parallel with the way in which Toto handled the material of his 'mother's' death by identification, without, of course, any manifestations of overt homosexuality.

In his behavior of doing good for all the people of the community we are able to see another tendency, in addition to that of identification. One has the feeling that Toto was doing this *for* his mother, as though he were attempting to satisfy some great ambition. What, after all, could be an expression of greater success than for a foundling, an orphan, to become the builder of a city? This accomplishment can then be presented to the woman of one's dreams. Freud has said: 'In young men egoistic and ambitious wishes assert themselves plainly enough alongside their erotic desires. But we will not lay stress on the distinction between these two trends; we prefer to emphasize the fact that they are often united. In many altar-pieces the portrait of the donor is to be found in one corner of the picture; and in the greater number of ambitious daydreams, too, we can discover a woman in some corner, for whom the dreamer performs all his heroic deeds and at whose feet all his triumphs are to be laid' (Freud, 177). In the film we see how, after he has possessed the dove, and has broken away from the demanding crowd, he goes to Edvige and offers her anything, 'even the moon.'

It is very interesting that if we follow this line of thinking we are confronted with the fact that Toto actually lays his deeds at the feet of his mother, when on the pole, but *at a time of his virtually complete defeat and surrender*. It seems strange that this should be so, unless we consider the fact that although he had in truth preached a great measure of success, his despair and disappointment that Mobbi should fail to keep his promise forced him regressively into the position of wishing for his mother's presence more than ever. He longs for her help and her guidance as he did during his childhood. The incident on the pole thus represents a fusion of three impulses: first, the desire to show his mother the extent of his accomplishments, that he had virtually built a city; secondly, that his triumph had collapsed at the very pinnacle of its glory, and that he needed her help and her consolation; third, and perhaps most important, was the gratification of the wish that his mother had not actually died, so that he would have been spared the painful, traumatic effects of separation from her.

His longing for his mother, the desire to have her back in life, is portrayed in a very skillful manner in another way in the film. A statue of a beautiful girl is discovered by two men in the debris during the construction of the city. They quarrel as to who is the rightful owner but Toto interferes, and the statue is placed in the centre of the little community. Later when Toto, with the help of the dove, is able to perform 'miracles,' he is asked to turn the statue into a live girl. He does this and she even subsequently kisses Toto, as has already been indicated. This sequence is especially interesting in view of the fact that it is here that Toto's wish to bring the dead back to life is gratified. There are some pertinent details which indicate a striking parallel with his own childhood. At the time of his 'mother's' death, he observed through a keyhole two men, physicians, holding the wrists of the dying woman, as they felt her pulse, while carrying on a voluble discussion. In the discovery of the statue, Toto participates in her disinternment, and *saves* her from the two men who argue about her. In his action of bringing the statue to life, he undoes the death of his mother. This sequence of events is demonstrated once more when he 'saves' the little community from the two millionaires who argue volubly as to its possession.

My impression is that the *true* miracle of this film has to do with Toto's 'raising the dead,' while the other 'miracles' are subsidiary to it. They express the thought: 'If I could bring my mother back to life, then I could do anything.' This wish stands out in sharp contrast to the wishes of the people, for their requests seem to be rather incongruous considering their lack of other, more important necessities. It is largely this theme and its elaboration which constitute the major appeal of the film. It permits the expression of the *fantasy* that the object relations of one's childhood can be revived and appear as beautiful and as vivid as ever before. This may be readily seen in the type of advertisements which are used for this film, such as those mentioned above. The fantasies are not altered in any way by the passage of time, and even the unconscious content of these fantasies can be expressed and gratified.

...

The psychological appeal of this little film may thus be understood from a number of different aspects, all of which deal with the possibility of gratification of one's wishes without any reproach or embarrassment. It approves the gratification of all manner of ego and reality wishes, ranging from whims such as a silk couch amidst the direst poverty, to the serious desire on the part of the Negro and White couple to change color, and such profound wishes as the fact that the dead can return to life. In many instances these wishes may be found to have their infantile roots. A powerful infantile wish, intimated in this film, is that, after all, there is no necessity to separate from mother, that she is omnipresent, and is ready to help in any moment of dire need. It is this aspect of the film which gives it its nostalgic character. On the deepest level, the film expresses the wish that instinctual strivings of all kinds, particularly one's Oedipal strivings, need not be abandoned because they too can be gratified. This is entirely in keeping with Rank's findings in *Das Inzestmotiv in Dichtung und Sage* where he demonstrated the ubiquity of the Oedipal complex in literature. In view of all of these themes, it is easy to understand the nature of the appeal which this production evokes.

A final question may, of course, be raised as to whether this film was deliberately constructed to portray just this, whether the author of the script consciously figured out a scheme for the detailed portrayal of such unconscious material on the basis of psychoanalytic understanding. Actually this makes little difference. Editha Sterba in answer to a similar problem writes: 'If, however, we remember that the creative process, the artistic transformation of the "naive day-dream" always takes place in the unconscious, then we may expect that even the creative artist who is under the influence of psychoanalysis will not be able to represent everything so clearly and make everything so conscious that no task is left for the psychoanalytic examination of the work of art' (Sterba, 307–20). It would, indeed, be very difficult to conceive of anyone being able consciously and deliberately to put together such a collection of details that are so consistent and so cohesive in their entirety, without the utilization of their own unconscious processes.

References

Cortesi, Arnaldo. 'De Sica on Miracle in Milan.' *New York Times*, 9 December 1951, sec. 2, p. 9, col. 5.

De Sica, Vittorio. 'De Sica Outlines His Steps to the Neorealistic Film.' *New York Herald Tribune*, 2 December 1951.

Freud, Sigmund. 'The Relation of the Poet to Daydreaming,' in *Collected Papers*. London: Hogarth Press, 1950. IV, 177–8.

Sterba, Editha. 'The Schoolboy Suicide of André Gide's Novel, *The Counterfeiters*.' *American Imago* 8 (1951), 307–20.

Pius Aeneas and Totò, il buono: The Founding Myth of the Divine City

HART WEGNER

Hart Wegner's 1977 essay sees Miracle in Milan *as something of a historical allegory, the founding of Rome being the mythic archetype for the founding of a new city of God. Wegner sees in Totò a reincarnation of the archetypical hero so well described in Joseph Campbell's* The Hero with a Thousand Faces.

The premiere of Vittorio De Sica's *Miracolo a Milano / Miracle in Milan* (1950), a film about the humble life and the ascension of Totò, the Good, caused a mixed critical reaction. By 1950 neorealism had been the predominant style in Italian film production since Luchino Visconti's *Ossessione / Obsession* (1942), the most acclaimed films of which movement were Roberto Rossellini's *Roma, città aperta / Rome, – Open City* (1944) and *Paisà / Paisan* (1946), and De Sica's *Sciuscià / Shoeshine* (1946) and *Ladri di biciclette / Bicycle Thieves* (1948). *Miracle in Milan* did not fit the naturalistic mold of these earlier films and critics feared that its thematic departure might signal the end of one of the few significant movements in the international cinema after World War II. Such fears, as it turned out, were justified, since, although De Sica in 1951 returned to neorealism in the creation of *Umberto D.*, this austere *Kammerspiel* on old age and dignity was to become the closing masterpiece of the movement. Like other neorealist films, *Miracle in Milan* depicts the lives of the poor, but it also introduces supernatural events; as a

Hart Wegner, 'Pius Aeneas and Totò, il buono: The Founding Myth of the Divine City,' *Pacific Coast Philology* 12 (October 1977), 64–71 consequence its critical reception was like that received in 1893 by Gerhart Hauptmann when he violated the naturalist canon by the introduction of the dream action in his drama *Hanneles Himmelfahrt*.

Miracle in Milan, adapted for film by Cesare Zavattini from his novel *Totò, il buono*, follows its aptly named hero from his foundling origin to his maturity as founder of a city of the dispossessed on a garbage-strewn plain by the railroad tracks. Joseph Campbell has outlined the standard path of the mythological hero as leading from separation to initiation and eventually to a return (Campbell, 30); *Miracle in Milan* concludes with the hero's ascension with his followers from Milan's Piazza del Duomo. Such an event as an ascension is obviously a departure from the documentary texture and the Zolaesque themes of neorealism. The statements made about contemporary society may be as harsh as those in De Sica's earlier films, but the fantasy elements are a defection from the neorealist aesthetic.

The reactions of reviewers and critics of *Miracle in Milan* have been mixed and, in some cases, guarded. One speaks of its use of 'compassionate and meaningful whimsy' (Casty, 252) while others find it a 'childlike view of Dostoyevsky's *The Idiot*' (Kael, 310), a 'metaphorical film' (Houston, 24), a 'likeable fable' (Kauffmann, 137), and a 'sociopolitical allegory in a fairy-tale dress' (Gregor, 27). A film encyclopedia judges the collaboration of Zavattini and De Sica as an example of the low state of the conventionally indifferent cinema, and adds an additional insult by quoting Jacques Rivette, who had found *Miracle* 'overstuffed, grimacing, puffed up' (Kurowski, 83–4). And although André Bazin senses in the film 'the most sweeping message of love that our time has heard since Chaplin,' (Bazin, 71), he feels the need to defend narrative inconsistencies within the film's structure. Some, seeking justification for their approval of *Miracle*, have found significance in the fact that the poor in their ascension fly to the East, or that the dove in the film is either a political or a religious symbol (Gregor, 27).

The problems faced by such critics of *Miracle in Milan* have in part been caused by their assumption that neorealist cinema (like that of all naturalist movements) is antithetical to historical concern.[1] The argument of this paper is that such problems can be solved through the use of a historical model and the recognition that concerns beyond the limitations of the concrete present can enter into the neorealist cinema.

If *Miracle in Milan* depicts the founding of a city, nurtured and aided through divine intervention, it appears logical to compare it to the myth of the founding of Rome, both as a model and simultaneously as a foil. As De Sica himself once stated, 'good film must represent the country of its origin' (Samuels, 144). *Miracle in Milan* is a political statement on the Italian condition in the post-war period and a ringing denunciation of the Fascist state of Mussolini with its self-conscious restoration of Caesarean trappings in rhetoric, pageantry, emblems, and architecture. As Umberto Barbaro has stated: 'We can never fully understand the neorealism of the Italian cinema unless we take ourselves back to the spirit and history of anti-fascism' (Cannella, 9). In *Miracle* De Sica and Zavattini attempt a revocation of the idealized Roman State of the *Aeneid*, where the supremacy of the State was proclaimed in an earthly city; however, they replace the mythical hero *pius Aeneas* with the fairy-tale simpleton Totò, il buono.

Totò shares with Aeneas one of the prerequisites of the Hero of myth and *Maerchen*, a miraculous birth and mysterious youth. Aeneas, conceived by Aphrodite on a couch of bear and lion skins, passes a rather obscure childhood and adolescence, reared according to differing sources either by his brother-in-law or nymphs on Mount Ida. Totò, whose birth is never revealed, makes his entrance as a lustily bawling infant found among the cabbages as the words appear on the screen, 'Once upon a time.' Lolotta, a kindly old lady, rears him and infuses her love into her charge, a feeling so sadly missing in Aeneas. 'Mother' and son share only one scene before she is shown on her deathbed (a fate which inevitably befalls good *Maerchen* mothers; only wicked stepmothers gain prolonged tenure). This scene celebrates love, which is to become Totò's guiding principle, and the building of a model city is introduced as a preview of Totò's mission. When Totò is alone and milk boils over and flows on the floor, Lolotta does not reprimand him, but instead builds with toy houses and trees a model community by the banks of the river of milk. Then, taking the boy by the hand, she leaps over the little city, exulting 'Oh, how big is the earth,' (De Sica, 20), foreshadowing Totò's leap over the city of Milan. After Lolotta's death, Totò, his youth obscured from us, is remanded to an orphanage, from which he emerges as an adult. Their futures are revealed to both Totò and Aeneas – to one in a simple childlike manner, to the other in the triumph of the stately poetry of Book VI of the *Aeneid* relating the vision of 'the glory to come.'

The city-states both men found are as opposite as their characters and the systems they represent. Certain defects of the ancient Roman state are reflected in its official hero Aeneas; as Herbert J. Muller has observed,

His high sense of duty is informed by no real love for its own sake; his deep piety is wanting both in simple humanity and spirituality. For the sake of Rome he was always prepared to sacrifice his happiness or the happiness of any other person.   (221)

Totò's city is founded under the ideal of unselfishness, a humanistic City of Good, where man and his needs are central, even if its inhabitants are all too human. Totò recognizes the needs of his subjects and he attempts to fulfill their wishes, however childish.

Both heroes continue to function under the divine guidance of their mothers, accepting their help whenever the situation demands intervention. Venus's appearances during her son's adventures are frequent, from the time when Aeneas asks in wonder 'O quam te memorem virgo' (1.327) to his battles in Italy, when Turnus angrily calls for combat: 'His goddess-mother will not be there, this time to hide him, running to the folds of her gown and cloud and empty shadows' (Virgil, 337). As Aeneas had earlier proclaimed so proudly, sure of his divine connection, 'I am known in heaven; it is Italy I seek' (Virgil, 17).

Totò is called 'angel' by one of the tramps inhabiting his city (De Sica, 86) and 'saint' by another (De Sica, 88), but he also receives divine maternal help, under circumstances which point directly to the Venus-Aeneas analogy. When Totò's city is besieged by the police, in a scene with a double indebtedness to Gilbert and Sullivan and Mack Sennett's Keystone Kops, the divine presence of his deceased 'mother' appears and offers help. She asks Totò: 'Do you want the moon?' and hands him a white dove, a bird sacred to Venus; in Virgil we find the passage: 'No sooner had he spoken than two twin doves came flying down before him and alighted on the green ground. He knew his mother's birds' (Virgil, 150). As long as Totò is able to safeguard the dove, he is able to fulfill any wish.

One of the distinguishing characteristics of the traditional Hero is his ability to bestow boons on his companions, and the white dove enables Totò to fulfill the wishes of the inhabitants of his city. The dove, essential for the survival of the community when Totò is the wisher, shows in true *Maerchen* tradition the foolishness of unlimited wishing if it is done by the wrong person or in the wrong spirit. The tramps try to outdo each other in obtaining the trappings of cartoon capitalists: fur coats, tails, and top hats; one wishes a wardrobe, another wants to be taller, a black man in love with a white woman wishes to be white; she, innocent of his change, turns black to be like him. And in a final aping of the outside society two tramps try to out-bid each other, each asking for millions in the futile desire to be the richest man in Totò's City of Good, a city in which Chaplin's final speech in *The Great Dictator* has come true: 'Greed has poisoned men's souls.'

The city itself, when founded and built, was to be a place of love, where each would receive according to the needs of his family and con-tribute as much as he could in the communal construction project. Totò singlehandedly converts an atmosphere of brutish self-interest into an enlightened community and serves as arbitrator in such disputes as that over Niobe, a plaster statue which the tramps found in the rubble. He stops the fighting for possession of the only work of 'art' in the commu-nity by buying off one [of the bidders] with a whistle from his pocket and placing the statue in the central square of the City of Love. When Totò is in possession of the magic dove, he is asked to give life to the statue in a scene which recalls Aphrodite's involvement in Galatea's metamorphosis as a result of Pygmalion's love. Totò's giving life to Niobe is a benevolent reversal of the cruelty of the petrification of the queen of Thebes in classic mythology. The newly awakened Niobe dances voluptuously with Totò and kisses him longingly, providing in miniature a Dido-Aeneas dilemma for Totò, who would fail his follow-ers were he to succumb to the temptress and be unable to lead them on their escape from the prison vans and to their subsequent ascension.

Totò's role as leader of an enlightened community appears much like Pierre Bezhukov's plan in *War and Peace* 'to secure the triumph of virtue,' to cleanse men from prejudice, to diffuse principles in har-mony with the spirit of the times, and to undertake the education of the young. Zavattini, the social utopian, creates Totò as an exemplary figure of the twentieth century just as Virgil created Aeneas as the ideal for his Augustan age.

Miracle in Milan thus appears as an original, even revolutionary neo-realist film, offering a militant alternative to what had become tradi-tional 'acceptance of fate' in modern films. Totò's people emerge from the ruins of Italy as indomitably as had Aeneas and his Trojans who refused to give up, an event noted by the disgusted Juno: 'Troy went down ... and they rose from the ashes' (Virgil, 187). As Pierre Leprohon has observed, *Miracle in Milan* was planned 'to go a step further, to do something else, to say more after earlier neorealist efforts' (Leprohon, 128). It constituted cinematographically and thematically a break with the past. Zavattini, echoing Horatio, has himself proclaimed: 'If one bridge has remained behind our backs, let's chop it down, to prevent our retreat from what we are' (Zavattini, 14), a challenge directed not only at the old Italian cinema, but also at the previous political regime and its roots set in the concrete past. *Miracle in Milan* proclaims the present. As Zavattini announced in 1952, 'The cinema should never turn back. It should accept unconditionally, what is contemporary. Today, today, today' (MacCann, 224). *Miracle in Milan* is, as De Sica calls it, 'a fable of our times' and in spite of its use of fantasy elements, the central character is 'closely related to the characters of the worker and child in *Bicycle Thief* and the boys in *Shoeshine*' (De Sica, 12).

Miracle in Milan does not, as De Sica assures us (13), praise poverty as the answer to modern social ills, but rather provides an attack on the 'State' as idealized in Aeneas who, according to Muller, 'was the symbol of a people who came to conceive the great ideal of *humanitas*, but were not humane enough to realize that this idea is a mere abstraction until it is embodied in a social order, imparted to all the human beings in that order' (Muller, 238). It is clear that De Sica's cinematic treatment of the poor in *Miracle in Milan* reveals the strong influence of the films of Chaplin and René Clair, not only in the depiction of social injustices accompanied by humor and sentimentality, but also in the manner in which all three artists visualized poverty by interlinking realism and fantasy. De Sica himself was aware that the influence of such predecessors as Chaplin and Clair presented a 'dangerous attraction' (De Sica, 14) and he tried to establish an independent vision by forming two 'defenses' against these strong models through his concentration on current Italian social problems, and above all – with the help of Zavattini – on the historical and mythological past of Italy.

The final scenes of the film illustrate De Sica's independent achievement. Through treachery and the temporary loss of the dove the Milanese have been able to drive Totò and his poor from their city and they are being taken to prison. As the convoy halts on the Piazza del Duomo, Totò, dove now in hand, bursts the walls of the prison vans and liberates his followers. The tramps wrest brooms from streetsweepers and follow Totò into the air, repeating the simple song which they had often sung in their city:

For us it's enough to have a hut to sleep and live in.
We need a little land to live and die in.
We ask for a pair of shoes, socks and a little bread.
Under these conditions we believe in the future.

This had been the inauguration song of the City of Good and now, exiled to a 'kingdom where good morning really means good morning' (De Sica, 120), it becomes the farewell of Totò's poor. At the beginning of the film when Totò had gone into the world wishing 'good morning' to the people he encountered he had been rebuffed, and all his later human contacts with 'outsiders' had been equally disappointing. Now his 'good morning' takes on a new meaning as he and his tramps leave for a new City of Good.

Interestingly, Zavattini planned a sequel which was to be called *Good Morning, Italy*. In his notes for this filmscript, Zavattini creates a nightmare scenario – again with characters from the past and present of Italy: Mussolini chased by Garibaldi and Mazzini, Paolo and Francesca rising from the *Inferno* where Hitler is devoured by the Prince of Darkness; executions at the end of the war (even Chaplin is gunned down) and scenes with Anna Magnani reminiscent of *Open City* tie the historic Italy to the present day. The camera was to emerge from its descent into hell on the very scene of Totò's departure, the Piazza del Duomo in Milan. Italy was again to be purged of the phantoms of its history and, as the script announces, 'dawn is about to break' (Zavattini, 122–6). It is clearly unlikely that Zavattini, who once spoke of neorealist film as cinema produced 'by many for many, a home-made Molotov cocktail' (Furhammar and Isaksson, 6), would create soothing religious allegories in his filmscripts, or celebrate poverty as an ideal state or see it as material for comedy in the manner of such Italian fare of the 1950's as *Bread, Love and Fantasy* (1954).

In *Miracle in Milan* Zavattini and De Sica attempt the cleansing of Italy from its past and they use the *Aeneid* as a foil. Aeneas and Totò are both group-oriented savior-heroes, rather than tragic-heroic in themselves; they share the mysteries of birth and adolescence and divine maternal guidance; in their city/state foundings, city models are revealed to both, and peace treaties and treacherous attacks figure prominently in their lives. But *Miracle in Milan* is an anti-*Aeneid*, because both De Sica and Zavattini believed the ideas of the ideal Roman state had been misused, just as Brecht wrote anti-Schiller plays because he felt that the applications of German classical-idealistic concepts were dangerous to the Germany of his own day. While the *Aeneid* is a future-directed work, *Miracle in Milan* points to the past for an answer to the problems of the present. Aeneas is weighed down by destiny and duty, while anti-Aeneas Totò's life is a series of impulsive acts prompted by kindness and compassion. The contrast of the heroes is underscored by the majestic stillness of the Latin account written, as Alain Renoir notes, in an essentially uncinematic style (Renoir, 154), and by the vivacious sequences of De Sica's film.

Totò's founding of the City of Good is therefore a rejection of the values praised in the *Aeneid*, a revocation of the heroic and a denunciation of the pseudo-Roman interlude in the more recent history of Italy. And yet, when Totò's army of the dispossessed marches and sings 'We need a little land to live and die in,' a faint echo can be heard of the Trojan refugees on the shores of Hesperia asking for a little land for their home gods and water and air free to all men.

Note

1 An exception is the *film-noir* directed by Anthony Mann in 1949, *The Black Book*, possibly the only historical film of this naturalistic genre. [Wegner's confluence of *film-noir*, historical film, and neorealism is problematic; his comments, however, at least suggest issues for further research. EDITORS]

References

Bazin, André. *What is Cinema?* Volume 2. Translated by Hugh Gray. Berkeley: University of California Press, 1971.

Campbell, Joseph. *The Hero With a Thousand Faces*. New York: Meridian Books, 1956.

Cannella, Mario. 'Ideology and Aesthetic Hypotheses in the Criticism of Neorealism.' *Screen* 14:4 (Winter 1973–4).

Casty, Alan. *Development of the Film: An Interpretive History*. New York: Harcourt, Brace Jovanovich, 1973.

De Sica, Vittorio. *Miracle in Milan*. New York: Orion Press, 1968.

Furhammar, Leif, and Folke Isaksson. *Politics and Film*. New York: Praeger, 1971.

Gregor, Ulrich. 'Kamera im Leben: Der Regisseur des Neorealismus.' *Die Zeit* [American edition], 48 (22 November 1974).

Houston, Penelope. *The Contemporary Cinema*. Baltimore: Penguin, 1963.

Kael, Pauline. *Kiss Kiss Bang Bang*. Boston: Little, Brown, 1965.

Kauffmann, Stanley. *A World on Film: Criticism and Comment*. New York: Dell, 1966.

Kurowski, Ulrich. *Lexikon Film*. Munich: Carl Hanser Verlag, 1972.

Leprohon, Pierre. *The Italian Cinema*. New York: Praeger, 1972.

MacCann, Richard Dyer, ed. *Film: A Montage of Theories*. New York: Dutton, 1966.

Muller, Herbert J. *The Uses of the Past: Profiles of Former Societies*. New York: Oxford University Press, 1957.

Renoir, Alain. 'The Terror of the Dark Waters: A Note on Virgilian and Beowulfian Techniques.' *Harvard English Studies* 5 (1974), 147–60.

Samuels, Charles Thomas. *Encountering Directors*. New York: Putnam's, 1972.

Virgil. *The Aeneid of Virgil*. Translated by Rolfe Humphries. New York: Scribners, 1951.

Zavattini, Cesare. *Sequences from a Cinematic Life*. Englewood Cliffs, N.J.: Prentice-Hall, 1970.

Umberto D.: Vittorio De Sica's 'Super'-Naturalism

VERNON YOUNG

Vernon Young's essay, published in 1956, disputes Umberto D.'s *position within the documentary aesthetic of naturalism and situates it, instead, within a formalist tradition of meticulous* mise-en-scène *symbology. Many of Young's essays, collected in* On Film: Unpopular Essays on a Popular Art *(1973), show him to be a committed formalist, several degrees more advanced than his contemporary film reviewers and scholars. Young (1912– 1986) had an excellent eye and a sharp wit, evident in his auteurist study,* Cinema Borealis: Ingmar Bergman and the Swedish Ethos *(1971). His criticism often anticipates in a cryptic way ideas that would emerge later in film criticism in a more fully delineated form. This essay is prophetic in its suggestion that we can detect in the style of* Umberto D. *an attempt at an erasure of 'authorial signature.'*

Sociological film criticism is forever mistaken because it is forever misled – on humanitarian principles or by self-righteousness or from color-blindness – into confusing ends with means. Asserting that importance lies in subject matter, it fails to recognize that no subject is important until awakened by art; assuming (to give its charity the benefit of the doubt) that love is greater than art, it fails to acknowledge that the art *is* the love. Vittorio De Sica's new film, *Umberto D.* (1952) ... provides a characteristic opportunity for confused judgment. To praise the film for its human appeal is as needless and as miserly as to praise a beautiful woman for her conspicuous virtue.

Reprinted by permission from *The Hudson Review* 8:4 (Winter 1956), 592–6. Copyright © 1956 by The Hudson Review, Inc.

Umberto Domenico Ferrari or Umberto D., as he prefers to call himself, is a retired civil-service clerk living on an inadequate pension and, as the film opens, facing eviction from a furnished room which, ghastly as it may be, is the only place he can call home. His sole companion is a mongrel dog, Flick. To maintain their precious, if contracting, haven (the landlady has taken to sub-renting his room to transient lovers while he is out), the old man joins other aged pensioners in a demonstration (unsuccessful) for higher allotments, sells his gold watch and his dictionary, tries to beg but is unable to support the shameful resolution, engages in frustrated transactions for boarding the dog or giving it away, and finally attempts suicide by standing in front of an oncoming train with the dog in his arms. Flick, in panic, escapes, and Umberto D., trying to recapture him, saves himself. The film closes on the old man trying to regain the dog's trust in a deserted park, with an occasional train speeding by.

So rehearsed, the film may easily be construed as an artless and unbuttered slice of life, a testimony of 'naturalism': ostensibly a method of expressing reality without inhibition, without overtones and as far as possible without style. Nothing could be further from the case. Like *Sciuscià / Shoeshine* (1946), or *Ladri di biciclette / Bicycle Thief* (1948), and with justification even more subtle, De Sica's *Umberto D.* – a masterpiece of compassion which he has dedicated to his father – might be termed *super*naturalism if this compound had not been pre-empted for another kind of experience entirely. The fidelity of De Sica's attention to the plight of the man Umberto, realistic in its living details, is enriched by a host of modulations working under and through the story line, so delicately registered as to be imperceptible save to that second awareness evoked from most spectators without their being able to define it. Cinematically created, these modulations are not arresting, since they accumulate from thematic relationships in the scenario. De Sica's use of the camera is clear-eyed, rather than ingenuous. As in his other naturalist films, his cinematographer (in this case G.R. Aldo, the same who was bewitched, with De Sica, into assisting David Selznick's Florentine hoax, *Stazione Termini / Indiscretion of an American Wife*, 1953) is not called upon to exhibit striking angles or movement; De Sica's compositions rarely startle one by their ingenuity. *What* he focuses on at a given point is more significant than the *way* he focuses. The way is never neglected, it simply isn't exploited; for it is to De Sica's purpose to move with un-elliptical life as closely as he dares without vitiating motion-picture technique altogether. To subordinate the essentially cinematic as he does is itself a technique of ineffable skill; and to efface his signature as a director from the style of a film argues a modest purity of aim.

In *Bicycle Thief*, De Sica developed the film's rhythm by a *pas de deux* of man and boy in their scouting expedition through the city, the boy nervously anxious to keep in time with his father's mood and intention. The adjustments of temper and of tempo, the resolution, the haste, anger and embarrassment, the flanking movements, the frustrations and periodic losses of direction: these constituted a form of situational ballet which gave the film its lyricism. There is no such springy movement in *Umberto D.*; the quality of its forms is established otherwise.

The possessive theme is time; its epiphanies are sounded in a scale of variations. Before even the credits have appeared on the screen, the bells of early Mass ring out as the pensioners gather in the street. After they have been dispersed by the carabinieri, Umberto D. offers his watch for sale to an acquaintance, murmuring his own pride in its workmanship with an imitative 'tick-tock, tick-tock.' As this scene is succeeded by one at a restaurant, where he resumes his attempt to sell the watch, the background noises of dishes and spoons seem to take up the clicking pulsations of time. Thereafter a tap dripping, footsteps, voices saying goodnight below Umberto's window, his alarm clock, the musical score itself and bells of one kind or another maintain this rhythm and reminder of the irrevocable. When, at the deepest moment of his despair, after he has failed to beg or borrow, Umberto D. returns to his room – already breached and dismantled for the landlady's new domestic arrangements – the clock ticks more loudly; it is virtually the only sound we hear besides the old man's breathing ... Intent now on self-destruction, he inquires first about boarding the dog. The haggling of the couple with whom he tries to deal, conducted in that fulminating rhythm of the back-street Roman, is intercut with a ferociously barking mastiff – the voice of all the world that opposes Umberto's need. He turns away, with Flick still unprovided for, and his retreat is mocked by a housewife who has flipped a carpet over her windowsill, which she then beats at a measured, doom-like pace. Time piles up. A beggar chants plaintively, 'Signora! I have two children ... Signor! I have two children.' As a well-dressed woman ignores his appeal, he repeats the plaint like a warning, between savagely clamped teeth, 'SIGNORA! I HAVE TWO CHILDREN!' ... Streetcar and railroad-crossing bells rattle and jangle. Umberto D. makes his futile attempt at self-extinction and is left with his problem as the train catapults by.

Sound, which is time, is always extraneous to Umberto D. It impinges; it does not involve him. The clatter of social life is beyond the fringes of his consciousness; he hears it but it isn't speaking to him. Maria, the landlady's adolescent servant-girl from the country, is ever ready to respond as far as her own preoccupation will allow, but she is pregnant (by whom she is not sure) and fearful that the landlady will find out and discharge her. With eyes misleadingly alive, she seems forever on the verge of communication with the old pensioner, only to escape into her private world of ignorance and fright. And Umberto D., on his side, is as incapable of saying the words that would unite them in their misery. (Beyond an ineffectual reprimand to one of Maria's 'seducers,' he operates within the circumference of his own pain.) As he lies in his bed, sweating, anxious, sick and alone, the landlady, her friends and her preposterous suitor sing pompous operatic choruses in the sitting-room. Music, badinage, whispers and coarse laughter announce, without reassurance, the life of others.

Visually the narration is equally cogent, taking in without appearing to emphasize the incongruities, the excrescences, the implacabilities of life at a level of civilization where the meretricious and the ugly are accepted or suffered, where in fact the vitality of a people cut off, by a superimposed culture, from its native modes, expresses itself by choice through a corrupt aesthetic. At the house of Umberto D.'s landlady the camera, with flat-lighted neutrality, exposes the importunate vulgarity of middle-class Italian decor: the mock-Imperial wallpaper, the cut-glass, the lambrequins like shrouds, the fringed table-scarves and (most horrible item of all!) a lamp in the form of a Grecian nymph, with naked light-bulbs sprouting from it. (The stilted terrors of the family photograph album.) There are some remarkable instances in this film of De Sica's sparing use of a background object as *direct* symbol. The old man's coat hanging lifelessly on a gigantic stand which looks like a monstrous underwater growth is analogous to the social situation in which man is an unbraced, drowning remnant in the ruins of a cheaply florid dream of empire – and when Umberto D. returns to his room the last time, a shot of the hallway gives prominence to a stuffed falcon among the bric-a-brac. The most impressive *vis-à-vis* is depicted in the painful scene of Umberto D.'s tentative rehearsal of begging (during which he tries using Flick to cover him until the humiliation of being encountered by someone he knows forces him to the pretense of teaching the dog a new trick). An overpowering classical column, cracked at the base, is the backdrop for this joyless act.

De Sica's balance between the lifelike and the cinematic is tenuous; if he had actors less responsive to the naked untheatricality he is commonly after, his muted formalism might suffer from the risks he takes. But he can afford to dwell at length on the faces and motions of Umberto D. and Maria precisely because Carlo Battisti and Maria Pia Casilio are sentiently, gravely, inside life. (Neither is a 'professional.' Where, but in Italy, can one find so much unconscious histrionic talent?!) Few directors could manage, without losing their hold on the continuity, the beautiful cadence in this film where the coming of day is enacted through the actions of Maria as she gets out of bed. The scene is wordless, leisured and almost unbearably intimate. There is little in it that could not be performed on a stage, but in its brief duration and its breathing nearness, in the particular placing of the camera for each view of the pregnant girl struggling to experience joy which gives way to fear and then to a daydream indifference, it is a marvel of movie timing and perspective.

Maria, while subordinate to Umberto D., is by an inspired implication complementary. Neglected youth and discarded old age. The girl and her involuntary burden-to-be; the man and his voluntarily assumed burden, Flick: girl and man subservient to the loud concerns of society, exemplified by the middle-aged landlady who is handsome in a brassy way, venal, pseudo-respectable and heartless – living in a world of opera, ormolu and broken-down technology. In *Shoeshine* the horse was a symbol, if you like, of the unattainable, a dream of power and freedom. The bicycle in *Bicycle Thief* was an occupational necessity which became a projection of the man's self-respect. Flick, neither ideal nor economic necessity, may be felt as representing the last thing a man will surrender: it is the love in the man, Umberto.

When De Sica and Cesare Zavattini (who wrote the story from which, with De Sica, the screenplay was shaped) avoided the easier termination, of suicide accomplished, by ending the film on an inconclusive (which is not to say indecisive) note – Umberto D. and the dog gambolling under the cedars – we can be sure they were saying very clearly: Life sometimes leaves you nothing but love, and in your deprivation and anguish you cannot bear to support even such a burden. But this is your only identity and until the day you die you must not put aside the little humanity left to you ... Umberto D. tries to entrust the dog to another; he tries to give it away; he tries to destroy it. In the end he is still, as our idiom says, 'stuck with it.'

Birth quickens in the unclaimed Maria; the venal landlady marries a

fool; Umberto is homeless but keeps his pet. De Sica's films in the naturalist vein have been accusations of the fascist aftermath; they take
their place with the most profound cinematic achievements by sounding vibrations in a dimension larger than the political ... When
Umberto D. twirls down the path under the trees with the jumping
dog, we recall not only the other De Sica 'conclusions' – Pasquale, in
Shoeshine, facing a lifetime of expiation; the frustrated 'bicycle thief'
and his son renewing the life-circuit by joining hands; the poor, of *Miracle in Milan,* flying away on their brooms to an unlikely heaven – but
also perhaps Baptiste, in *Les enfants du paradis / Children of Paradise*
(1945), striving against the tide of revellers cutting him off from Truth,
the woodchopper in *Rashomon* (1950), undaunted by fearful disclo-
sures of moral ambiguity, deciding to adopt the abandoned baby – and
Chaplin disappearing into a California horizon (the *first* time!).

The Subversive Potential of the Pseudo-Iterative

MARSHA KINDER

Marsha Kinder is well known for her many writings on film which explore issues of self and culture, words/images, and post-structuralist methods of criticism. In this essay, excerpted from a longer study of the pseudo-iterative published in Film Quarterly, *Kinder explores the use of critical concepts drawn from French theorist Gerard Genette.*

The *iterative* was introduced into contemporary narrative theory by French narratologist, Gerard Genette, in his ground-breaking work, *Narrative Discourse,* where he considers '*narrative frequency,* that is, the relations of frequency (or more simply, repetition) between the narrative and the diegesis [the fictive world],' which, he claims is 'one of the main aspects of narrative temporality' (Genette, 113–17). He describes the iterative as a type of narrative 'where a single narrative utterance takes upon itself several occurrences together of the same event (in other words, ... several events considered only in terms of their analogy)' – as in the example, 'every day of the week I went to bed early' ... [H]e defines the iterative as '*narrating one time* (or rather: *at one time*) *what happened n times*'; as opposed to narrating one time one time (the *singulative* – as in the example, 'yesterday I went to bed early,'); or narrating *n* times what happened *n* times (the *anaphoric,* as in 'Monday I went to bed early, Tuesday I went to bed early, Wednesday I went to bed early, etc ...' which is merely a multiple form of the singulative); or

From Marsha Kinder, 'The Subversive Potential of the Pseudo-Iterative,' *Film Quarterly* 43:2 (Winter 1989–90), 2–3, 7–9, 11, 16, by permission. © 1989 by the Regents of the University of California narrating *n* times what happened one time (the *repeating* narrative, as in 'Yesterday I went to bed early, yesterday I went to bed early').

Usually signalled in verbal discourse by the use of the imperfect tense ('I used to go to bed early') and normally limited to a subordinate descriptive function in classical literary narrative, the iterative aspect, according to Genette, can be traced all the way back to Homer, but was first liberated from 'functional dependence' by Flaubert in *Madame Bovary* and most fully expanded in 'textual scope, in thematic importance, and in degree of technical elaboration' by Proust in *A la recherche du temps perdu* where it becomes a key component of his radical innovation. What I intend to do in this essay is to explore how the elaboration of the iterative functions in filmic narrative and the filmic means by which it is signalled, particularly in works that attempt to make a radical break from existing narrative conventions.

Italian Neorealism: The Pseudo-Iterative as Narrative Rupture in *Umberto D.* and *Il Posto*

Within the neorealist aesthetic, rich photographic detail frequently functions to express, not the singulative (as in Hollywood classical cinema), but the iterative. Although the iterative is sometimes signalled by voice-overs (as in films like *La terra trema*, *Paisà*, and *Amore in città*), it more typically is marked by visual operations, particularly through spatial determinations.[1] The referential interplay between the singulative event and the paradigm it represents is frequently played out spatially in terms of foreground and background. Yet, the iterative background is not merely 'descriptive' or subordinate as in Hollywood classical cinema, but at least co-equal, normative, and determinant in ideological terms – relations that can be established by spatial or temporal continuity through depth composition or long takes punctuated by ellipses. Individuals and their actions are chosen precisely because they are representative and typical in an iterative sense; the anonymous characters in the background are not used merely as backdrop against which to distinguish the singularity of the protagonist (a singularity which then is invisibly transformed into a norm as in classical Hollywood cinema), but rather as a means of explicitly acknowledging the iterative aspect and the slippage between it and the singulative dimensions of this particular occurrence within the series.

For example, the singular protagonists of De Sica's *Bicycle Thief* and *Umberto D.* are introduced within a crowd, from which they are visibly selected for foregrounding during an habitual event (a daily hiring of workers, or one of the frequent impromptu demonstrations in postwar Rome).[2] Yet it's the typicality of these characters and their events that is valued and repeatedly emphasized, not their singularity. Similarly, the multiple protagonists of Rossellini's *Open City* and *Paisà* emerge from events involving large numbers of people, events that are already in progress and that are presumed to be illustrative of a common series that frequently occurred during a specific historical period in a specific location. The precision of detail in the image helps identify the paradigm to which the particular characters and events belong; the long take and depth focus, and even the montage structure at the opening of *Umberto D.* and *Shoeshine*, continue to acknowledge the connection between the individual and the paradigm, between the singulative and the iterative aspects.

Umberto D. (1952)

The use of visual codes to express the neorealist intoxication with the pseudo-iterative and to control the slippage between the iterative and the singulative can be demonstrated in a celebrated sequence from *Umberto D.*, which is frequently cited as the 'purest' example of the neorealist aesthetic. The sequence where the pregnant maid does her morning chores seems to contribute nothing whatever to the advancement of the narrative line; rather, it merely presents her ordinary daily moves. Bazin calls it 'a perfect illustration of [the De Sica–Zavattini] approach to narrative, ... the exact opposite of that "art of ellipsis" ... [which] presupposes analysis and choice.' He defines it as 'the succession of concrete instants of life, no one of which can be said to be more important than another, for their ontological equality destroys drama at its very basis' (Bazin, 81).

By presenting the maid's ordinary morning routines, this totally nonverbal sequence clearly foregrounds the iterative. Yet, perhaps even more important for my argument here, it also trains the spectator in how to read the familiar moves both of the maid and of the camera and the editing, and to thereby deduce what she is probably thinking. Moreover, these cognitive tasks will be required later in the two singulative events that *are* crucial to the narrative line – the two moments when the old man Umberto contemplates suicide. Thus, in this sense, the sequence *does* contribute to the narrative by renegotiating the relationship between the iterative and the singulative, a relationship which proves essential to our understanding of what happens in the film.

In the representation of this particular morning our attention is first drawn to the old man Umberto who stands in the foreground, phoning the ambulance to take him away to the hospital, arranging a singulative event that will distinguish this day from all others. The maid appears behind him in the background, as part of the ordinary context against which Umberto's singulative event is to be read. When the film cuts to the maid, lying on her back in bed, there is a noticeable slippage to the iterative, which now takes over the foreground. Her ordinary morning routines fill in the time (or temporal gap in the narrative) that it takes the ambulance to come for Umberto. As Bazin suggests, this sequence rejects narrative ellipsis.

Yet Bazin fails to notice that the way her actions are represented visually is not always consistent with what we normally identify as the neorealist aesthetic. For example, this sequence does not rely on the long take, but has at least seventeen intra-sequence cuts. In the very first shot, the maid rubs her eyes, drawing our attention to her gaze. Then there's a cut to the object of her gaze – an upward angle longshot of a cat walking across the roof seen through a screen-like surface with a striking graphic design. This shot stands out, not because it depicts an unusual event (undoubtedly, like the maid, the cat is pursuing its daily morning routines), but because the almost abstract formalism of the visuals is not characteristic of the neorealist aesthetic. This shot is followed by a cut back to the maid, which then moves in closer to her gaze, anchoring it firmly within the suturing structure (shot/reverse shot/shot) normally associated with classical Hollywood cinema. This suture works toward the kind of emotional identification that is also typical of De Sica and Zavattini. Then the camera follows the maid into the kitchen where we see her performing a number of household tasks in a series of long and medium shots more typical of neorealism. Three shots later there is a medium shot of her through the window, and then she and the camera move toward each other, a convergence which again calls our attention both to her gaze and to our own. The reverse shot reveals the object of her gaze in an exterior longshot – a white cat walking along the slanted roof, evoking the earlier more abstract image of the cat through the screen, and then there's a cut back to her gaze through the window.

Despite Bazin's claims that no one instant in this sequence is more important than any other, the formal repetition (of the shot/reverse shot suture, of the camera moving in closer to her gaze, and of the cat imagery) privileges these two moments. This repeated pattern leads us not only to identify with the young maid, but also to speculate on her thoughts: perhaps she, too, is identifying with the feline, envying its freedom, particularly in light of her pregnant condition. This hypothesis is strengthened a little later when she looks down at her slightly swollen belly, and the camera moves in tighter, almost to a close-up of her face, which reveals her eyes blinking, as if to ward off the tears that will appear a few moments later. What's really at stake here is not whether we reach a 'correct' interpretation of what she is thinking, but rather that we learn how to read the phenomenology of her moves and how to recognize the filmic codes that elicit such speculations.

All three of the visual codes that have been foregrounded in this sequence through repetition – the shot/reverse shot suture, the striking camera movement (or zoom) that closes in on the gaze, and the accelerated tempo of the cutting – are used again later (and intensified through the accompaniment of dramatic non-diegetic music [commentative sound tracking]) in the two melodramatic sequences where Umberto considers suicide: first, when he stands at his window staring at the streetcar tracks below, and finally, when he carries his dog to the railroad tracks and nearly lunges in the path of an on-coming train. In both cases he is prevented from acting out his suicidal impulse by the presence of the dog, another inarticulate creature (like the cat in the maid's morning sequence, or like the anonymous poor backgrounded by the narrative) whose readable gestures serve as the basis of emotional identification for spectators trained by the neorealist aesthetic. If we are *unable* to read these silent moves and gestures (or what Pasolini would later call *im-signs*), then we prove to be less trainable than Umberto's clever little mutt whose ability to decipher these nonverbal signs saves both himself and his master.

...

In these sequences from *Umberto D.* ... the neorealist *intoxication with the iterative* immerses the spectator, not in the emotional intensity of personal memory as in Proust, but in the ideological relations between individual and collective experience.

...

Though perhaps less radical in their demands on the spectator, the two neorealist films discussed in this essay also require a similar shift in reading, one that de-emphasizes the narrative line and that leads one to interpret gestural language and rich perceptual detail. It's as if one to interpret gestural language and rich perceptual detail. It's as if the foregrounding of the slippage between the iterative and the singulative helps one to see both the distinctiveness of the present image and its deep immersion in a system of representation. And it's the duality of this perception that helps empower one as an active spectator who is capable of resisting the singular closed reading and of perceiving the iterative traces of collective history and dominant ideology.

Notes

1 Edward Branigan develops this kind of argument in *Point of View in the Cinema*, where (explicitly echoing Genette) he observes that ... 'in a verbal narrative the temporal determinations of the narrating act are more salient than the spatial determinations. By contrast, this dissymmetry is exactly reversed in pictorial narration ... The spatial properties of a picture are at least initially more important than other properties and, hence, may serve as a reference with which to measure the general activity of narration.' Edward R. Branigan, *Point of View in the Cinema: A Theory of Narration and Subjectivity in Classical Film*. New York: Mouton Publishers, 1984, p. 45.
2 EDITORS' NOTE: Kinder is in error here: Ricci is introduced in *Bicycle Thieves* sitting alone, at a considerable distance from the crowds at the employment office, revealing not his commonality or participation in human solidarity but his singulative dissociation.

References

Bazin, André. *What is Cinema?* Volume 2. Translated by Hugh Gray. Berkeley: University of California Press, 1971.
Genette, Gerard. *Narrative Discourse: An Essay in Method*. Translated by Jane E. Lewin. Ithaca, N.Y.: Cornell University Press, 1980.

A Home in the Ditch of Saint Agnes: De Sica's *The Roof*

HOWARD CURLE

The Roof *(1956) was the final neorealist collaboration between De Sica and Zavattini and has received the least critical commentary. It was developed from a sketch that Zavattini wrote in 1952 for an episodic documentary about Italy. At the time of its first screening in Cannes (1956) Lindsay Anderson remarked that De Sica and Zavattini had 'reached a point in their works in which they are exploiting rather than exploring the effects of poverty' (Wakeman, 234), but considering that the film had no audience or supporters, it is difficult to see any exploitation in De Sica's work. In fact, in this original essay Howard Curle argues that the film is one of the most realist films – emphasizing plain people without embellishment – De Sica or anyone else ever made. Indeed Arlene Croce found the weakness of the film to be the plainness of the characters: 'It fails ultimately, because the two people it tells you it cares about remain merely a pair of pleasant looking nonentities' (Croce, 50). But, more significantly, Curle notes that the film is an exploration not so much of poverty as of solidarity, and thus it becomes one of the few De Sica films in which the characters actually solve a problem. In his comments on* Umberto D. *De Sica remarked repeatedly that* Umberto *is a story of a failure to communicate (see 38 above). In that light one might see* The Roof *– like* Umberto D. *its focus is the quest for habitation – as a story of the success of communication. Neorealism was not dedicated to stories of failure* a priori.

Curle demonstrates how embedded The Roof *is in the neorealist tradition, as, for example, in De Sica's use of carefully researched details such as the housing laws of the time. Curle also shows that there is a consistency between* The Roof *and De Sica's earlier films, although it differs from them in its formalist experimentation, which reminds one of Antonioni's work of the same period.*

In most films, the adventure of two people looking for somewhere to live, for a house, would be shown externally in a few moments of action, but for us it could provide the scenario for a whole film, and we would explore all its echoes, all its implications.

CESARE ZAVATTINI

I

If, as Kristin Thompson suggests, neorealism adumbrates the acceptance of art cinema by altering the conception of realism from a mere social-problem discourse to one validating ambiguity, despair, and open-endedness, then Vittorio De Sica's *Il tetto / The Roof* (1956) may be considered a casualty of that achievement (Thompson, 217). By the time it was released in North America in May 1959,[1] two years after its Italian premiere (it was first screened at the Cannes Film Festival in 1956), the film was easily overshadowed by neorealism's art-house successors. Satyajit Ray's *Aparajito* and Ingmar Bergman's *Wild Strawberries* were both in New York at the time, and the arrival of the *nouvelle vague* was just months away. Although critical response to *The Roof* was generally positive, American reviews at the time tended to be condescending in their praise: '[a] good little picture ... made to a sure formula,' remarked the *Nation* (Hatch, 484); and the *New Yorker* commented: 'With broad sympathy and gentle humor [De Sica] follows the Zavattini blueprint' (McCarten, 82). Not every reviewer, however, assumed De Sica and Zavattini were merely rehearsing a formula; indeed Arthur Knight of the *Saturday Review* saw in *The Roof* a debased form being refurbished: 'Over the past decade, neorealism has taken many a sorry turn. Actuality was translated into sensationalism; for the true stories of simple people were substituted highly colored fictions about dope addicts, prostitutes, and wayward girls.' However, *The Roof*, Knight continues, 'is a confirmation of the power of neorealist principles to create an awareness of people and their problems far more affecting than fiction ever could be. The apprentice bricklayer and his young wife, the protagonists of this lovely film, are so affecting because they are so real; and they are so real because De Sica has seen to it that every incident, every detail in every shot contributes to a sense of unstrained, unforced actuality' (Knight, 23).

These critics' accommodation to the film notwithstanding, *The Roof* was not a success with audiences and quietly folded. Infrequently revived thereafter, and largely ignored in surveys of De Sica's career –

it goes unmentioned in Peter Bondanella's *Italian Cinema: From Neorealism to the Present* – the film has slipped into obscurity. If Knight's concern about the sensational films spawned by neorealism now sounds too moralistic and his view of the original neorealist aesthetic strikes us as problematic, his words can, nevertheless, provide a way back into the experience of the film. It is 'the power of neorealist principles' and the 'affecting' quality of *The Roof* that I want to examine here. Now available on videotape,[2] *The Roof* deserves reconsideration for its place in the development of neorealism and in De Sica's career, and particularly for its portrait of working-class marriage and aspirations.

Although there is evidence of an alteration in De Sica's camera style in *The Roof* from that employed in his earlier neorealist films, the movie demonstrates an essential aspect of the neorealist aesthetic, that quality which, in André Bazin's celebrated phrase, 'give[s] the illusion of chance, to result in giving dramatic necessity the character of something contingent' (Bazin, 68). Encouraged to look not at just the foreground drama but at unfolding events touching upon and surrounding that principal drama, the spectator sees a far different Rome from that of *Shoeshine* or *Bicycle Thieves*, one in which the war-battered is renovated and the new rises up beside the ancient.

Like most of western Europe, Italy underwent major economic and social reconstruction after World War II. This transformation was concurrent with a 'metamorphosis' in the cultural realm as well,[3] neorealism in both literature and film being one of its most honoured, yet within Italy itself most contested manifestations. With the victory of the Christian Democrats in the 1948 election came social legislation that, while ostensibly offering reform, re-entrenched the power of status-quo groups. For example, Thomas Angotti in his book *Housing in Italy* notes that the Turpini law (passed 2 July 1949) provided low-interest loans and tax incentives to developers, and consequently house building rose sharply. However, as is often the case with such stimulus, the primed market led to a proliferation of middle-class dwellings to the detriment of low-cost housing. The result was that from the mid-1950s – the period dramatized in *The Roof* – up to 1961, Italy had the second-highest (after Turkey) per-capita housing shortage of all European Economic Community and Cominterm countries (Angotti, 2–9).

Like Fellini's *Nights of Cabiria* made the following year, *The Roof* acknowledges the nascent economic boom that would lift at least middle-class Italians out of the deprivations of the war years. The

Rome of the via Veneto jet-setters, celebrated in Fellini's *La dolce vita*, is but four years away. Yet De Sica had already seen the beginning of these changes and examined their effect on the Italian character and culture. One of the events in *Umberto D.* (1952) is the renovation Umberto's landlady perpetrates on her tenants. Less interested in obtaining Umberto's back rent than in ousting the old pensioner from the premises altogether, she does her utmost to make him leave, everything from arranging afternoon trysts for couples in Umberto's room when he is absent to having workmen punch holes in the walls of his room while he is in the hospital. In both cases Umberto just happens to intrude on these events when he opens the door of his apartment. The landlady's desire is not so much to renew as to completely cast off the old, and in so doing she betrays Umberto, who had given her financial help during the war. This indifference towards others on the part of the builders, the renovators of Italy's economic recovery, asserts itself again in *The Roof*, but whereas in *Umberto D.* it resided in the middle class, in *The Roof* it affects the behaviour of the working class as well. It is, for De Sica, part of the price paid by the working class in their attempt to grasp the new prosperity.

> Nothing is so hard as to understand that there are human beings in this world beside one's self and one's set.
>
> WILLIAM DEAN HOWELLS, *Their Wedding Journey* (1871)

II

Throughout *The Roof* the noise of jet planes competes with the sound of commerce below. Rome bustles with the energy of new construction (high-rise apartments appear over the opening credits), street traffic, people eager for the new consumer goods who crowd storefronts to watch television commentators make confident predictions about journeys to the moon. 'Now that's a big help,' Natale, an apprentice bricklayer, responds to the television speaker as he passes. Here is a new verbal expressiveness in a De Sica hero: sarcasm breaking through the boosterism of TV commentary. (Natale is played by Giorgio Listuzzi, a footballer De Sica found after a considerable search, who has about him a brashness not unlike Renato Salvatori, the star of Monicelli's *Big Deal on Madonna Street*.) Unable to afford one of the apartments of the type he is building, Natale and his new wife Luisa (Gabriella Pallotta, a fisher's daughter – a relationship poignantly reproduced in the film) stay briefly with her mother after their marriage, then longer but less comfortably with Natale's brother Cesare and his expanding family. After a quarrel with Cesare, Natale and Luisa find themselves out on the street with a cart of meagre belongings when the apartment they reluctantly had resigned themselves to accept is condemned.

The film's action after this incident hinges on one of those absurd Italian laws that seem created to spur Zavattini's imagination. In *Umberto D.*, for example, a city ordinance forbade pets on public transport except for hunting dogs. Umberto, desperate to find a home for his dog and only companion, Flick, boards a tram, and when the conductor seems about to insist he get off, he spontaneously declares the little pooch to be a hunting dog. In *The Roof* it is a law that permits the permanency of a shelter built on municipal land so long as the inhabitants have a house with a door and a finished roof that enables the young couple to solve their problem.[4]

What distinguishes Natale and Luisa in their pursuit of this improvised solution to their homelessness from De Sica's earlier sufferers, even more than Umberto, who surmounts tram regulations, is their determination not to be victims. Their ultimate victory, in fact, makes *The Roof* unique among De Sica's neorealist films. Specifically, Natale and Luisa reveal the strength of their marriage and their capacity to extend a sense of connection to selected others, and thus break a pattern of resignation. The tragedy of Ricci in *Bicycle Thieves* and Umberto, in part at least, is a measure of their obstinacy, a kind of fixedness on their state of being. Ricci's blinkered search for his Fides bicycle exposes a 'faith' in the vehicle as symbol of his breadwinner status and hence his manhood. As exposed by the search, this faith is held onto to the neglect of his son Bruno, whom he fails to see tumble onto the wet pavement during the downpour or nearly be hit by a passing car as he is crossing a piazza. Umberto's class-bound distance from the maid Maria – stronger ultimately than the effect of the age gap – leaves him blind to a potential circumstantial kinship. Natale and Luisa, however, have youth and energy – they are born into the film at the moment of their marriage – and the early scenes denote a strong conjugal intimacy. In addition to a new brashness in his characters, this sensuality too is a new quality for De Sica, no doubt partially attributable to a relaxing of strictures on the representation of sex in films by 1956. In *Bicycle Thieves* the representation of sexuality is restricted to an emotional flash during a domestic scene. Ricci responds to Maria's remark that his new cap makes him look like a cop by off-handedly slapping her. Jostled slightly, she smiles, pushing back her hair; her eyes and body communicate a striking sensuality. In contrast to the daytime setting and the vertical position of the couple in *Bicycle Thieves*, *The Roof*'s comparable but considerably longer intimate scene takes place at night with Natale and Luisa in bed. They touch one another as they whisper their apprehension about being guests in Cesare's home. The sexual tension is increased by the knowledge that Cesare's kid sister is spying on them; seeking privacy, the couple leave the bed to embrace more passionately in the hall.

Commensurate with the bolder depiction of intimacy is the more forthright behaviour of the characters in the creation of their new home. Natale must convince his sceptical fellow workers and neighbours that the task can be done surreptitiously. Solidarity proves workable here as compared to the disintegration and self-recrimination of the protestors at the beginning of *Umberto D.* or the sadly comic ineptitude of the bicycle-market searchers in *Bicycle Thieves*. Despite the betrayal of some neighbours, and the delay necessitated by finding a new site in the dark, the brigade holds together and finishes the job. Moreover, Luisa plays a crucial role. Unlike Maria in *Bicycle Thieves*, who is marginalized by the father/son story, Luisa temporarily quits her merely supportive role to persuade her brother-in-law Cesare to join the crew of bricklayers.

Following the all-night building session, *The Roof* climaxes with an episode that reworks one of the key confrontations in De Sica's work: that between obdurate authority and desperate powerlessness. In turn, the episode generates an event characteristic of the film-maker's art, that moment when the comic and the painful co-exist. The morning reveals a ramshackle structure – reminiscent of Cabiria's wasteland bunker – that still needs finishing touches to make it a legal if minimally acceptable home. In order to delay the approaching police Natale has two co-workers stage a domestic quarrel. This burlesque amounts to nothing more than a comically lacklustre rehearsal of the authentic arguments that have punctuated the action in Cesare's home. The policemen break up the quarrel without missing a stride. The police in De Sica's neorealist films are not often deliberately injurious – just dutiful and unimaginative. They are functionaries of what appears to be an indifferent state, but one which upon more rigorous examination operates in hegemonic support of the power elite. One thinks of the policeman in *Bicycle Thieves* who wipes his hands after inspecting the freshly painted bicycle, thereby dismissing Ricci's accusation of theft and cover-up; or the newspaper reporter earlier in the film who, aroused by Ricci's pleas to the police inspector, is told that there is no story here – 'just a stolen bicycle.' This last incident, in which the police tell the media what constitutes news, functions as one of the most explicitly Gramscian moments in De Sica's oeuvre.

Continuing the improvised theatrics, Natale quickly thrusts a neighbour's baby into Luisa's arms (she is herself pregnant) and strategically directs her into a hurriedly positioned bed inside the house so that she will be framed maternally by an open window when the policeman comes by. Here De Sica eschews the option of the fantastic available to his squatters in *Miracle in Milan* and, interestingly, also abdicates the option of wilfulness he has been practising with his characters here as well. Rather, Natale and Luisa face the policeman in a fashion that recalls an earlier scene in the film notable for its modesty and tenderness. In that episode the young couple face Luisa's mother for the first time since their marriage. Luisa almost immediately runs off to the nearby beach where she fruitlessly tries to make contact with her unforgiving father. Natale is left in the street with Luisa's mother who is doing laundry. Although brief, the scene is instantly enveloping, one of the plainest validations of Welles's claim that with De Sica the screen seems to disappear to reveal life itself, or, acknowledging De Sica's own qualification, to reveal the poetry of life. Disarmed by the woman's worn but benign face, Natale hesitates; then, stealing a glance past her to Luisa's retreating figure, he simply says, 'your husband should see I'm human.' Are these words not Zavattini's testament, and does not De Sica's rendering of the scene – the camera placed directly in front of each figure, tilted slightly upward to their faces – elucidate a naked appeal for compassion? Luisa's mother recognizes Natale's essential goodness and welcomes her son-in-law into her home. The father however, as often in De Sica, remains obstinately implacable; standing in his fishing boat, tending the nets that define his working self, he remains separated from Luisa by the sea.

In the comparable episode between Natale, Luisa, and the patrolling policeman, physical and legal distances are bridged. Natale, confronting the male authority figure he has not previously been able to overcome hostility towards in the persons of Luisa's father or his own brother, is for once able to make contact. The policeman views the crude structure, emblematic of the couple's attempt to flout the law, but sees past it to the appeal of their circumstance and, more importantly, to their faces. One recalls the victim of Ricci's thievery, now the arbiter of Ricci's fate – a man with his own hard story etched in his face and hands as he glances from Bruno to his humiliated father to the unyielding faces of Ricci's captors. The policeman's authority is entirely different, of course, as is his physical appearance – well-fed, smooth-skinned – but his decision is a similarly generous one, releasing Natale and Luisa from the grip of an indifferent legalism. The couple pay a small fine. The officer retreats and the film ends with Natale and Luisa joyously celebrating their new home.

Appearances would suggest then an optimistic conclusion, certainly the first De Sica and Zavattini have permitted themselves among their neorealist films. For whereas the homes in *Miracle in Milan* and *Umberto D.*, for instance, are abandoned, the couple in *The Roof* make a home of their own and by film's end occupy it. Moreover, they are part of a tentative community of like builders for they have a neighbour who plans to expand his house. He tells Natale and Luisa that they have built in the Ditch of Saint Agnes, named for the fourth-century maiden who refused marriage because of her dedication to Christ. With a comparable dedication and perseverance Natale and Luisa have gained a home of their own. The film's title makes these qualities resonate. Explicitly in the film it is a roof that gives a human structure to the dwelling that Natale, Luisa, and their compatriots have built. Even as the morning arrives with the knowledge that the authorities will soon appear, Natale stubbornly insists upon a slanted roof, not a flat one that would make their dwelling no more than a rabbit's hutch: an aesthetic choice that privileges human imagination and will thus becomes a measure of working-class resistance to the inexorable forces of nature and society.

The issue of structure is significant in another way too. With its keen eye for the technology and material culture of a burgeoning Italy *The Roof* asserts a neorealism of greater formality. Shots of Natale receding from the camera after saying goodbye to Luisa before she boards a tram recall comparable moments in *Bicycle Thieves* and *Umberto D.*, but share a greater affinity still in composition and dramatic intent – the search for a new life – with Antonioni's *Il grido* (1957) as Aldo (Steve Cochran) undertakes his road journey. Further, and equally Antonioni-like, as befits a story about the building of structure in a couple's life, De Sica's camera discovers new structures everywhere in contemporary Rome: high-rises under construction, signal-regulated crosswalks (which momentarily confuse Luisa in one scene), and giant construction derricks which, sliding along tracks, seem capable of engulfing the human figure, but which Natale appears to negotiate with ease.

Yet in imagining a formidable hero for a new urban environment De Sica refuses triumphalism – the film is no proletarian version of *The Fountainhead*. Neither is *The Roof* optimistic in the sense of the *neorealismo rosa* films like Comencini's *Pane, amore e fantasia / Bread, Love and Dreams* (1953), its sequels and imitators, by this time the dominant form of the movement and the cause of Arthur Knight's (and others') disdain. Rather, the morning light puts Natale and Luisa's achievement – and the new dawn of working-class accomplishment – in ironic perspective. What the couple actually possess De Sica's long shot reveals: not a rabbit's hutch admittedly, but still a hastily assembled shelter, edged on one side by a swamp and on the other by a dirt incline topped by a railway track. A ditch is still a ditch, even one graced with the name of a saint.

Contributing to the sense of only qualified optimism is the couple's last act. Luigi, the little boy who the night before had been lamplighter and pathfinder for Luisa in her search for Cesare, still clings close to the new home. Quite deliberately Luisa shoos him away as if he were a stray dog. 'Nobody's waiting for me,' the boy had matter of factly informed Luisa when she urged him to go home. Now he is rejected and becomes a cousin to the *Shoeshine* boys of De Sica's first postwar film. Interestingly, his status finds an echo in Luisa's other brief companion, her girlfriend Gina, who like Maria in *Umberto D.* (the two characters are not unlike in their delicate demeanour) is also cast off. In the face of this difficult evidence of human indifference, André Bazin's words are again appropriate: 'In the universe of De Sica, there lies a latent pessimism, an unavoidable pessimism we can never be grateful enough to him for, because in it resides the appeal of the potential of man, the witness to his final and irrefutable humanity' (Bazin, 74).

The Roof connects sympathetically yet not uncritically with working-class aspirations amid the burgeoning prosperity of 1950s Italy. Yet the film was perceived as merely a late entry in a form De Sica and Zavattini had mastered years before and to many it looked passé in comparison with new films, which had assimilated the modernist aesthetic inherited from neorealism. Although filmmakers like Ermanno Olmi (*Il Posto / The Sound of Trumpets, I Fidanzati / The Fiancés*) and Vittorio De Seta (*Banditi a Orgosolo / The Bandits of Orgosolo*) would inherit De Sica's humanist principles and quiet observational style, the more politically radical and stylistically disruptive films of Pier Paolo Pasolini (*Accatone, Mama Roma*) and Francesco Rosi (*Salvatore Giuliano*) received more enthusiastic attention. De Sica passed on the neorealist mantle to this younger generation of film-makers and retreated to his own Neapolitan origins with the comic audience pleasers, *Yesterday, Today and Tomorrow* and *Marriage Italian Style*.

Notes

1 Curiously, the *New York Times Magazine* for 8 January 1958 published a short pictorial article on *The Roof*, suggesting, perhaps, that a North American release was imminent, although this did not occur until over a year later.
2 *The Roof* is available on VHS from Budget Video Inc. in California. Unfortunately, the transfer has resulted in a certain murkiness in Carlo Montuori's otherwise attractive monochrome photography, especially in the night-time sequences.
3 The reference is to *The Italian Metamorphosis, 1943–1968*, an exhibition of paintings, design, literature, cinema, and fashion at the Guggenheim Museum in New York, 7 October 1994 to 22 January 1995. The exhibition catalogue – in printed version and CD-ROM – is published by ENEL and the Guggenheim Museum.
4 I have been unable to locate the exact piece of legislation, but it may have its source in planning legislation passed in 1942 as Law # 1150 (see Angotti, 17).

References

Angotti, Thomas. *Housing in Italy*. New York: Praeger, 1977. My thanks to Markian Babij for making me aware of this book.
Bazin, André. *What is Cinema? Volume 2*. Translated by Hugh Gray. Berkeley: University of California Press, 1971.
Croce, Arlene. 'Il Tetto.' *Film Quarterly* 13:2 (Winter 1959), 49–50.
Hatch, Robert. 'Theatre and Films.' *The Nation* 188:21 (23 May 1959), 483–4.
Knight, Arthur. 'Raising *The Roof*.' *Saturday Review* 42:19 (9 May 1959), 23.
McCarten, John. 'Winning Team.' *New Yorker* 35:14 (23 May 1959), 82.
Thompson, Kristin. *Breaking the Glass Armor*. Princeton: Princeton University Press, 1988.
Wakeman, John, ed. *World Film Directors. Volume 1: 1890–1945*. New York: H.W. Wilson, 1987.

The Case of De Sica

JAMES PRICE

This article by James Price from London Magazine *(1964) is ostensibly a review of* Yesterday, Today, and Tomorrow; *however, Price uses the occasion to speculate on the nature of De Sica's authorial input in his own films. Price's notion that it was neorealist theory that galvanized De Sica into becoming an* auteur *remarkably anticipates issues of authorship and text that Michel Foucault was to raise in subsequent years. Although Price's speculations are tentative, we find his thesis unique and fascinating.*

When not long ago the hoardings went up in Lower Regent Street for *Ieri, oggi, domani / Yesterday, Today and Tomorrow* (1963) (Mastroanni chewing his nails and a beefy Loren removing a stocking) I remembered catching sight for the first time of a poster of *Ladri di biciclette / Bicycle Thieves* (1948). It was in Paris in the summer of 1949, and the poster was a coloured blow-up of that still from near the end of the film showing the father and son sitting disconsolately on the kerb. The boy is turning questioningly towards his father, and the man is looking away, to the right of the camera. Behind them pass the hurrying feet of strangers. It is one of those frozen moments which can be analysed in very much the same way as one discusses an example of genre painting, since it contains the essential ingredients of the film: the son's dependence upon his father and his desire to help him, the father's desperation and his horror of betraying that desperation to his son, the cold and indifferent city, the busy movements of those bent on business, the poverty and deprivation. You can ask all sorts of questions

James Price, 'The Case of De Sica,' *London Magazine* 4:9 (December 1964), 76–9 about it, and most of the answers will mean something. This doesn't only apply to this still, of course. *Bicycle Thieves* is a film which you can stop at almost any point and the images on the screen will be found to relate to the central concerns of poverty, solitude, alienation and solidarity.

Beside *Bicycle Thieves*, De Sica's *Yesterday, Today and Tomorrow* is such garbage that it would be hard for an occasional visitor from Mars to connect the two to the same individual. For us, alas, it isn't so difficult. Critical opinion hasn't yet agreed upon the relative merits of *Bicycle Thieves* and *Umberto D.* (1951), but from one or the other of these it is generally held that De Sica and Zavattini went into a swift decline. Perhaps we are all mistaken about this. It may be that later audiences will recognize the differences between early and late De Sica, as they do the differences between English and American Hitchcock, and prefer the later: it's at least possible. *Yesterday, Today and Tomorrow* does have virtues, extravagantly beautiful colour photography by Giuseppe Rotunno, and a masterly comic performance by Mastroianni (last episode) being the most obvious. It isn't an isolated work either. It connects with the other Sophia Loren vehicles, in particular *Oro di Napoli / The Gold of Naples* (1954) and De Sica's contribution to *Boccaccio '70* (1962); in content and technique it is carefully tailored to proven box-office requirements. The name De Sica now means at least four things: the Neapolitan pastoral represented by *Yesterday, Today and Tomorrow*; the cumbersome histrionics of *La ciociara / Two Women* (1961) and *The Condemned of Altona* (1962); the comic actor [*Men Are Such Rascals* (1932), *Pane, amore e fantasia / Bread, Love and Dreams* (1954), Andy Warhol's *Dracula* (1972)]; and *Bicycle Thieves*. Which of these four De Sica's is the true one?

If authentic cinema is personal expression by the director, the answer to this question matters. Not all these personae can be valid. The first to go, obviously, must be the De Sica of *Two Women* and *Altona*. The case of both of these adaptations is the same: they have the wrong director. Like Fellini, De Sica makes criticisms of the old order of society yet remains a party to it, profoundly orthodox; a critic of clericalism, but one of the traditional sort, entrenched in the Catholic and humanist position. Moravia and Sartre, on the other hand, begin from totally non-Christian premises. In *Two Women*, consequently, the naturalism and lack of emphasis in the Defoesque original is blurred by direction which is constantly forcing the pace towards what De Sica sees as the big scene, the rape of Cesira and her daughter by a horde of

Moroccans in a church, and from this point through a kind of purgation to a final vignetted reconciling. De Sica's and Zavattini's strong sense of dramatic tempo is connected with their redemptive view of life; and this view of life is quite alien to Moravia. Applied to Sartre, the confusion is even greater. The central subject of the play *Altona* is guilt: in the film it becomes Germany's economic revival.

De Sica as an actor, however, is on safer ground. He was a light romantic actor before the war, appearing in about thirty movies never seen over here; but the actor we know best is the figure of the toothy, grey-templed Don Juan of *Bread, Love and Dreams* and countless other films made primarily for domestic consumption. The basic role is of a well-fed man, meticulous about his own dignity and aware of his good looks, extremely sensitive to ridicule and yet somehow always being made to appear ridiculous, the kind of man who digs a hole and then falls into it himself. He would make a good Malvolio. In Rossellini's *Il Generale della Rovere* (1959) the character was taken further: the charlatan finds himself having to die a hero's death, and solemnly rises to the occasion. The point about this role is that it represents certain characteristics of stock Italian comedy. One can go further and say that it stands for certain aspects of the Italian character; further still, that it mocks the ideas of e.g. the Italian lover, the Italian husband, the Italian official and the Italian hero. How far the motif of pretence in all these parts is connected with a disillusioned assessment of Italy's military grandeur or of falsity in Fascist society I find it hard to judge, but I feel sure (particularly in *Il Generale della Rovere*) that the connection is there. The *Pane, amore* films, in which De Sica was juxtaposed with the nubile earth-goddess Gina Lollobrigida, could stand analysis in this direction.

It is the conformity to a national kind of comedy which links De Sica's acting performances with his handling of films like *Ieri, oggi, domani*. Here again, deep in the spaghetti belt, an earth-goddess reigns. The first episode, 'Adelina of Naples,' reads in synopsis like a parody of a chapter from *The Golden Bough*. Threatened with imprisonment for selling black market cigarettes to support her unemployed husband Carmine and their family, the pregnant Adelina is overjoyed to learn of a legal loophole; she cannot go to gaol until six months after the birth of her baby. So she goes on having babies until, after the seventh, her exhausted husband fails to get her pregnant again in time. But her prison sentence is short, for Carmine, burning with renewed desire, contrives to get her a pardon. The episode is full of babies' bottoms and Sophia Loren's mountainous pregnancies, as national a brand of humour as a Whitehall farce. Loren, like De Sica, commits herself to it wholeheartedly, showing no hint of the reserve one senses in Mastroianni's performance.

The second episode, 'Anna of Milan,' is a short story about a rich woman driving out of Milan in her Rolls with a prospective lover. It is slighter than the other two and the humour is drier. The third, 'Mara of Rome,' concerns an expensive call-girl (Loren), one of her regular clients (Mastroianni), and a novice priest: it ends with Mastroianni and Loren intoning Hail Marys on their knees in self-imposed celibacy. As always in De Sica's comedies, a morality of human kindness is glutinously observed. Loren may be a black marketeer or a call-girl, but she is a good-hearted black marketeer and call-girl, and if she makes a vow, she keeps it. If her attractions lead a young priest astray, she puts matters right again. If an old woman, her enemy, comes to her in tears, she consoles her. In an ideal, formalized way suitable to the conventions of this kind of comedy, these values are De Sica/Zavattini constants. The message is the kind which can appear profound if uttered with conviction, but trite and banal if delivered without it. All De Sica's films try to steer a path along the edge of banality; and only too often they have toppled off this edge into wish-wash of the worst kind (*Stazione Termini*, *Il tetto*, parts of *Miracolo a Milano*).

The films we most admired at the time (*I bambini ci guardano*, *Sciuscià*, *Bicycle Thieves*, *Miracolo a Milano* and *Umberto D.*) are the ones we still admire now; but now people tend to admire them less fervently, and their reasons for doing so may be different from what they were originally. All these films, at any rate, have conviction. They are made with passion, and this alone raises them above the level of De Sica/Zavattini's work since.

Bicycle Thieves and *Umberto D.* were, of course, films made to fit a theory. That the theory was mistaken (a confusion between realism and naturalism), or that the label *neorealism* was unjustifiable, is really beside the point: De Sica and Zavattini believed the theory was true, and after they had built their edifice and the neorealist sands shifted away, the edifice remained there, a work in its own right. It is true that *Bicycle Thieves* is less a statement about poverty in dispossessed Rome (as strict neorealist criticism would have it to be) than a myth about spiritual death and regeneration; but at this point in time this doesn't seem to matter any more. However errantly, the theory had performed its task: it had brought *Bicycle Thieves* into existence.

'Theory' is a bleak way of referring to what has been described as a

religious revival. One has only to read the film magazines of the time
to catch at once that extraordinary fervour. In an article in *Sight and
Sound*, for example, Zavattini wrote that neorealist cinema 'would not
be easy to achieve. It requires an intensity of human vision both from
the creator of the film and from the audience. The question is: how to
give human life its historical importance at every minute.' And again:
'Life is not what is invented in stories; life is another matter. To understand it involves a minute, unrelenting and patient search.' The human
eye must be made to see the human truth: not the truth of literature or
of Aristotle, but the *truth*: 'A starving man, a humiliated man, must be
shown by name and surname; no fable for a starving man, because that
is something else, less effective and less moral. The true function of the
cinema is not to tell fables, and to a true function we must recall it.'
Neorealism was a kind of 'domestic universal judgement,' as Zavattini
said on another occasion.

The well-known fact is that from this last trump only three films
were made approaching the conditions Zavattini was striving for.
They are: *Bicycle Thieves*, *Umberto D.*, and Visconti's *La terra trema*
(1948). And the differences between Visconti's work and De Sica's are
so radical as to invalidate any but the most general talk of correspondence between them. Without the theory, moreover, we would have
had only *La terra trema*; it was the theory which drew from De Sica/
Zavattini something which they could not otherwise have produced.

Umberto D. and *Bicycle Thieves* are deeply pessimistic films. It is often
an elegiac, rather self-indulgent pessimism (most notably on the sound
track, in Cicognini's music); and this slots into place with what we
know of De Sica from his other films. But, countering this, *Bicycle
Thieves* has a harsh quality which is all its own: a visual harshness, rest-
ing much in the choice of faces, especially in that of the leading actor,
Lamberto Maggiorani. Maggiorani has none of the self-consciousness
which characterizes the old man in *Umberto D.* or the boys in *Sciuscià*.
He is nakedly what he is, a Roman workman: his face is a kind of tragic
mask, conveying the pain and despair appropriate to the role while at
the same time preserving a secrecy and dignity. It is an anonymous
face, and it is an anonymous performance.

Is *Bicycle Thieves* perhaps an anonymous film? It would be a convenient way of disposing of De Sica if one could deprive him of its
authorship. And in a quite serious sense this is one way of regarding it.
What is trivial and predictable about other De Sica work is here sub-
dued inside a structure which rises above his personality. Analysed as

a pattern of loss, death and rebirth, it fits into the Christian pattern we would expect of him; but from the outside it is an object whose surfaces are unusually hard and unyielding.

Bicycle Thieves is more interestingly and more usually discussed in relation to neorealist theory than it is to De Sica's other work. And the fact that this is so tells us something about De Sica's artistic character. He is not an originator, but he is, or was, acutely sensitive to the mood of his time. It seems to have been a matter of chance that he was able to rise to the opportunity when it occurred after the war. Now, nearly twenty years later, we neither need – nor do the circumstances exist which could bring into being – a Bicycle Thieves. Our themes are less concerned; and as far as De Sica goes, the mood of the time has deserted him. Or has it? Perhaps Yesterday, Today and Tomorrow is what we deserve. At any rate, it demonstrates only too well the impasse into which the true artist in the cinema can find himself.

References

Zavattini, Cesare. 'Some Ideas on the Cinema,' Sight and Sound 23:2 (October 1953), 64–9. The essay is included in this volume, 50–61 above.

Hiding in the Light:
De Sica's Work in the 1960s

STEPHEN SNYDER

Stephen Snyder's original essay toys with the notion that De Sica's least-liked films from the 1960s are thematically continuous with the more serious neorealist works. These films present a De Sica wavering between a modernist and postmodernist sense of 'self.' They are useful in their provision of a deliberate critical model by which we can, to some degree, read De Sica's earlier films. As well they seem to point towards a psychological peculiarity of De Sica's, the man who loses himself at the point of his greatest visibility – or conversely seems to become himself most completely in an adopted role. One thinks of De Sica's role in Rossellini's film **General Della Rovere** *in which the character comes to identify with, and indeed becomes, the role he is given to play in the text within the text of the film. Snyder suggests that the focus in these films, no less than in the neorealist works, is the insulted, even assaulted, eyes of the protagonists, which embody or betray a self beyond social construction, which see, suffer, and seek their confirmation in the eyes of others.*

> But emptiness, too, has its value and somehow resembles abundance.
>
> CLARICE LISPECTOR

Let me start by indulging in a reader-response kind of criticism, and confess that I enjoy *After the Fox* (1967). The reason, however, has less to do with Peter Sellers, or De Sica (or Neil Simon's screenplay) than it does with Victor Mature (1915–99). That chiselled-in-stone face was a part of my childhood. *The Robe* (1953) was the first cinemascope film I can remember seeing. I was taken by my grandmother and we subsequently went eagerly to *Demetrius and the Gladiators* (1954), after which I was allowed to read part of the original book by Lloyd C. Douglas. I quickly conflated 'mature' with Mature. The Mature face was the cornerstone for endless biblical epics (and endless discussions in my family). That face left no emotion in doubt: Fear, Love, Anger were writ large in neon letters on his brow. Looking at that face now I am struck by the waves of panic that seem to roll across it unchecked; yet I also sense the ability of that panic to convert itself into an empathy for 'like' creatures instantaneously. Mature's is a face whose eyes speak both existential angst, even true terror, and the hope for a redemption of the world he is in. Mature has a gaze that betrays an almost tragic degree of concern for all that it rests upon; a gaze that wants protection for itself, protection for all suffering beings across whose eyes it slides for a signal of recognition. That gaze conveys a sense of utter impotence to protect either the gazer or anyone he sees. It is a gaze, perhaps, that registers a continual non-comprehension of the world in which it finds itself. I would like to explore the notion that Victor Mature's eyes are part of the subject of De Sica's film *After the Fox*. I contend, in fact, that they resemble De Sica's own eyes as they appear in an episode of his film *L'oro di Napoli / The Gold of Naples* (1954). Both faces look at the audience with a sense of pain that blurs easily into compassion. The gaze reaches out to the objects of the world for assurance and probes other eyes for protective approbation. These are eyes that can be blind to all sorts of rigamarole, because, in fact, like an infra-red telescope they are attuned to one span of the light spectrum, the contract for mutual protection. Mature's eyes do not want to draw you into their interior gloaming; they want to jump out of the sockets and hide in you, to see their way to invisibility.

My description of Mature's dilemma invokes the spectre of Jacques Lacan, especially his description of the human condition as being comparable to imprisonment in a hall of mirrors. For, indeed, part of the human contract that the eyes of De Sica's characters seek is a reflected commonality. Although one hastens to add that if the world is a line of mirrors, De Sica's world is a line of broken mirrors, a string of failures made melancholy by their ineffectuality. But perhaps Lacan is the man to employ as the envoy into De Sica's world, for he is the psychologist who has most conflated the act of seeing with the act of being seen (Lacan, 'The Mirror Stage,' 734–8). The premise of Lacan's psychology is that our individual sense of identity arrives via reflection, from the outside (Lacan, 'Of Structure,' 186–95). The term 'the mirror stage' can denote an actual physical occurrence of an infant seeing itself as an image in a mirror, or the term can denote a perpetual psychological condition in which one's sense of identity has come to one as an ego ideal from the approbation of others: how I see myself is how I see myself reflected ideally in the eyes of my parents; my eyes will glide across the eyes of others throughout my life seeking the reflection of my own image as though it were hidden and protected in the gazing eyes of others. One might say I both exist as a subject and hide as a self in the light of the other's gaze. In Lacan's sense the subject, which he understands as the only self that exists (Lacan, 'The Mirror Stage,' 738), is that which is seen in another's seeing (Silverman, 147). Such at least is the circumstance of our life that De Sica meditates on in *After the Fox*; whether we are to see this meditation as a break with modernist notions of self-liberation or a humanist retrenchment within modernism is difficult to say. Clearly the 1960s films of De Sica demarcate a transition in implied faith: implied faith in a 'soul,' implied faith in something called reality, faith in human progress, faith in the very modernist Marxist belief that history will produce human liberation, faith in the existence in each human subject of some small degree of identity that reaches beyond and reclaims the symbolic order of culture in which it is embedded. But, by suggesting that De Sica's middle-period films depart from the relatively modernist/humanist position of his neorealist works, I do not want to claim that they either leap into or are easily aligned with a postmodernist vision, particularly since it is possible to find something postmodernist in everyone. Still, one cannot avoid the fact that a number of these 1960s films are immersed in issues of self-mirroring and the potential lack of any essence in the human subject, immersed as it is in the mechanics of identity construction. Without turning De Sica into a postmodernist, I wish to point to the relentless undertow of doubt that permeates these 1960s comedies, doubt which manifests itself in a kind of Lacanian visual paradox without necessarily taking its final rest in the Lacanian bed. For while De Sica's protagonists do indeed attempt to lay claim to a sense of identity in the mirrored gaze of others, they also see, suffer, and seek confirmation of their suffering in the eyes of other people. The identification of oneself with the scarred or broken condition of another human being is a form of mirroring which is something more than the sort of mirrored identity detailed by Lacan.

After moving, gradually, from tragic to comedic stories in his films of the 1950s, De Sica in the 1960s manufactured a series of light comedies which have been consigned by critics to that part of limbo called 'lame.' *Ieri, oggi, domani / Yesterday, Today, and Tomorrow* (1963), *Matrimonio all'italiana / Marriage Italian Style* (1964), *Un monde nouveau* (1965), *After the Fox* (1967), *Woman Times Seven* (1968), and several other films have few fans and have occasioned almost no interesting commentary. I think there is a general consensus that these 1960s films present a De Sica who had 'sold out' to the demands of industry filmmaking, whose films are miles away from his neorealist art, produced only because they were the kind of films for which De Sica and Zavattini could get enough funding to pay the rent, etc. And, as De Sica has admitted, these circumstances are to some degree true (see 44–6 above). Still, within the context of the required conformity to industry codes of bourgeois entertainment and the compound authorship of the scripts, the films offer an ongoing meditation upon the nature of textuality, which seems to anticipate Foucault's question 'what is an author?' (Foucault, 138) and to suspend before us a mirage-like critical discourse on how we have seen, or might see, De Sica's own work. More specifically, these 1960s industry films turn, again and again, to issues of vision and to the counterpart of that issue, the invisibility of one's self. *Seeing* and *being seen* have a shared thematic axis in most of the De Sica work of his so-called middle period.

De Sica's concerns with seeing and being seen have as their first reference point De Sica himself, for he occasionally places himself in the films or represents himself in the role of either actor or director. In expanding upon some of Cannistraro's ideas on De Sica's acting career (Cannistraro, 86–93 above), we may be justified in recognizing a not uncommon psychological aspect in De Sica the performer, what we might call the wish of the artist to become visible within his work (confirm something of himself for himself) while at the same time losing something of himself in it: the desire of the director to disappear, as he does in *After the Fox*, to become invisible and protected, behind a mask of spectacular public visibility. One can argue with Cannistraro that De Sica the director is an evolution of De Sica the actor, that as a director he retains his position as the star of his films, a man who seems to display his deepest self in public, through his characters, but who remains, nevertheless, rather enigmatic and stands outside his work. After looking at De Sica's films one may wonder if self-display does not function, periodically, as a means of achieving total self-disappearance, and thus, perhaps, as a way of self-preservation. I believe De Sica has allegorized this tendency for us in *After the Fox*. The need of the director is to become invisible at the very moment that he is burdened with the need as an actor to make a display of himself; or with the need as a director, meeting the demands of the medium, to make something visible, something that emerges either from a dimension of his own soul or from the nature of inscription: to embody emotional crises in terms of authorial invisibility. De Sica's rather hard-nosed ironic twist to the drama of self-preservation is, I suggest, the result of his realization that the strategies for saving the self through invisibility serve to destroy that self, and that the strategies for saving the self through total public self-dramatization may also serve to destroy that self. A De Sica character, perhaps De Sica himself, is propelled by a wish to find a way of disappearing from the world while inscribing her/himself within it – hiding in the light, as my title suggests.

It is possible for a film critic interested in formal themes to make any film seem to be rich in material. I would, accordingly, like to place the discourse on vision in De Sica's films in context for a minute. For example, one may easily identify Lacanian issues of mirroring and seeing in *Ladri di biciclette / Bicycle Thieves* (1948). When Bruno stands beside his father on his father's first work morning, he takes pains to resemble his father, even making sure his wrapped lunch is placed in the same pocket of his work suit as Ricci's is in his. Clearly, at the film's end Ricci's failure has been an insult to Bruno's vision of Ricci to the degree that the original mirror he made of his father is broken. Bruno takes his father's hand, anyway, and, although the two still reflect each other, their shared, mirrored, identity is a sharing of a mutual shattering. The Lacanian mirror has been replaced by something that exceeds Lacan's sense of the mirror as a nexus of self-identity. With a different turn the crisis of mirroring is presented in the late film *Il giardino dei Finzi-Contini / The Garden of the Finzi-Continis* (1971), wherein the need of the Jewish family to be 'invisible' is countered by their equally strong urge to live in 'style.' The act of retreat practised by the family eventually serves to make them more vulnerable to the very visible dangers (Fascism) of the world; yet, they are attached to that world as a confirming mirror of themselves and deny its true danger. They cannot see the danger, perhaps, taken up as they are by the Lacanian need for confirmation. The effort one makes towards one's own visibility is propelled by a sense of the fragility of one's self-image and by a fear of disappearing at one end of the spectrum or the other – hypervisibility or utter anonymity: 'we are the Finzi-Continis/we are not here.' Yet at the end Micòl's comforting of her grandmother, like Bruno's of his father, is something more than the kind of identity mirroring that Lacan talks about. It is as though Micòl is seeing the world of other people, as others, for the first time. Her eyes, which are one of the more prominent visual aspects of the film, register something more than the self-enclosed hardness which they maintain for most of the narrative.

The issues are foregrounded again with a different twist in De Sica's early comedy *L'oro di Napoli / The Gold of Naples* (1954). Here he parodies himself in the role of a gambler who is reduced to pursuing his addiction, invisibly, among children. The role within the film is intended, I think, to be an ironic comment by De Sica on the public figure of himself, a man who was known to squander money all too often at the gambling tables while manufacturing films on the ills of poverty. The self-representation, it strikes me, like Chaplin's in *City Lights* (1931), looks to us for forgiveness for the small vices of mankind. In a small comedic way De Sica apologizes and seeks the approbation of *our* gaze. There is a peculiar gesture of self-revelation here; by hiding in a role he uses the movie screen as a mirror to elicit identification of the audience with the weaknesses of the man De Sica.

In a number of De Sica narratives to be visible is often correlated with the ability to see. Visibility is shown to be as perilous as being utterly invisible: perilous especially to De Sica's mind because visibility readily converts itself into a condition of self-loss. To allow oneself to be seen is to lose oneself to a public performance which severs one part of one's self from another. To have nothing in reserve as one turns one's sense of who one is over to public approbation quickly changes one's desire for approbation into 'duty,' and what were once variable possibilities of feeling or action in the arena of art now become contracted gesticulations, concentrated into a unitary fixed persona, depleted of life and emotionally diminished. Thus to be *seen* may be to allow oneself to be appropriated in some way, to lose one's power of choice (or sense of that power, since *choice* may be delusional in De Sica's world) and thus one's freedom: one's very self. To be seen may amount to living for someone else's gaze only, a gaze that will command a suppression of tonalities in the chromatic scale of human melodic possibility. Thus, self-expression, as an act of making one's self visible, may be a prelude to one's own self-destruction. For example, Totò *il buono* experiences exactly such a fate as he rises to the rank of leader of a 'labour' movement; his identity is made progressively more rigid by the society in which he lives; finally, as a modern Jesus, he can only fly off into clouds. What he holds in reserve is the liberty of a Thoreau-like retreat.

In De Sica's 1960s comedies this compound issue of mirroring and invisibility is not fraught with the emotional baggage of the earlier 'serious' films. One finds it displayed, here, with a certain good-natured humour, as for example in the cameo scene from *After the Fox* in which De Sica appears as himself, directing some sort of exotic beach-blanket biblical epic. One may recall that the scene shows the director trying to photograph a sandstorm. As he calls for ever more sand and wind, he disappears into the duststorm he has generated, becoming invisible in a cloud of dirt. Here De Sica is, on the one hand, clearly laying out a parody of the history of his own post-neorealist career, a man who was gradually obliterated by the system of commercial cinema in the industry – or perhaps a man whose distinctive features were obliterated by his very success. On the other hand, one may note that it is the director himself who summons forth this self-erasing sandstorm. In a sense that Foucault might sanction the author presents his authorial role as a locus where other zones of power overlap. He disappears into the context, or the text, of his work. The act of inscription, a self-assertion by the artist, is also the moment of his evaporation into his text, of his disappearance as a self. De Sica as text unfolds into the De Sica text.

Although De Sica credits Neil Simon for everything in *After the Fox* (see 45 above), we cannot completely discount De Sica's role in the film. In a most detailed fashion the film advances the issue of invisibility dealt with in De Sica's other works, and it supplies us with different versions of the relationship of self to seeing. The protagonist Vanucci (played by Peter Sellers), a so-called mastermind criminal, breaks out of jail at the beginning of the film because of his Oedipal, possibly mirror-like and incestuous, interest in his own sister. The premise of his escape is his ability to remain invisible to the police (in the public realm) while being in plain sight. To this end he disguises himself as a carbiniere, a priest, and other visibly public forms of identity. Vanucci is everywhere and nowhere, mirroring himself in everybody and thus preserving his freedom. The demands of his sister to be in a movie, to become a publicly visible sex symbol, coupled with his own greed to steal gold, lead Vanucci to discover the ultimate mode of self-effacement: the role of film director. Here his public performance can almost perfectly conceal his real identity. And, as if that were not enough, Vanucci chooses as his model the film's director, Vittorio De Sica himself, who makes a cameo appearance (along with John Huston) as himself. Ricci, the almost disappearing, would-be family man of *Bicycle Thieves* emerges twenty years later as De Sica in disguise. At film's end Vanucci must escape from prison one more time by substituting himself for the prison physician. When one of the Vanuccis is finally outside, neither we nor he knows which person he is. The little musical refrain which comes up repeats the question, 'who is anybody?' Seen from Vanucci's point of view, the film is a postmodernist exercise on the instability of identity and the disappearance of the self in a sort of symbolic public realm. Hiding in the light amounts to disappearance, and disappearance amounts to preservation, holding something back.

On a parallel course with Vanucci is Victor Mature playing himself, but posing as that self was fifteen years earlier. Mature hopes that his visibility in Vanucci's film will do nothing less than take twenty years off his age, make invisible all those years of hard living. Mature, masquerading as himself in the 1949 movie *Easy Living* (which is seen for a moment in the film), sweeps the world of the film with his lacerated eyes as though looking for a refuge and a real self. His poignant gaze, it seems to me, really testifies to a modernist/humanist sensibility that sees the real self as some ill-defined reservoir concealed beneath the various public performances of self. Mature's tragedy, if we can call it that, is his sense of loss of anything left undefined in himself. Through his point of view the film is less postmodernist than it is humanist. He wants to be loved, yet he retreats from physical contact with Vanucci's sister for fear of being discovered. (His cheap hair dye comes off on her face.) His adopted role of lover inhibits his ability to be a lover. The real self is the only one through which he could claim love, but that self can be found, for the most part, in his need for love itself. In some sense he is the person he seeks, for without dropping the role that he thinks will attract love, he cannot experience the love he desires. His condition resembles that of Vanucci, but it is given, I think, a much more humanist slant. 'Give me a hit in the stomach,' he says to Martin Balsam, only to collapse utterly when the blow is delivered. The sequestered powers of life have been squandered. You disguise yourself in order to be seen and in the process you lose yourself or the figure from whom you want love. Such was the great lesson of Chaplin's *City Lights*.

At times, the trick of *After the Fox* is not that things are not what they appear to be, but rather that they are. In Mature's case, the eyes with which he looks are the objects for which he is looking. Our final view of him in the film is a close-up of those agonized eyes as Vanucci tells him, 'true talent will never be diminished by the passing of years.' Their very visibility makes them hard to recognize, or, if not to recognize, to accept, since they are scarred with the ineradicable passing of time.

In Vanucci's case one must hide in the light, so to speak, on the public square. Here he must repossess the world in a fraudulent way in order to avoid being possessed by it. He risks losing all sense of identity while aiming to protect it. For De Sica, the director within the film, self-liberation seems to be equated with choosing invisibility. He can at best use Vanucci or Mature as surrogates. These three male figures present different variations on a theme: in one case the variant strikes me as being postmodernist (Vanucci), but in the other cases the point of view seems to invoke the perspective and the values of De Sica's neorealist humanism: true talent, or the true self, will not be diminished by time (Mature); the role of the director may empower one to act, but the actions must propel human awakening (I see Vanucci as speaking for De Sica in his final confessional speech in the courtroom).

Also true of the film's situations, especially the confusion at film's end, is its insistence upon the implication of character in text. If Vanucci disappears into himself at film's end, he dissolves into the very text he has created. In the writing scene Vanucci opens the cultural text and opens himself to only an absence. There is no Vanucci; he exists in the endless free play he opens. The zone in which he works is so broken down that his chosen double, his signifier, melts into a series of possibilities in which the gap of difference closes temporarily. The other main figures, De Sica and Mature, present experiences which affirm the need and the possibility of establishing a gap between oneself and others.

While *After the Fox* is the 1960s film that most blatantly presents invisibility as its theme, *Yesterday, Today, and Tomorrow* covers some of the same ground. On the one hand the film, composed of three episodes from different periods, is a social satire that explores Italian attitudes to maternity. Not far from the surface of the film lurk the cultural archetypes of women as *mother* and *whore*. The first episode portrays Sophia Loren as a baby factory while the third episode, a highlighted Oedipal drama, deals with the fusion of the roles of prostitute and mother, and suggests, in addition, a symbiotic relationship of the two with the Catholic Church. One can see De Sica already playing with the issue of visibility here as a kind of cultural joke. Loren's monumental production of text (the string of look-alike children) in the first episode liberates her from the law and gives her a legitimate textual status in her culture. Her visibility as a producing mother frees her, in some sense renders her invisible, to the claims of law. Her independence is a function of her vast undefinable reserves of possibility. In the final episode of the film Loren's powers of production are metamorphosed into her act of giving birth to a priest, a figure whose symbolic value sanctions motherhood itself, while his required celibacy looms as a peculiar effigy of the contradictions of the culture. The film, as text, makes a deconstructive gesture towards the culture in which it is inscribed.

The first disturbing dimension of *Yesterday, Today, and Tomorrow* that is likely to strike a De Sica fan is the fact that the film, set in 1953 – the world of *Umberto D.* (1952), or even *Miracolo a Milano / Miracle in Milan* (1950) – seems to be a total vulgarization of the very situations that provoked De Sica into making his best films. Suddenly, instead of real people, we have Italian stereotypes, forking down plenteous bowls of pasta and gesticulating wildly over the most trivial matters. The financial and emotional poverty of *Il tetto / The Roof* (1956) is replaced with a Himalayan insistence upon fecundity and prosperity. The world circa 1950 is crowded with images of fertility in contrast to the earlier films where the landscape was occupied by alienated old men and pregnant girls who faced immense emotional and financial problems. In *Yesterday, Today, and Tomorrow*'s 1963 vision of 1950 the earlier period is presented as a sit-com fertility rite in which no one really needs to work because food is so plentiful; the only problem is finding a way to sell it on the black market. It is as though a large screen painting of overflowing fruit bowls has been placed in front of *Umberto D.*, rendering the world of that film effectively invisible. Is De Sica himself deconstructing his own extended text?

Either De Sica in his comedic mode is redressing the bleakness of the earlier films or he is cementing that bleakness with a very cynical satire on Italian culture. A quick plot summary of the three episodes demonstrates how difficult it is not to consider the film a brutal satire. In the first episode, 'Adelina of Naples' (*Yesterday*), Sophia Loren has cheated her creditors but discovers she can avoid arrest indefinitely by being in a state of perpetual pregnancy. So she balloons up with one child after another until her vacuous husband, played by Marcello Mastroianni, can stand no more. She spends some time in jail, but is released to a heroine's welcome for which all of Naples turns out. (Is this some sort of grotesque homage to working-class solidarity?) The point of the first episode seems to be the absurdity of the Italian insistence upon producing enormous numbers of children (all boys). However, the second episode, 'Anna of Milan' (*Today*), inverts the satire by making fun of a superficial bourgeois woman whose failings may be measured by her failure to be big with child. This episode goes to great lengths to parody the cinematic style of Michelangelo Antonioni, to whom De Sica applies the term *aesthete* (see 36 above), and in so doing complicates the issues of satire. The Loren and Mastroianni characters are infinitely more interesting in the first episode than in the second. Is the satire in the second episode directed only at Antonioni, or does it serve to reverse the cynicism of the first episode? – is profligate childbearing better than the upper-class superficiality of the contemporary (1963) scene?

The third episode, 'Mara of Rome' (*Tomorrow*), locates the characters in much the same world as the *Today* episode. The future holds no major changes. Loren, a high-class prostitute, becomes the object of love of a student priest who looks as though he floated off the set of a Robert Bresson film. Loren manages to become a mother figure to this sensitive wraith, eventually taking a vow of short-term celibacy herself in order to spirit him back to his celibate path. This third episode presents itself as a satire on the common cultural stereotype of the maternal whore, or rather the misogynistic stereotype of woman as whore and mother. The mother/whore figure gives birth to a priest, setting carefully into place the cornerstone of the Italian cultural conscience. This episode is obviously saturated with Oedipal themes. The priest has a grandmother whose attachment to the young man is almost unnatural. Yet the attachment is peculiarly repressive insofar as her investment lies in maintaining her grandson's virginity. The priest is presented as some sort of cultural scapegoat ('we'll keep one of us clean') for all the busy extramarital sexual activity of a culture whose nature and essence are condensed in the image of the Loren prostitute. Yet we never see Loren engaged in any consummated sexual activity. Her gestures toward such consummation are always interrupted by her maternal/sexual interest in the neophyte priest. Meanwhile the Mastroianni character is equally distracted from gratifying his sexual desires by his obsessive attention to the demands of his father. He wants to be a 'good' son, and achieves this dream by remaining a child in perpetuity, a sort of Oedipal fiction of his father, who remains invisible throughout the movie.

Each of the episodes invokes the issue of invisibility in some subtle way. The first episode turns on the matter that Adelina (Loren) is invisible to the law only as long as her pregnancies are visible facts. She is required to show and tell in order to avoid a prison sentence. The second episode opens with a long shot taken through the windshield of a moving car, thus rendering Anna (Loren) invisible for several minutes of the film. By the end of the episode she is indeed an invisible figure by virtue of being a cipher, a non-person. More to the point, her invisibility is a by-product of her barrenness; one would like to claim that hers is a culturally induced transparency, but the rough treatment given to her by De Sica suggests, rather, that her real problem is her childlessness. The third episode derives its force by its constant allusion to invisible agents of law: the absent father of the Mastroianni character, the abstract vows and cultural codes that bind the Bresson-clone to his priestly celibate life, the culturally sanctioned code of the sacrificial victim. Indeed, the looming moral injunction of the third episode is to save one's self by dropping out somehow, becoming culturally invisible. For the characters in this film seeing is pretty much defined as seeing your identity mirrored for you in your culture. It seems to me that, while the film satirizes this Lacanian mirror relationship, it does not in any way break the mirroring process. It engages postmodern themes without moving wholly into them as does *After the Fox*.

Marriage Italian Style (1964), like *Yesterday, Today, and Tomorrow,* is conceived of as a satire on Italian culture. It is, of course, a follow-up to the very funny Pietro Germi film, *Divorzio all'italiana / Divorce Italian Style* (1961), also featuring Marcello Mastroianni. Both films, one might argue, pull the veil off sexual desire as an unending Lacanian chain of metonymic substitutions (men and women engorge each other hungrily, one eye out to the next significant other before the last is fully digested). De Sica's film opens in the present, but moves quickly into a flashback in which the issue again is presented as a problem in visibility and identity. The Mastroianni character meets the Loren character in a bordello during an air raid. She is hiding in a closet, and in opening the door he looks momentarily at an image of himself reflected in the door's mirror. When asked why she is hiding, Loren explains that she does not want to be seen and identified by the other people there. She wishes to maintain her personal sense of self, which is not that of a whore, by refusing a public appearance. The scene evokes the persistent De Sica theme of the need to hold something in reserve. She rejects the mirror society offers, and in the course of the film she continues to reject that mirror as defining the totality of herself by raising a family in private. The film ends with a parable on the difficulty of establishing a parent-child mirroring process. Loren has three sons, only one of whom has been fathered by Mastroianni. He desires to know which is his in order to establish a mutual mirrored identity with his real son. But this mirroring is now impossible. The authenticity of the real son is invisible. Each one is the possible mirror. Mastroianni must adopt all three to insure his prerogatives as a parent. The identity of the real son has been blurred to indistinctiveness. In *Bicycle Thieves* the parent-child bond of Bruno and Ricci is undermined by doubt and rendered arbitrary. In a certain sense the signifier of Mastroianni's fatherhood in *Marriage Italian Style*, the frame in which he wishes to see his own image, is unavailable, or at least multiple. *Marriage Italian Style* takes a definite step towards the incertitude of *After the Fox*.

Another variant upon the issue of seeing is found in *Amanti / A Place for Lovers* (1968), which is not a comedy. Julia (Faye Dunaway) recognizes Valerio (Mastroianni) on a television program as a man who approached her for a date in an airport. So, improbably, because he gave her a card with his telephone number, she is able to call him and initiate an intense love affair. What is interesting here is that Valerio becomes visible only when zoned off by the television screen; he gains presence through his virtual absence, inscribed in the television text. Valerio breaks off the affair when he becomes disgusted with Julia's penchant for orgies, group sex, pornography. Julia pursues him, however, and eventually persuades him to forgive her. They live in an Alpine chalet for a while. Valerio learns that Julia is terminally ill and that her behaviour has been a compensation for her impending disappearance. In this serious but positive work De Sica expresses a faith in the ability of some sincere aspect of the human being to break through the disguises which society has imposed upon it.

In various ways these later films raise the same questions one sees in De Sica's neorealist films: a human being needs protection from his own helplessness. This is a fundamental theorem of *Bicycle Thieves*, for example, a film that proves nothing if not the utter helplessness of Ricci, the protagonist – and, by extension, our common helplessness in the face of overwhelming circumstances. And could the same not be said for the protagonists of *Umberto D.* and *Sciuscià / Shoeshine*? But from what well-spring of the human heart can some sort of mutual reciprocal protection be summoned in a De Sica universe? From what source other than the nebulous depths of one's own potential empathic imagination? If I understand Lacan, there is no such thing in his account of mankind. Human solidarity, as the Marxists envisioned it, is probably not entirely congruent with De Sica's vision of solidarity. Numbers, alone, are not the issue. Rather, what is at stake is the imaginative extension of one human being into the imaginative space of another: my protection for myself must be part of my willingness to offer the illusion of protection to you too – perhaps a form of Lacan's notion of love as the giving of something you do not have to someone who is not there (Lacan, 'Of Structure,' 186–200). And yet, in the De Sica world, it works; in fact, it is the only thing that works – Bruno reclaiming his father to himself by taking his hand; the alienated brother in *The Roof* showing up to help the younger brother complete his fantasy space; or all the suffering wives in *Woman Times Seven* (1968) trying to reclaim themselves by claiming a piece of some man's fancy. My invisibility may become, in the empathic moment, your coat. *Woman Times Seven*, though made from a script by Zavattini, seems to me the weakest comedy of the 1960s period. For my purposes the film can be summarized as a catalogue of the various ways wives become invisible to their husbands. The most interesting aspect of it may be that, while Shirley Maclaine plays seven roles, she is a variant of the same lovelorn character in each. Her efforts to be loved culminate narratively in the question of suicide. Mirroring is reduced to self-annihilation. We begin with the death of the 'man' and end with the near-death of 'the woman.'

In De Sica's serious films imagination, more often than not, fails its characters. He refers to these films as Egoism #1, #2, etc. (De Sica, 38 above). In the comedies, however, imagination, when invoked, is almost always entangled in issues of identity, frosted with a thick layer of irony. We can certainly say that the 1960s comedies are essays on the nature of imagination, even if the results of imaginative action seem, at best, problematical. The emotional protection generated is confused and barely tangible. The sort of communal protection which emerged, however fragile, from the collective empathy of people in *The Roof* now finds its expression in the desire and ability of the characters to find a way of disappearing more or less into each other, or into utterly fabricated roles they may invent for themselves.

All in all, De Sica's work of the 1960s, whatever its value as comedy, forms a lengthy meditation by De Sica on the nature of textuality and the position of a 'creating' subject within it. The play for visibility on the part of the characters is a play for a more substantive life within a human community; the motion towards invisibility is a characteristic result of the desire for more life, or even, at times, the peculiar result of the subject's re-inscribing of her/himself within the film. I would say, in fact, that the movement towards absence in the 1960s films is an index of the longing for a greater sense of *presence*, a sense of the hereness of self and world that the author cannot, in fact, pin down. The endless piercing gazes of De Sica's characters, sliding across the eyes of the viewers, are not gazes creating a subject position for that viewer but rather looks that testify to the unfastening of any present world from the gaze that seeks to behold it.

The gaze of so many De Sica characters has a lacerating quality (for me, that is), from that of the child in *I bambini ci guardano / The Children Are Watching Us* (1942) to Victor Mature's eyes which hover above the landscape of *After the Fox* like those of a suffering martyr. These gazes do not so much gather strength from their narrative contexts as work to empower or even redirect those narratives. The eye, in these De Sica films, is both symbol and touchstone: that point at which our own humane eyesight, as well as our visibility, brings itself into momentary focus: our desire to behold and our desire to be held by another's vision become confused or frustrated. The eye is looking for itself endlessly, afraid of what it will or will not find. While De Sica's 1960s films celebrate the power of images, they convey with equal force his persisting humanist belief in the power of the invisible.

References

Adams, Hazard, and Leroy Searle, eds. *Critical Theory since 1965.* Tallahassee: Florida State University Press, 1989.

Cannistraro, Philip. 'Ideological Continuity and Cultural Coherence.' *Bianco e nero* 36:9–12 (September–December 1975) 14–19. Reprinted in this volume, 86–93 above.

Foucault, Michel. 'What Is an Author?' In Adams and Searle, eds. *Critical Theory since 1965.* Translated by Donald Bouchard.

Lacan, Jacques. 'The Mirror Stage' (1937). In Adams and Searle, eds. *Critical Theory since 1965.* Translated by Alan Sheridan.

- 'Of Structure as an Inmixing of an Otherness Prerequisite to Any Subject Whatsoever.' In *The Structuralist Controversy*. Edited by Richard Macksey and Eugenio Donato. Baltimore: The Johns Hopkins University Press, 1972.
Lispector, Clarice. *The Hour of the Star*. Translated by Giovanni Pontiero. New York: New Directions, 1986.
Samuels, Charles Thomas. *Encountering Directors*. New York: Putnam's, 1972.
Silverman, Kaja. *The Subject of Semiotics*. New York: Oxford University Press, 1983.

In Love and War: Vittorio De Sica's *Two Women*

FAYE McINTYRE

Faye McIntyre's original essay is a reading of Two Women *through the lens of* The Garden of the Finzi-Continis. *Both films feature characters whose sense of identity is derived on the one hand from a delusive fantasy of idealized childhood, and on the other from an image of themselves as living a guilt-permeated adulthood. McIntyre sees the metaphor of architectural construction as operating in both films.*

In what seems a small concession to cinematic realism Vittorio De Sica opens his film *La ciociara / Two Women* (1960), with a series of photographs which depict 'real life' in wartime Italy. This collection of images appears to be all that is left of a commitment to an aesthetic, and perhaps also to the corresponding moral vision, that took as its primary subject Italy's years under Fascism, the war, and the resistance. Many of the images of Rome seem randomly chosen shots of crowds of people and of empty streets, rows of cars and buildings seen from a remote, unspecified, or depersonalized vantage point. During the presentation of these photographs, however, the camera begins to insinuate itself into the image. In the penultimate image we see a grouping of people, perhaps a family, seated around a table, apparently poor, perhaps, judging by the too thin arms of the children, destitute, all of them looking complacently, despairingly, or cheerfully at the dispassionate camera. Closer to the end of the credits a lone woman is isolated in the shot, evidently stopped on her way to or from work: she wears a uniform and carries a bundle of papers. She also seems to confront the camera, albeit weakly. The final scene of people walking along a street in Rome becomes a tableau as sound is added over the image while the image, for a brief interval, remains a still, silent, and undisturbed picture. The addition of sound has the effect of suggesting a potentially threatening outside to the photograph, an observing authoritative agency which seemingly becomes offensive when the scene is animated and we see the people of the formerly still shot begin to scatter in fear as they hear an air-raid siren. Images that might have served to memorialize the war years, which this film looks back to retrospectively (Marcus, 28), are opened up by the camera, as it were. The beginning of the narrative seems, in effect, to terrorize the 'real' image, and the people who, seconds earlier, were safely consigned to history.

Apart from the opening images, in many obvious ways *Two Women* veers away from the aesthetic tradition of neorealism, especially in its use of famous actors (Sophia Loren and Jean-Paul Belmondo), its studio settings, and its ideal or progressive narrative which is built upon the biblical paradigm of redemption that also underlies the novel by Alberto Moravia that is the literary source for the film. Yet if the style of *Two Women* seems to suggest De Sica's turning away from the neorealist tradition, thematically, at least, the film shows an ongoing dedication to the ethos of the movement. One cannot help noticing, in this regard, that the method used in the credit sequence of *Two Women* and the forestalled crisis that opens the narrative resemble the film that screenwriter Cesare Zavattini proposes in his 'journal,' *Scenes from a Cinematic Life*. In an entry marked 'Italy, 1944' Zavattini discusses a new creative project that he has in mind:

> We stop in a destroyed village where the people are slowly beginning to resume life among the ruins. We talk with them in the square; I'll say I'm guilty of this and that, at first they'll consider me a monster; but this is the only way I'll be able to act also as accuser, attribute to each one his responsibilities, drag them out of their anonymity like Marsyas from the vagina of his limbs, ... here and there are unhinged doors, others lie in the dust, buried behind you, all that could be heard was the sound of doors slamming after nice Italian families. Some of those present try to justify themselves and they don't realize I'm offering them a chance to get it all off their chests ... then I'll have a plane appear over their heads, releasing bombs. The bomb is about to fall: I stop it in the midst of the sky ... shall we make the bomb fall? They all start yelling 'No, no,' I let it drop another two hundred yards, then I stop it again. During the fall of the bomb along these two hundred yards which we follow in slow motion, I have time to ... savour their terrified faces, I force

them to return in their thoughts to a year ago, ... to ten years ago, to a point in their childhood, then move to the future, to when they'll be dead. It's extraordinary how changeable they are and how these men ... looking at me and the camera, who listen to me with indifference, can do so many things, become pale in a fraction of a second, jump over a hedge like hares, or give a shove as they run to an old woman who – look at her there – has fallen to the ground, showing the hem of her drawers; if I make the house collapse and their children are trapped under it, they start digging in the rubble like dogs. I interrupt the digging, and now there they are, listening to my sermon, and they say they had nothing to do with it, they're innocent ... We set up a primitive screen in the centre of the square and we show some bits of film we've shot in other places, ... The narrator (me, in other words) tries to make the people in the square understand that these other men also weep, die, kill, run off, go to bed with women; that they aren't very different from others.   (Zavattini, 11)

Assigning himself the roles of Old Testament judge and destroyer, but also of confessor and redeemer, Zavattini sees himself as interrupting his 'audience' in the process of postwar reconstruction, explicitly understood here to mean both the rebuilding of destroyed architecture and the restoration of shattered identities. Zavattini's projected film extends the apocalyptic moment of the war, making possible a fortuitous immediacy of vision in which the barrier between spectacle and audience is annihilated and the spectator is therefore forced out of hiding, and exposed, as it were, as subject of his own story. That is, cinema, undoing the idealizing work of self-reconstruction in memory, prevents the spectator's nostalgic return to a unified memory-image of the self, a self that Zavattini sarcastically describes as one conforming to a sentimental version of social responsibility and connection, 'doors closing on nice Italian families.' With the achievement of the 'continuous and perpetual attention' (Marcus, 116) that Zavattini demands for his film the spectator witnesses the incongruities and discontinuities of the self when, as during the war, 'the pressure of the usual codes' of behaviour are removed, and it finds itself to be a character abandoned to 'a plot without law' (Sypher, 64–9). Zavattini offers, as a kind of painful existential redemption, 'a chance to get it all off their chests,' the escape from the narcissistic enclosure depicted as an opening up or wounding that is both a rebirth out of the suffering body, Marsyas flayed alive as a version of the passion, and the death of the ideal ego-identity, concomitant with the destruction of the fragile façade of civility and humanity. To the 'innocent' audience that would, like Narcissus, fail to recognize its own countenance in the image of the other ('these other men also weep, die'), Zavattini metes out cinema as a scourging of perception, a primal narcissistic crisis of vision.

De Sica concerns himself thematically in many of his films, whether or not they adhere to the characteristic style of the neorealist tradition, with this crisis of vision to which Zavattini's ideal neorealism ultimately aspires. Consequently, his characters are often seen trying to avoid or deny this moment of self-recognition, trying to shelter the self against exposure by retreating into a socially conferred identity that is revised and idealized or 'intended' in memory.

With these ideas in mind, and before turning to De Sica's *Two Women*, I would like to look first at his later film *Il giardino dei Finzi-Contini / The Garden of the Finzi-Continis* (1970), in which this abiding theme of self-reconstruction and its accompanying architectural metaphors of enclosure and shelter are explored again in the context of the historic catastrophe of World War II, which for De Sica, as for many other twentieth-century artists seemingly marked the end of the nineteenth century (Ross and Freed, 91). Perhaps by virtue of the film's greater temporal distance from this period, De Sica seems to have given a firmer delineation to the self that he sees as emerging from, or rather being forced out of, a nineteenth-century consciousness. The fortified garden world of the Finzi-Continis, to which the protagonist Giorgio is seeking entrance at the start of the film, and from which he is evicted at its end, is one in which the exclusiveness of social privilege is conflated in his mind with a romantic ideal of Platonic love. Accordingly, the garden is an exclusive site both in the sense that its inhabitants are aristocrats and also in the sense that it is isolated from the flux of time, the world of physical desire and the historical/political changes taking place in Ferrara. Hence Giorgio's relationship to his beloved, Micòl Finzi-Contini, is defined in the film not by present interaction as much as by memories of the loving glances which they surreptitiously exchanged as adolescents. De Sica ties what is essentially their prolonged state of childhood to a stagnant nineteenth-century idealism through Giorgio's and Micòl's shared love of novels from the romantic period, which, significantly, Micòl remembers reading during childhood illnesses, and through the image of the Finzi-Contini library, which houses an extensive, seemingly unread collection of nineteenth-century poetry texts behind its barred, prison-like doors.

De Sica's films look beyond the nineteenth-century vision of self-hood, and his characters accordingly are not isolated individuals whose lives are given 'purpose, unity and direction' by passion (Sypher, 63). In contrast, De Sica depicts the walled Finzi-Contini garden of Giorgio and Micòl's Platonic devotion as a deathly world that metaphorically speaking is without 'inspiration' or vital passion, as is indicated by the fatal respiratory illness from which Micòl's brother, Alberto, suffers. It is an enthralling milieu of suffocating nostalgic sentiment which is kept contained and meaningful by incestuous agreement between Micòl and Alberto: 'It's nicer when we're alone.'

The sickness at the heart of the love relationships in the garden world is characterized by the unhealthy contrariety of the body and the self's 'unalterable sanctified history' in memory (Ross and Freed, 3). Hence, Giorgio and Micòl are in love, as Kristeva says, 'with what resembles an ideal that is out of sight but present in the memory' (Kristeva, 269). De Sica's garden is not a prelapsarian realm of innocence, for De Sica gives the idea of 'innocence' and 'before' a negative or ironical refiguring; nor is it an inviolable sanctuary for the self, as we are reminded from the start by the presence of the ancient family dog, Jor, the toothless defender of the gate. Here, the lovers are bound by the imaginary relation and its inherent lack described by Lacan. Consequently, an immanent as well as imminent sense of loss permeates the garden and is manifest in the self-conscious melancholy of the characters, who like Giorgio and Alberto are hopelessly intent on 'recovery.' Their desire, as De Sica depicts it, 'rests on narcissism and its aura of emptiness, seeming, impossibility, which underlays any *idealization* equally and essentially inherent in love' (Kristeva, 267).

De Sica suggests that the self-deception at the core of one's relationship to reality finds itself 'rehabilitated, neutralized, normalized' in the loving relationship (Kristeva, 21). For the lovers, like Narcissus, 'in love with unbodied hope' (Kristeva, 104), the narcissistic regard is all that covers over 'the gaping hole' of the mirror stage, as Kristeva calls it (Kristeva, 23). Accordingly, in the second of two scenes in which Giorgio tries to assert his physical desire for Micòl, De Sica, by filming the couple at one remove, as it were, through a mirror in Micòl's bedroom, makes the viewer feel that Giorgio's is a desperately awkward, even strangely unimpassioned effort to realize his love. Micòl's eventually successful efforts to repulse Giorgio are paralleled by the camera's moving from where it is remotely watching their reflection in the mirror 'through' the mirror into close proximity with the pair on the bed. The camera metaphorically asserts the mirror as the barrier to the expression of passion.

Micòl's endeavours to open up her walled-in being to difference, to the outside, to the body and history, and to all that seems to be implied in her stated desire to 'be a woman,' are something of a camouflage. When she openly claims to want to escape the place where her childhood is preserved (as is the carriage in the gymnasium of her school days) and where she feels inhibited by the protective gaze of her parents, she is misperceiving the boundaries of her imprisonment, assuming that her chaste body, as it is circumscribed by the gaze of her parents, marks the limit of her self's confinement and her freedom. Despite what might seem like a liberating assertion of her sexual autonomy then, Micòl is inevitably limited, not only by the tightening civil restrictions on her as a Jew, but also by her wilful tendency to repeat or dictate the terms of her relationships in order to secure her sense of self as it has been established within the bounds of the garden. Her relationship with Alberto, for example, falls into the pattern of parent and child as she humours and pampers him, even ordering him off to bed with a hot water bottle and a motherly kiss on the brow. Furthermore, her love affair with Bruno, whom she initially describes as being repellent to her because he is 'too communistic,' too business-oriented, 'too frank,' and 'too hairy,' suggests a decision on her part to espouse that which is in radical opposition to the aristocratic decorum and inherited ideals of her garden home. But significantly, her trysts with Bruno never take her farther than the cabana beside the garden wall, which, rather than the body, marks the boundary of her exclusive identity.

Intriguingly, her friends describe Micòl as 'unpredictable,' yet, in truth, Micòl cannot imagine her own being except in terms of a likeness secured from the past. In musing about old age to Alberto, she asks him if she will look like their Granny Josette, who planted the palms in the garden; she claims for herself the same fate of spinsterhood that Emily Dickinson knew; she experiences a thrill which evokes her only passionate gesture towards Giorgio, imagining that it was Lucrezia Borgia who planted the plane trees in the family garden. Ironically Micòl aligns her destiny with creative women and originators, female authorities of the past. Yet finally even her choice of Bruno as lover seems less a daring transgressive gesture and more a decided effort to subvert Alberto's own admiration and desire for Bruno, thereby keeping her brother to herself. In the end, though Micòl seems to make an effort to open up the garden compound and herself to the world of spontaneity and change, to the vagaries of desire, in actuality she assumes complete authority in order to ensure that she and Alberto remain in a place where their conferred/intended identity is reflected back to them, where they can, as Alberto says, 'choose the faces [they] meet.'

The outbreak of war in *The Garden of the Finzi-Continis* is coincident with Giorgio's expulsion from the exclusive, self-reflective world of childhood memory that he too would inhabit with Micòl. The third and final time he departs from the garden follows upon his surreptitious viewing of the primal scene between the lovers Micòl and Bruno in the cabana. The anguish that this vision occasions for Giorgio, as Kristeva describes this exclusion from the illusory union with the self's ideal, opens up 'a psychic space,' the space of subjectivity (Kristeva, 116). As Giorgio is banished from the walled garden, he steps out into a street where Italians are thrown into a state of panic as they await Mussolini's historic declaration of war. This moment brings about a disillusionment akin to the death of identity, both in his personal life and in his public life, in which, following the newly instituted racial laws and the outbreak of war, he will be without the status of citizen or even of person in the eyes of the law. For De Sica it seems it is necessary to experience, both in one's public life and in the deepest reaches of one's inner life, the destruction of one's illusory sense of connection to and identity with others. For, perceiving the disparity between the self's ideal history and its larger social history in process, which Giorgio does when he acknowledges that his broken heart is absurd, makes possible what De Sica has spoken of as the salvation of freedom from 'complicity with a corrupt moral order' (Marcus, xiv, xv). Gramsci's exhortation 'to participate actively in making the history of the world, and not simply to accept passively and without care the imprint of one's personality from outside' might be applied here (Gramsci, 58). Gramsci and De Sica both suppose the necessity of being subject of, rather than subject to, a cultural discourse.

Like *The Garden of the Finzi-Continis*, *Ladri di biciclette / Bicycle Thieves* (1948) and *Two Women* propose the necessity of experiencing the death of an identity that is no longer truly representative of the nature of one's connection with others as this is embodied or made manifest in action; Gramsci speaks of the 'contradiction between [one's] conception of the world and [one's] conforming norm of conduct' (Gramsci, 61), and in accordance with this idea we can see each protagonist as being progressively stripped of the security and safety which a received identity, with its connection to both familial and civic and religious orders, provides. In this sense at least the De Sica version of self is a particularly modern one, which can only endure or 'stand out from under' in an existential sense (Ross and Freed, 3) in spite of perceiving the flimsiness of the self's habitation in the world and its loose and permeable boundaries. One way, a more hopeful way, of seeing this is to say that in De Sica's films the self is enlarged in sympathetic identity with others and as a result it potentially increases its moral vision and understanding, but it also remains defensive and vulnerable to the terrifying destruction of the ego's boundaries and its sovereignty. Innocence or wholeness or integrity can only be re-established when the I relinquishes its illusory authority over the idealized Other. 'I am helpless,' Giorgio says when he takes leave of Micòl after failing to win her love. In *The Garden of the Finzi-Continis* De Sica shows the dependence on the empty authority conferred by a received idealized identity as symbolically resulting in a familial rift which is subsequently repaired as the parent and child eventually claim a shared perspective of loss. In this case Giorgio's father mends the breach between himself and his son when he equates his 'death,' his disenfranchisement as a Jew under the Italian Fascist government, with Giorgio's rejection by his beloved Micòl.

De Sica's *Two Women* shares with *The Garden of the Finzi-Continis* and with the earlier *Bicycle Thieves* the emotional and dramatic emphasis on the destruction and reparation of the bond between parent and child. In both films the alienation between the two reaches a crisis point at the end of a process in which the parent has lost the security of public status, the identity and respectability associated with bourgeois civic life. In *Bicycle Thieves* we watch through Bruno's eyes as he witnesses his adored father chased, apprehended, and publicly humiliated after he has tried to steal a bicycle. Both films focus on the event of the parent's defeat as a crushing disillusionment for the child, suggest a crisis of vision entailing the child's loss of faith in an idealized image of the parent. In *Two Women* De Sica shows Cesira's inability to prevent her daughter's rape from occurring 'under the eyes of the Madonna' in a bombed and desecrated church where they have sought refuge, and therefore the film more clearly conflates the powerless parental gaze with the lost idealized regard of the Other.

As in *Bicycle Thieves*, everything in *Two Women* depends on the child's reclaiming a lost kinship with the parent from within a collapsed, 'inhuman' perspective. So Bruno symbolically restores the identity of his father, renewing his identity as 'father' and resisting or denying his identity as 'thief,' by retrieving Ricci's old hat for him from among his tormentors. Similarly Cesira depends on her daughter to acknowledge her as 'mother' following their period of estrangement, not as a sign of Rosetta's deference to her as protector and authority over her, but as an indication that her daughter has not finally capitulated to the amoral environment of the war and the forces that would objectify them both. For the despair that Rosetta initially gives in to following her rape leads to her abandoning herself to her destiny as fallen woman, circulating her body in the postwar black-market economy, a fate that has been imposed on her as an extension of the objectification of her body by the Moroccan rapists, for whom her virginity is part of the claimable spoils of war. Yet this destiny is perhaps only a more brutal version of that implied in Cesira's own prizing of her daughter's beauty and her virginity. She is, for example, amused by and seemingly proud of the effect that the sight of Rosetta's nude body has on their friend Michele when he inadvertently looks in on the girl while she is bathing. She is also subsequently reluctant to honour Rosetta's modesty and her wish never to see Michele again following the incident, arguing that they 'must be nice to Michele' because his father has the largest stock of provisions in the village. Rosetta's reaching out to her mother in the final moments of the film, after hearing of Michele's death, is an indication to Cesira that Rosetta, and she herself by implication, might be absolved from complicity in their imposed destiny. It seems important to qualify this argument and to suggest that it is not the violation and subsequent devaluation of the child's body in the mother's eyes, nor is it simply the shared experience of loss that follows the rape, that make possible or define the significance of this reunion. Rather, it is the mother's being able to divine likeness, to see in her child's renewable feelings of grief the hope of her own escape from the isolating stupor of a life lived only for material gratification.

In *Two Women* the relationship between parent and child initially involves a mutually idealizing regard. The narcissistic union of mother and child, like that of brother and sister or of lovers in *The Garden of the Finzi-Continis*, circumscribes a world outside of time that is designated metaphorically by De Sica as an enclosure or shelter for the self, a home that is transfigured by memory and longing. Moravia's *Two Women* also connects the themes of nostalgia and narcissism. The novel begins with the narrator, Cesira, remembering the days when she was a young bride, leaving her life as peasant behind and becoming a middle-class home owner, shopkeeper, and mother in Rome. She is proud to say that her house, which is both domestic residence and place of business (suggesting the materialism of her marital contract), shines like 'a mirror.' In the novel, as in the film, Cesira's home is both a self-reflecting sanctuary and a sign of her status and identity (Moravia, 6).

The initial sequence of De Sica's film of *Two Women* shows Cesira emerging from her home/shop to scan the sky for approaching bombers, and when she hears them, pulling shut the door. This is the first of a series of scenes in which Cesira is besieged by forces of greater and lesser threat and is seen to close windows and doors in an effort to protect herself and Rosetta: the futility of this action is implied by De Sica in this first scene because the door has become warped in the bombing and is, therefore, unclosable. De Sica's imagery here and in several subsequent scenes suggests the connection between the narcissistic enclosure of the mother/child relationship, the world that Cesira tries desperately to preserve, and her own bourgeois respectability as she imagines it to be beheld, or kept safe, in her daughter's eyes, a projection in fact of her daughter's own 'innocence.' Rosetta's body is invested by Cesira, and by her culture, with a symbolic history of 'before' and 'after,' with its related hierarchy of value that is primarily and in the long run economic: following her daughter's rape, Cesira, seemingly without regard for Rosetta's feelings, refers to her as being 'ruined forever.' However, both the novel and the film suggest the need to interrogate the notion of innocence and its too frequent association with respectability; to this end they seek to dissolve the connection between spiritual and physical virginity. Hence Rosetta's 'innocence,' as this term also designates her devout, obedient, and selfless behaviour prior to the rape, comes to be seen by Cesira as a fragile façade, something, perhaps, like Milton's 'fugitive and cloistered virtue'; furthermore, it is illusory and false as Cesira herself has constructed it, to the extent that she has conflated it with the value of her own bourgeois middle-class respectability.

That Cesira's identity as a chaste widow, who lives a morally circumspect life devoted to her daughter, is a false remembering, a forgetting of life lived in the body and of desire without economic or domestic end, and also a reflection of her daughter's symbolic virginity, is suggested by the sequence in which Cesira goes to Giovanni's shop to ask him to protect her business and belongings while she is in the country. During their ensuing discussion Giovanni and Cesira both acknowledge the accusations of hypocrisy made by the other, each revealing that while she/he presented the outward appearance of devotion to her/his spouse, in actuality, each was sexually repulsed. But, immediately afterwards, Giovanni's behaviour belies his apparent acknowledgment of hypocrisy when he methodically closes all the windows and doors in his shop as a preparation for their lovemaking. When Cesira is leaving, she makes clear her intention to exclude their meeting from her recollection and angrily exhorts Giovanni never to tell Rosetta what has happened between them for she herself considers this episode never to have happened: 'We are as we were,' she says in parting.

As in *The Garden of the Finzi-Continis*, however, the search for a refuge in an idealized identity forged in memory becomes a trap. Cesira's retreat into the countryside of her girlhood, is undertaken, first of all, as a kind of adventure in which she intends to participate as a tourist, adopting temporarily the role of peasant and being delighted to share her memories with Rosetta and teach her the seemingly exotic skills and traditions of her former way of life. When they disembark from the train carrying them away from Rome, Cesira coaches Rosetta on how to carry her suitcase on her head, since they will be walking a long distance to the village of Cesira's birth. Their preparations for the trek are watched by the other travellers from the windows of the train. Rosetta and Cesira are observed by both the Italian citizens and the German soldiers, who all cheer them on their way and hoot good-naturedly at Rosetta's difficulty in bearing the heavy unbalanced load, seeming to appreciate the awkwardness the women display in their efforts to take up these unfamiliar roles. However, De Sica suggests the necessity of destroying nostalgia when the benevolent gaze of their audience is replaced by the murderous eye of the fighter pilot who tries to shoot them down as they begin their walk to the village.

The disparity between the reality of Cesira's former life as a peasant, which she had earlier described to Giovanni as being very grim and desperate, and the gaiety with which she recalls how she used to ride a mule when she was a child, anticipating that Rosetta may soon be able to do the same, suggests that in casting her as surrogate protagonist of her nostalgic return to the past she has indeed encumbered her daughter, not merely with their belongings, but also with the sacrificial burden of her own hypocrisy. I am reminded here of De Sica's *Indiscretion of an American Wife* in which the heroine (Jennifer Jones) makes the decision to abandon her lover, whom she has met on holiday in Rome, return home, and resume her duties to her husband and daughter. Before boarding her train, however, she purchases a peasant costume as a souvenir for her daughter, a costume which seems clearly to signify the mother's compensatory desire to reinvest in her child her secret and forsaken hope for a shared life with her lover in his rustic country home.

The figure of the child in De Sica's films seems not only generally to represent the renewable possibilities for social feeling, but, especially in *Two Women*, to embody the 'uncontradictable' self 'left behind' in the parent's move to the realm of adult experience. What is suggested by Cesira's exclusive devotion to her child, which seems to be a chosen compensation or substitution for a more outwardly directed, though perhaps socially unsanctioned, sexual or romantic love, is also, then, the lingering faithfulness to a conception of the world that is not reflected in one's actions (Gramsci, 61), a world to which one will be restored when one has successfully negotiated the present harsh and corrupting existence wherein one is obliged to prostitute oneself, and in which, one hypocritically tells oneself, one is forced to do business with those nameless 'bastards,' as Cesira calls them in the novel, who are in control of government and authority (Moravia, 31). The child embodies the inviolate part of oneself kept safely hidden from such a world, one's privately cherished possession, a sort of dowry kept secure until one becomes 'free' to marry one's unrealized vision of life to life itself. Though suspicious of a self-destructive withdrawal from life, De Sica also seems sympathetic to this attempt to sequester and redeem something of one's self from the world's sullying objectifying gaze.

In De Sica's *Two Women* the child is wrongly perceived by the mother as the extension or embodiment of the self that has not yet been possessed by the world and has been secreted away from its encroaching eyes. Cesira spends much time in the first half of the film trying in vain to ward off or escape the eyes of men, whose gaze increasingly threatens to divide her from that of which she believes she is possessed, her money, her matronly reputation, and her daughter. Once in the country, she and Rosetta stay at a house occupied by a mother, named Concetta in the novel, who is also at pains to conceal her children, her two deserter sons. Concetta's circumstances provide an ironic context for Cesira's protective measures on behalf of her daughter insofar as Concetta's loyalty to her sons is evidence of a mother's love that is unconscionably exclusive, and ruled by a self-protective and mercenary instinct. For, although she harbours her own children, with whom she shares a criminal black-market partnership, Concetta is apparently quite willing to hand Cesira's daughter over to the Fascists (who want the girl to 'help in the kitchen' at their headquarters) if it will mean that the officials will be less bothersome in future about searching for her sons. The interlude at Concetta's helps to define the absurd moral landscape of the war which Cesira and Rosetta are entering as one characterized by the corruption of the primary and traditionally most sacred human bond, that between mother and child (Freed and Ross, 97). In addition, this episode provides the context for Cesira's implication in the 'sacrifice' of her daughter, the child's rape. It is she who hurries Rosetta away from their refuge in the hills in her impatience to be back in Rome and watching over her shop, 'damning' the girl for her hesitation to leave. The rape itself, which is presented as an invasion of alien male eyes, results most significantly in the destruction of the enthralling narcissistic bond of mother and daughter, bringing about a tragically ironic 'liberation,' but also leaving them each in isolation, drawing inward and away from one another. Accordingly, when they leave the church the pair are seen from high overhead, a point of view that reveals them to be on opposite sides of a hitherto unseen bomb crater, a visible sign not only of the devastation that Rosetta has suffered but also of the emotional and symbolic gulf that now divides them.

Cesira's failed nostalgic return to her origins is thematically parallel to Michele's idealization of the peasant life, which he believes holds promise of a regeneration of the Italian consciousness, and his faith in a new order which would come about as a result of the Allied victory over Germany. Thus, Michele's love for Cesira, which has been criticized as being a sentimental deviation from the novel (Prigozy, 78–88), may also be seen as De Sica's subjection of Michele to the same scrutiny as his other characters. For Michele's dissenting philosopher's voice (which honours the peasant in theory while he is contemptuous of his parents and openly hostile to all of the peasants and evacuees waiting out the war in his village home) and his self-imposed isolation from the other evacuees is presented by De Sica as comparable to Cesira's detachment from life insofar as both have chosen to devote themselves to the ideal of family and community and 'sacrifice' love in the meantime, as Michele says. Their chastity is thus artificially invested with an elevated significance that justifies their retreat from the common dangers of openness and intimacy. Michele's studious political convictions and Cesira's proud widowhood are both found wanting by De Sica insofar as each is characterized by an alienating and impotent passion – a rhetorical sacrifice.

Together Michele and Cesira come to recognize the extent of their hypocrisy. Michele's stilted admiration for Cesira is born of his tendency to romanticize the image of the peasant that he conjures up in his desire to fashion a new, more civilized world in touch with reality and the senses and human feeling. However, it is not until Michele leaves the safety of his intellectual constructs and abandons himself to his desire for Cesira that he is able to benefit from an altered and self-revealing perspective. Accompanying Cesira on her quest to find food in the valley town of Fondi, Michele is caught in an air-raid attack while he and Cesira are at the home of a wealthy friend there. As they are running outside to the bomb shelter, Cesira encourages him to take off his glasses. When he obeys her, he must rely on her to guide him, holding her hand like a child as they take cover in the garden. After the hail of bullets has stopped they raise their heads from the ground and De Sica's camera reveals a changed point of view; it is, literally speaking, extremely close, and from ground level we watch a ladybug meandering along a blade of grass. As Michele becomes figuratively absorbed in this worm's eye view of things, he 'discovers' his hand on Cesira's back and finds himself following through with an embrace involuntarily begun. But this earthy romantic moment is short-lived and unrepeated. Furthermore, the image of the mother and child that De Sica suggests here by virtue of their hand holding and the ostensible age difference between them contributes to the complexity of meaning in this embrace and its uncomfortable aftermath. The heightened moment that culminates in a picture of a passionate kiss in an idyllic garden setting is subtly belied by the suggestion of an incestuous transgression, even though the kiss paradoxically seems to be a potentially healthy correcting of Cesira's substitution of child for lover.

As elsewhere in his films, what begins as an invitation to indulge in a private romantic sentiment is spoiled for the characters and the viewer by De Sica's reinstatement of another point of view, that of the outsider, the stranger or the child. Such a moment occurs in the scene from *Indiscretion* in which the mother becomes aware that her dreamy fondling of her daughter's peasant costume is regarded with curious amusement by another passenger sharing her coach on the train. The glance that dispels the sentimental reverie has the effect of allowing the person succumbing to the dream to be granted a view of himself/

herself in the third person as it were, and to see what this behaviour must look like from the outside. Coming upon Cesira and Michele are another mother and son, Michele's friends, who emerge from the bomb shelter to find this scene of passion in their garden. The effect of Michele's friends seeing the embracing couple, who had moments earlier denied any suggestion of romantic interest in each other, is to recontextualize Cesira's and Michele's behaviour, allowing it to be seen as duplicitous and absurdly frivolous given the larger seriousness of the war. As a result it subjects Michele to the point of view that he has previously taken in relation to his own parents, whom he has condemned for lavishly celebrating their wedding anniversary in the midst of wartime deprivation and death. The structuring of this scene suggests that De Sica does not intend this love to be a sentimental addition to the story; rather for De Sica the arena of love itself is a theatrical proving ground in which one has the opportunity to measure one's desire for community against its mistakenly sentimentalized or idealized object. As in *The Garden of the Finzi-Continis*, romantic love is both a nostalgic evasion of the nature and consequences of this desire and also the primary means by which one discovers the extent to which one is outside the garden, shamefully dislocated.

The rape of her daughter leaves Cesira, like the mad mother whom she and Michele meet in Fondi, not only separated from her beloved child, but also removed from a world that has at the war's end absurdly resumed its old ways, without seeming to take notice of her pain. De Sica pictures Cesira's alienation through her exposure to the uncomprehending stares of the villagers where they spend the night on their way to Rome. After Rosetta, without her mother's knowledge, goes out with Florindo, an amoral black marketeer, Cesira appeals to the villagers to help her search for her daughter. Cesira is shown to be in the centre of a circular space, surrounded by houses whose occupants come to the window at the sound of her cries. She is told by the inhabitants, who do not understand that her concern is for her daughter's spiritual rather than physical well-being, that Rosetta went willingly with Florindo, and that she should not fear for her daughter who is, they say, absolutely 'safe.' Cesira, in effect, is isolated in the midst of her own community; emerging from the cocoon-like enclosure of the evacuees' life in hiding, she is subject to a new and painful sensitivity or vulnerability to the familiar world that leaves her suffering the pain of the exile (Slater, 3). This estrangement puts Cesira outside the reach even of the common language and meaning of her society. Her new distance from her spiritually benighted neighbours is accordingly measured in terms of a semantic disparity. 'Your daughter is safe' is a statement that can hold none of its intended consolation for Cesira, not even that which irony might provide.

The final image of *Two Women* recalls and completes the opening sequence. In *Two Women*, as in *Bicycle Thieves*, De Sica seems to leave parent and child in their shared isolation at the film's end. In *Bicycle Thieves* father and son disappear into the moving mass of city-dwellers, their pain only momentarily acknowledged in the film before they return to 'real life' and obscurity. In *Two Women*, however, the camera allows mother and daughter to be 'merely' photographic subjects, eventually overshadowed in the composition by the peasant's cart in the foreground left. By slowly withdrawing from the scene the camera seems to grant an iconic significance to the pair and also to dignify their reunion with privacy.

References

Gramsci, Antonio. *Selections from the Prison Notebooks of Antonio Gramsci.* Translated by Quentin Hoare and Geoffrey Nowell-Smith. London: Lawrence and Wishart, 1971.

Kristeva, Julia. *Tales of Love.* Translated by Leon S. Roudiez. New York: Columbia University Press, 1987.

Marcus, Millicent. *Filmmaking by the Book.* Baltimore: Johns Hopkins University Press, 1993.

Moravia, Alberto. *Two Women.* Translated by Angus Davidson. New York: Farrar, Strauss and Giroux, 1958.

Prigozy, Ruth. 'A Modern Pieta: De Sica's *Two Women* (1961).' In *Modern European Filmmakers and the Art of Adaptation.* New York: Ungar, 1981.

Ross, Joan, and Donald Freed. *The Existentialism of Alberto Moravia.* London: Feffer and Simons, 1972.

Slater, Philip. *The Pursuit of Loneliness.* Boston: Beacon Press, 1976.

Sypher, Wylie, *The Loss of the Self in Modern Literature and Art.* New York: Vintage Books, 1962.

Zavattini, Cesare. *Sequences from a Cinematic Life.* Translated by William Weaver. Englewood Cliffs, N.J.: Prentice Hall, 1970.

De Sica's *Garden of the Finzi-Continis*: An Escapist Paradise Lost

MILLICENT MARCUS

Millicent Marcus has written widely on Italian cinema, including essays on Bicycle Thieves, Umberto D., *and* Two Women. *In this essay she discusses Giorgio Bassani's novel* The Garden of the Finzi-Continis *and De Sica's film and provides a useful exploration of the literary tradition of the garden. Whereas Bassani's novel makes personal memory itself the centre of the story, Marcus suggests that De Sica's film directs the audience's gaze towards a larger history, a larger memory, especially of the Holocaust, but as well towards the redemptive legacy of neorealism.*

At the centre of Giorgio Bassani's novel (1962) and Vittorio De Sica's film (1970) is a garden, a natural, physical space so replete with poetic, theological, art historical, and philosophical significance that it rightly dominates the titles of both works. The garden, called the Barchetta del Duca, is, 'to be more precise, the vast park that surrounded the Finzi-Contini house before the war, and spread over almost twenty-five acres to the foot of the Mura degli Angeli on one side, and as far as the Barriera of Porta San Benedetto on the other' (Bassani, 11). But Bassani's decision not to call his book *The Park of the Finzi-Contini* or even simply *The Finzi-Contini* reflects as much the intertextual wealth invoked by the garden as its greater euphony. By virtue of this title, then, the book insists upon its relationship to an entire history of textual gardens, from Eden through the love gardens of medieval romance to the enchanted

Millicent Marcus, 'De Sica's *Garden of the Finzi-Continis*: An Escapist Paradise Lost,' in *Filmmaking by the Book: Italian Cinema and Literary Adaptation* (Baltimore: Johns Hopkins University Press, 1993), 91–110 gardens of the Renaissance epics written in the Este court of the novel's Ferrarese setting. This history suggests, too, a variety of literary ancestries for Micòl Finzi-Contini, the tutelary spirit of the novel's garden, in the Beatrices and Mateldas of Dante's earthly paradise, in the Laura of Petrarch's *locus amoenus*, as well as in the Alcinas and Armidas of Ferrara's own Ariosto and Tasso. Finally, the garden constitutes a psychological metaphor for the Finzi-Continis' passivity and withdrawal in the face of Fascist anti-Semitism – a response that invites fruitful comparison with Freud's category of neurotic denial.

Nor is De Sica's [film] a literal-minded transcription of this central textual image, whose Edenic and romantic associations are adapted in cinematically appropriate ways. Thus his *Il giardino dei Finzi-Contini / The Garden of the Finzi-Continis* (1970) plumbs film history to find medium-specific analogues for the paradise lost and the enchantresses of Bassani's textual garden, while ultimately rejecting mainstream cinematic convention by disrupting its traditional alignment of gazes. If Bassani's garden is also an exposé of the state of mind that shuts out history and abdicates any moral responsibility for its progress, De Sica's film refuses to be a garden by renouncing any easy withdrawal into the cinematic consolations that typified his postneorealist years. Thus in adapting this novel to the screen, De Sica had to accommodate not only the material differences between the two media but the ideological demands of his own postneorealist agenda. Before exploring this complex process of transformation, however, let us consider the poetic image on which so much of Bassani's historical vision is based.

It should come as no surprise that the archetypal garden of the Judeo-Christian tradition lends its iconography to the Barchetto del Duca, whose first Edenic attribute is its remoteness and its consequent difficulty of access.[1] Enclosed by high walls, the Barchetto del Duca is a veritable *hortus conclusus* that only admits the protagonist into its inner reaches after nine years of waiting – a delay simulated by the textual distances that the reader must traverse before finally entering the garden in part 2, chapter 3. Edenic, too, is the garden's prodigious botanical wealth and variety, which make it an arboreal microcosm in its 'lindens, elms, beeches, poplars, planes, horse chestnuts, pines, firs, larches, cedars of Lebanon, cypresses, oaks, ilexes, and even palms and eucalyptuses' (Bassani, 11), so that the five-hundred-year old plane tree offers a Finzi-Continian equivalent to the Tree of Life, and Micòl's fund of arcane information, both vegetal and human, makes her the honorary custodian of the garden's numerous Trees of Knowledge.[2]

As prelapsarian Eden was a place of absolute leisure whose soil gave spontaneously of its abundance and precluded the necessity of work, the Barchetto del Duca is a locus of pleasure and beauty, free of utilitarian concerns. In Italian, the distinction between *giardino* (ornamental garden) and *orto* (vegetable garden) emphasizes its Edenic leisure, as does the topographical centrality of the tennis court, itself a miniature *hortus conclusus* in its fenced-off cultivation of recreational pursuits. Eden's timelessness, its blissful repose in the luxuriance of eternal spring, finds its Finzi-Continian equivalent in the *estate di San Martino*, or Indian summer, which blesses that series of tennis-playing afternoons. 'We were really very lucky with the season. For ten or twelve days the perfect weather lasted, held in that kind of magical suspension, of sweetly glassy and luminous immobility peculiar to certain autumns of ours' (Bassani, 56).

The garden mentality is thus, by necessity, ahistoric. It acknowledges neither time, nor change, nor the encroachments that history may make on its privileged domain. Accordingly, it stands as a metaphor of the Finzi-Continis' passivity in the face of the anti-Semitic threat. In psychological terms, such behavior is a function of neurotic denial – the procedure 'whereby the individual refuses to recognize the existence of a painful anxiety-provoking external reality or internal demand' (Walrond-Skinner, 92). Like the garden wall that excludes unwelcome influences, neurotic denial screens out all threats to the individual's psychic equilibrium. As a collective psyche, the Finzi-Continis practice a common art of denial, ignoring all signs of Alberto's increasing debilitation, Micòl's transgressive sexuality, and the ever-tightening noose of racial persecution. The quintessence of Finzi-Continian denial is the plan to improve the family tennis court – a project that originates in response to filial complaints, but that comes to assume thaumaturgic proportions in its promise of an Edenic future dedicated to eternal play, presided over by a healthy Alberto and an untainted Micòl. The film uses a powerful visual metaphor to reveal how dysfunctional this defense mechanism is – how denial invites the very death it seeks to obliterate. As Ermanno watches over the tennis court improvements, the mise-en-scène bears a striking resemblance to a fresh grave site with mounds of dirt piled high on each side, as if awaiting the arrival of the dead.

Though the Finzi-Continis' withdrawal from external reality represents the most extreme form of historical denial, their refusal to resist the course of Jewish persecution is typical of most of their coreligionists whose obliviousness to impending doom took the form of early and massive collaboration with the Fascist regime. Convinced that their liberation from the ghetto during the Risorgimento campaign of the 1860s had been an invitation to full citizenship in the newly formed Italian state, Jews had enthusiastically participated in the civic life of their fatherland. Thus, when the Infornata del Decennale of 1933 opened up Fascist party membership to the population at large, Jewish enrollments were high, reaching the ninetieth percentile in such cities as Ferrara. And though the 10 percent of noncompliants included the Finzi-Continis, such resistance represented as much the family's aristocratic distaste for all partisan politics as its rejection of Fascism per se.

Because of their previous Fascist allegiances, most of the Jews in the novel must practice more subtle and complex forms of denial. Freudians associate this defense mechanism with *splitting*, the 'simultaneous experience within the ego of two contradictory responses to reality, acceptance and denial, without the ego needing to produce a compromise between the two or repress the one or the other' (Walrond-Skinner, 324). Examples of such splitting abound in the story, where characters both accept their persecution and deny its virulence by citing a series of mitigating circumstances. One of the novel's most accomplished splitters is the protagonist's father, who manages to find ingenious ways to convince himself that the racial laws, onerous as they are on paper, do not substantially alter the quality of Jewish life as lived in Ferrara. The ban on obituary notices in the press has not been burdensome because no one of consequence has died in the month since the edict was handed down – only two old women in the rest home on Via Vittoria, and of these, only one was a real Ferrarese. Nor has the ban on phone listings been enforced, as the old directory has yet to be replaced with a purged one, while Jewish employment of Gentile domestic help continues despite its official prohibition, and Jews have been allowed to maintain their membership in the various business and sports clubs to which they belong. Of course, the very cataloguing of leniencies proves the existence and the potential ferocity of the list of prohibitions it seeks to disprove. Like all parodies, the protagonist's father's exercise in denial becomes a backhanded affirmation of the very truth against which he rebels.

Adriana Trentini and Bruno Lattes engage in variant forms of splitting in their response to anti-Semitism at the Eleanora d'Este Tennis Club. On the verge of winning a tournament, the couple is interrupted in midset and the contest postponed until the next day – a stalling device that would allow time for Bruno's letter of expulsion to arrive by registered mail and thus avoid the embarrassment of a Jewish victory. Adriana, herself Gentile and unscathed by the mass expulsions, is incensed less about the principle of discrimination than its style. 'Did they have something against Bruno? If so, they could easily have forbidden his entering the tournament ... But once the tournament had begun, or rather, almost ended, moreover, with his winning, by a hair, one of the competitions, they should never have behaved the way they had. Four to two! What a lousy trick! A lousy thing like that was worthy of savages, not of well brought-up, civilized people!' (Bassani, 53). For Adriana, mixing politics and sports is 'bad taste' (53) – she is far more concerned with etiquette than with ethics and is indifferent to the human consequences of her partner's expulsion from the club.

Bruno's indignation is similarly misplaced. Refusing to address the overarching issue of social injustice, Bruno projects his anger onto the person of one Gino Cariani, secretary of GUF (Gioventù Universitaria Fascista), whose sycophantic desire to please the local leadership and thus further his own political ambitions dictates such anti-Semitic zeal. Bruno's response to discrimination is to give it a name and a face, to reduce it to the level of personalities, rather than to acknowledge it as an example of the larger, more universal and terrifying operations of Nazi-Fascist inhumanity. To contain this experience by limiting it to the malevolence of a single, inconsequential young man is to engage in the kind of splitting that both accepts and sanitizes an intolerable reality.

A more subtle form of denial typifies the narrator's account of his expulsion from the municipal library. Narrated in one of those interminable afternoons spent in Alberto's study, the episode is exploited for polemic purposes that have nothing to do with the real issue of racist persecution. Since Alberto's suite has become a stage for a political struggle between the protagonist and Malnate, nothing said in that forum is exempt from partisan appropriation. The narrator's particular axe to grind is Malnate's Marxist faith in the masses, and he tells this story not to attack the Fascist leadership responsible for promulgating racist policy but to revile the plebeian Poledrelli, the janitor who orders the protagonist to leave the premises. All the victim's bile is reserved for evidence of Poledrelli's vulgarity: his inability to speak in anything but dialect, his immoderate consumption of *pastasciutta* and consequent obesity, his pompous delight in one-upping a social superior. Like Bruno, the narrator is reductive in his outrage, personifying the abstract phenomenon of social injustice in one despicable antagonist, himself devoid of power, whose ancillary attributes become the mis-placed object of the victim's rage. 'However, he, Malnate, should be very careful ... not to be taken in by the false appearance of good nature on that broad, plebeian face. Inside that chest, thick as an arm-oire, there was housed a heart this tiny: rich in folk humors, all right, but not at all to be trusted!' (Bassani, 113).

In a politicizing move typical of De Sica's adaptive technique, as we shall see later on, the film reverses the protagonist's splitting operation by shifting his anger from Poledrelli, the plebeian instrument of the anti-Semitic order, to its authoritarian source. Unlike the novel's narra-tor, the film's protagonist (called Giorgio) does not submissively leave the premises but demands to see the director, Dr. Ballola. As the film cuts from the library reading room to the director's office, the sound track reports Ballola's answer to Giorgio's unvoiced *why*. We hear Ballola well before we see him, so that his feeble explanation, 'I'm sorry, dear boy. I'm sorry but it's not up to me,' seems to come out of nowhere, in keeping with his disavowal of all personal responsibility for his Fascist compliance. But De Sica's camera sabotages Ballola's attempt to deny his complicity by panning left and revealing the cor-poreal source of the disembodied voice of his disclaimer. 'Directives are directives,' he explains in a formulation whose tautological equiva-lence of subject and predicate makes authority a self-sufficient, self-reflexive syllogism needing no recourse to external principles of justifi-cation. 'If it were up to me' ... 'If it were up to you?' Giorgio chimes in, and though his face remains off screen, we can well imagine its look of cynical impatience. 'Personally,' Ballola continues, 'I'd be delighted for a talented young man like you, also for the old friendship between me and your father ... [you are] our hope for national literature,' but he does not complete the thought, appropriately enough for a man who is absolutely unprepared to act on his own personal recognizance. Ballola also cannot complete the sentence because he has inadvertently slandered the Fascist cause by implicitly opposing it to a series of unimpeachable ideals: the acknowledgment of artistic genius, the sanctity of old friendships, the future of Italian letters. At this point, the camera pans back to Giorgio so that the viewers share Ballola's dis-comfort in having to face the concrete object of Fascist racial policy.

In an attempt to divert the protagonist from his outrage and shame, Ballola abruptly shifts rhetorical gears. 'By the way, how are we progressing with the poetry? Are you still writing?' Here the personal pronouns are strategic. In the editorial 'we,' Ballola presumes to reincorporate Giorgio's literary accomplishments into the national cultural arena from which he has just been banished by Fascist decree. In fact, the very next verb reaffirms Fascist hegemonic control in its insistence that the 'tu' and 'Lei' of second person informal and formal usage, respectively, be replaced by the uniform 'voi,' according to the Reform of Custom Act of 1938. In the question 'Scrivete, scrivete sempre?' (Are you still writing?), the Fascist verbal form used by Ballola excludes the protagonist from the national literary patrimony to which he is supposedly being recruited. At this juncture, the contradictions in Ballola's rhetorical performance reach such a pitch of absurdity that they risk rupturing the fictions of civilized exchange. As he breaks off the interview, the director is placed in the paradoxical position of pleading with his victim: 'Be patient, but I ...,' and here Giorgio completes the predictable excuse. 'I know, you have a family. All Italy has a family.' In his insistence on using the non-Fascist form of address ('Lei') and in his contemptuous rephrasing of the Fascist slogan 'Patria e famiglia,' Giorgio commits a double, if futile, gesture of resistance. Where Mussolini's propagandists would make the state into a kind of superfamily whose organic unity and ties of loyalty would find their best analogue in blood kinship, the Ballola interview implies the most cynical of continuities between public and private spheres: that obedience to the one can best be achieved through threats to the other.

If the garden condition is one of exclusivity, of being closed off spatially by walls and temporally by exemption from historical change, then the novel's first gardens are the cemeteries that punctuate the prologue and the opening pages of part 1. Once established as important examples of the garden theme, cemeteries recur throughout the text – in Micòl's translation of the beautiful sepulchral poem by Emily Dickinson, in Ermanno's funerary cult of the Italian Jewish past, and in the tennis court excavations that promise a future foreclosed by illness and deportation. It is the narrator's visit to the Etruscan necropolis of Cevetri in 1957 which inspires the novel's writing – a commemorative impulse whose built-in *a priori* revelation that the Finzi-Continis have suffered tragic, premature deaths endows the text with a double epistemology that locates us both inside and outside time.[3] By sharing the protagonist's mystified perspective and the narrator's *ex post facto* omniscience, we are granted a twofold perspective that informs our judgments of all Micòl's actions, even her most callow and calculating ones, in the light of the death that awaits her. Bassani's novel comes to fulfil a specific funerary function by the end of the prologue, which concludes with a rhetorical question that makes this act of writing an exercise in classical *pietas* (see Bon, 58). 'Whereas for Micòl, the second born child, the daughter, and for her father, Professor Ermanno, and her mother, Signora Olga, and Signora Regina, Signora Olga's ancient, paralytic mother, all deported to Germany in the autumn of '43, who could say if they found any sort of burial at all?' (Bassani, 7).

What Holocaust history denied the Finzi-Continis will be provided by this writing, which will give burial to the dead so that they may speak the mortal truths that funerary literature pronounces, from Foscolo to Carducci to Emily Dickinson (through Micòl's translation). In contrast to the architectural monstrosity of the Finzi-Continis' mausoleum, this novel will provide appropriate Etruscan burial in its dignity, its delicacy, and its plentitude of life. The Etruscan analogy is significant not only for the temporal distance that it interposes between the narrator and the object of his own commemoration but also for suggesting a certain theory of death which characterizes the narrator's own memorialist aspirations.[4] 'We entered the most important tomb, the one that had belonged to the noble Matuta family: a low underground room that contains about twenty funeral beds set inside many niches in the tufa walls, and heavily decorated with polychrome stucco figures of the dear, trusted objects of everyday life: hoes, ropes, hatchets, scissors, spades, knives, bows, arrows, even hunting dogs and marsh fowl' (Bassani, 5–6). The spectacle of the intact Etruscan family whose second life is seen as continuous with the first, accommodating the 'dear trusted objects' of its days on earth – such a spectacle presents the greatest possible contrast to the fate of the Finzi-Continis, dispersed, dispossessed, and dismembered by Holocaust history. Indeed the objects that the Matuta take with them in death are full of contrastive significance for the Finzi-Continis. Fiercely functional and assertive, these objects affirm the family's will to domesticate a hostile environment and to shape the world in its own image in opposition to the garden mentality, which passively awaits history's verdict. So positive and life-affirming an approach to burial provides a model for Bassani's commemorative project. Etruscan self-assertion will counteract the very *forma mentis* that invited Finzi-Continian doom. Thus Bassani will proceed by giving his subjects burial in the fullest Etruscan regalia – a goal facilitated by the family's own enthusiasm for the creation of exquisite, personalized domestic spaces.

It is the literariness of this novelized epitaph of the Finzi-Continis that prompted so much leftist criticism of the novel as an abdication of the postwar imperative to politically committed art.[5] But I would argue that Bassani's literary strategy, and particularly his intertextual characterization of Micòl, is what propels us into history, forcing us to take into account the concrete material circumstances of a death that so violently distinguishes her from her sisters in the lyric, romantic, and epic tradition of Italian letters. Indeed, her role as muse, whose inspirational function is predicated on inaccessibility, as Marilyn Schneider so compellingly claims, places Micòl in a long literary tradition of women who had to die to inspire conversions (and the impulse to write about them) in their poet-lovers.[6] But *donne angelicate* invariably die natural deaths, expiring quietly of disease or childbirth in ways that do not shatter our calm. Micòl, instead, dies the most unnatural death imaginable, a fact which Bassani relegates to the extra-narrative apparatus of the prologue and epilogue because it has no place in a story about a stilnovist lady[7] who inspires a conversion and a memorialist writing. 'My story with Micòl Finzi-Contini ends here,' the narrator concludes, because such a fiction, by dint of its literary pedigree, cannot accommodate a death whose unnaturalness would derail the poet's journey toward personal, lyric fulfillment. But this is precisely Bassani's point in juxtaposing two such discordant genres as the novel of sentimental education and that of Holocaust chronicle. It is this juxtaposition that propels us into history and keeps us there throughout the course of the entire narration.[8]

There is a second literary tradition that informs the novel and provides an equally powerful push toward historical consciousness, though it offers sharply contrastive analogues to the figure of Micòl. Indeed no 'garden' novel so self-consciously set in Ferrara could fail to acknowledge the enchanted gardens of the *Orlando furioso* and the *Gerusalemme liberata*, whose Alcina and Armida each serve to divert their warrior-lovers from military pursuits. Though devoid of the moralizing Renaissance judgment of these false gardens, which exploit their Edenic exemplar by manipulating the gap between appearance and essence, Bassani's text nonetheless recognizes the mortal danger they pose as temptations to withdraw from history and embrace their invitation to oblivion.[9] Micòl, like Alcina or Armida, entices the narrator into the garden of historical forgetfulness where, like the crusading knight, he sheds his armor and ignores the inevitable signs of impending doom. Bewitched by this enchantress, the narrator is lulled into the same ahistorical stupor that keeps the Finzi-Continis from taking the necessary steps to stave off Apocalypse, or at least to escape it. Significantly, the moment of disenchantment, when the spell is broken and the protagonist is freed from bondage to his erotic obsession, coincides with his return to historic consciousness. As the narrator's sexual curiosity leads him toward the Hütte where he is sure that Micòl and Malnate are trysting, his summons to the watchdog, Jor, meets an unexpected response.

> But then, as if in reply, a faint sound, heartsick, almost human, suddenly arrived from very far away, through the night air. I recognized it at once: it was the old, beloved voice of the clock in the square, striking the hours and the quarter hours. What was it saying? It was saying that, once again, it had grown very late, that is was foolish and wicked, on my part, to continue torturing my father in this way, who, surely, also that night, concerned because I hadn't come home, was unable to fall asleep: and that finally it was time for me to resign myself. Truly. Forever.   (Bassani, 197).

What breaks the protagonist's spell is the call of time, and the fact that it issues from the piazza clock makes this an intensely public voice, the collective voice of the *vivere civile* which he had so long ago ceased to hear in his romantic monomania. The weakness of this voice, and the distance it must traverse, is a measure of just how far the protagonist has withdrawn from the public sphere, but the fact that the sound is old and dear makes its summons a return and a recuperation of lost values. This disenchantment is a freedom not only from erotic obsession but also from its attendant self-absorption, so that now the narrator is able to participate in another's suffering and to take responsibility for its alleviation. It is his father's voice, then, which calls him back to the world of public accountability in the name of the history that threatens the garden from without.

But the protagonist is not the only character to suffer a disenchantment that banishes him from an illusory paradise, for the father who calls him back to the public sphere must himself undergo a painful reckoning. 'In life,' his father tells him,

> if one wants to seriously understand how the world works, he *must* die, at least once. And, since this is the rule, better to die young, when you still have so much time ahead of you to pull yourself together and resuscitate ... To understand, when you're old, is bad, much worse. What's to be done then? There's no time left to start over again from the beginning, and our generation has made so many mistakes!   (Bassani, 190–1)

In this confession, the father explicitly compares his political disappointments with his son's romantic ones. Blind Fascist allegiance and adolescent infatuation are both gardens that benumb the critical intelligence and paralyze the will to act, so that only the death of the deceived self can insure survival. Critics who fault the novel's withdrawal into sentimental trivialities, or who argue for the irrelevance of the love plot to the persecution chronicle, fail to see the convergence of political and romantic themes in this climactic father-son encounter that reveals, retrospectively, how the romantic narrative has functioned allegorically for the Jewish 'garden' mentality all along, signifying the historical obliviousness that had allowed the Jews to suspend their disbelief in Fascist betrayal.[10] It is significant that Bassani's protagonist makes his nocturnal garden visit *after* reconciling with his father, as if his parent's admission of political disenchantment were necessary to the protagonist's act of self-emancipation. The fact that the Micòl-Malnate tryst is the protagonist's *self-generated* fantasy reveals the protagonist's psychological readiness to experience the liberating effects of the primal scene in the Hütte.

De Sica's film has been faulted for its explicit rendering of the sexual epiphany that the novel's protagonist fantasizes but never verifies. Such explicitness has been seen as a surrender to the medium's voyeuristic appeal and as an excuse for gratuitous erotic display. But I would argue that the scene is eminently justifiable as a cinematic expression of the novel's enchantment-disenchantment theme, done in a medium-appropriate language that brilliantly approximates Bassani's intertextual technique. De Sica's strategy is to find cinematic equivalents of the Armidas and Alcinas of Renaissance literary history, and he does so in the *femmes fatales* of the prewar film industry, the enchantresses and seductresses of the silver screen who epitomize the narcotic, diversionary power of Hollywood cinema. Several critics have compared Dominique Sanda's performance in *The Garden of the Finzi-Continis* to that of the young Greta Garbo, and I think that Joseph von Sternberg's fetishized treatment of Marlene Dietrich is also a model for Micòl's representation.[11] Dietrich's influence is especially powerful in the primal scene, whose rhetoric of disenchantment warrants close visual analysis.

It is night when Giorgio climbs the garden wall in a final desperate attempt to reach Micòl. As he passes all the familiar landmarks – the tennis court, the *magna domus*, the Hütte – Giorgio finds them transformed by the night into ominous signs of the spectacle that awaits him. The light issuing from Micòl's bedroom window is just such a sign – it directs his gaze to the Hütte where Jor's custodial presence acts on him with the force of revelation. De Sica's camera zooms in on the dog and cuts back to Giorgio's sombre expression as the music stops and is replaced by the portentous sound of hooting owls. After Giorgio runs to the Hütte, we see him from within, shot through the grating on the window, whose constrictive framing and protective bars provide a perfect visual metaphor for his psychic enslavement to obsession. A cut shows us what Giorgio himself has just seen: Micòl in eery chiaroscuro, her illuminated face tilted upward in revery, her lower body enveloped in shadow. After another cut to Giorgio, the camera returns to Micòl as her sight line converges with his, signalling her awareness of his presence. At this point Micòl throws off her covering, and the camera pans to Malnate's face, asleep in profile, softly illuminated. Heightening Micòl's drama of self-disclosure, she turns on the light, exhibiting the cold, clinical beauty of her naked torso. But the cruelty of this exhibition is not unalloyed – by shooting Micòl through the same window bars that had figured in Giorgio's erotic entrapment, De Sica's camera denies her the status of free agent. Herself incapable of intimacy – victim of elaborate psychic defenses or of a tragic foreknowledge that precludes sentimental attachments – she will be consigned to a series of future incarcerations: deportation centres, cattle cars, and finally, Dachau or Buchenwald. Thus the climactic close-up of Micòl, framed by window bars that anticipate her doom, is a powerful representational paradox. On the one hand, she is the archetypal *femme fatale*, the diva who visits destruction upon others but herself remains unscathed, while on the other hand, she is history's quintessential victim, the innocent object of Nazi genocidal rage.

But the demystification of the diva is not the only unmasking that occurs in this scene. Though it is Micòl who is literally unmasked in her nudity, it is she who unmasks Giorgio by switching on the light, throwing off her covering, and returning his gaze, making explicit her status as visual spectacle, and his as voyeur. By shattering his illusion of invisibility and reversing the subject-object relationship, Micòl breaks the spell of narcissistic projection on which Giorgio's erotic fantasy is built. The return gaze, along with the sight of a nudity that preempts the need for imaginative speculation, forces Giorgio to accept that Micòl is indeed *other*, a separate subject able to make him, in turn, into its object of consciousness.[12] In her cold, stony beauty, Micòl is the Medusa who depetrifies her lover by breaking the trance of her sensual appeal even as that appeal is most fully displayed. Her return gaze also has important implications for Micòl's relationship to conventional feminine portrayals in film. If visual pleasure in mainstream cinema derives from viewer identification with an active male agent who in turn directs a fetishizing look on the passive female object of desire, then any interruption of such alignments will challenge our complacency and call into question the traditional systems of representation on which our spectatorship is based.[13] It is significant that Micòl reverses the conventional alignment of gazes at the moment when she is most diva, when her representation comes closest to the image of the fetishized Hollywood star. With her return gaze, Micòl renounces her membership in the sisterhood of cinematic sirens and its attendant narrative invulnerability. 'There is always a certain excessiveness, a difficulty associated with women who appropriate the gaze, who insist on looking,' writes Mary Ann Doane. 'Woman as subject of the gaze is clearly an impossible sign,' and as a result, such a woman either takes off her glasses or gets punished (Doane, 83–4). The second, tragically, is Micòl's fate – a fate whose foreknowledge may be precisely what compels her to disenchant Giorgio, to banish him from her false paradise and liberate his energies to act in self-defense.

De Sica's iconoclasm in the primal scene is also a moral *prise de position*. Like the novel, which reveals the dangers hidden in the garden mentality, De Sica's film will not be a garden – it will refuse the easy escapist pleasures so expertly provided by the 'cinema of consolation' (including his own postneorealist production). Indeed, the temptation to make a 'garden' film is there in the lush musical score composed by the director's son, Manuel, in the visual appreciation of the Finzi-Continis' botanical wealth, in the elegiac treatment of 1930s-style dress, decor, and taste captured by the sepia tones of the photography and the recurrence of such pop music as 'Sentimental over You,' and in the poignant spectacle of a youth for which there will be no old age.[14] The film could easily wallow in sentimentality, nostalgia, and a self-pity that identifies with the victims and abdicates any responsibility for their historic plight.[15] But the film renounces its own temptation to escapism and pleasurable withdrawal by insisting on the cinema's realist vocation – not in any literal, documentarist sense but in the moral imperative, enshrined by neorealism, to historical accountability.[16] Film's mission, according to the neorealists, is not only passively to record reality but actively to forge it by enlightening and arousing the public to undertake corrective social action. In filmic revisitations of Fascism and war, the realist purpose is twofold: to reveal the hidden continuities between present and past in order to counteract any tendency to disown Fascist history, and to instill a sense of personal responsibility that precludes the kind of moral abdication required for authoritarian control. In an interview with Charles Thomas Samuels, De Sica acknowledged the moralist impulse that drew him to Bassani's novel and explicitly contrasted his film to the previous 'consolatory' productions for which he is now seeking absolution. 'After the disaster of *Sunflower* [a Carlo Ponti enterprise starring Loren and Mastroianni] I wanted to make a true De Sica film, made just as I wanted it. I accepted this subject because I intimately feel the Jewish problem. I myself feel shame because we all are guilty of the death of millions of Jews ... I wanted, out of conscience, to make this film, and I am glad I made it' (De Sica, 47 above).

When Giorgio says to his father early in the film, 'We stood by silently when it wasn't happening to us,' his indictment of public tolerance for persecution explains De Sica's own return to a cinema of moral accountability. Given this ethical impulse to make *The Garden of the Finzi-Continis* it should come as no surprise that De Sica would shift Bassani's emphasis from inside to outside the garden, where the Holocaust chronicle takes place. This change in emphasis has important consequences for the comparative structuring of novel and film, for it requires that the circular movement of the text be replaced by the film's linearity, thus riveting our attention on the *what* of history, on its relationship of cause and effect, and on its sequential unfolding of Holocaust logic. The novel, instead, inscribes its end in its beginning so that our curiosity about plot is replaced by an interest in the process by which *then* becomes *now*, by which persons and events become commemorative texts. For example, the passage at the opening of part 1, chapter 6, arrests the narrative flow in order to foreground the novelist's act of imaginative revocation. 'How many years have gone by since that far-off afternoon in June? More than thirty. Nevertheless, if I close my eyes, Micòl Finzi-Contini is still leaning over the wall of her garden looking at me, and speaking to me' (Bassani, 33). Such a stop-action technique serves to call our attention to the process of writing itself and to the back-and-forth movement of consciousness which produces the first-person narration.

Bassani's repudiation of the film is well known, and one of his quarrels with it concerns De Sica's failure to honor the novel's twofold temporality. As the collaborator on an earlier version of the screenplay that was radically modified, to Bassani's great chagrin, the novelist had included a series of black-and-white flashforwards of the roundup of Ferrarese Jews following the Nazi takeover of September 8, 1943.[17] Such a technique would have served to remind the viewers of the narrator's *ex post facto* perspective, while it would have obviated the need to include such obvious didactic devices as the little Nazi flag on the basket of the newsboy's bicycle in the scene of Giorgio's fleeting encounter with Bruno Lattes. But, with the exception of the film's flashbacks to 1929, De Sica chooses to respect the time-space continuum of the realists' code and to focus our attention on the *what* of Holocaust history, rather than on the *how* of its representation. In the two scenes where De Sica makes explicit his cinematic self-consciousness, the net effect is less to dramatize the artistic process than to emphasize its historical-moral accountability. Appropriately, the two scenes are set in a movie house, and each insists on the relevance of what is occurring on-screen to what is transpiring in the streets. In the first such metacinematic episode, Giorgio and Malnate witness a newsreel of burning wreckage along with footage of Hitler and Goebbels haranguing the German masses, followed by clips of Mussolini's attempts to imitate his Nazi exemplars. Unable to restrain his contempt, Giorgio erupts in a string of invective that provokes his viewing neighbors' irritation. 'Dirty Jew,' they retaliate, and when a scuffle breaks out, Malnate intervenes to remove Giorgio from the fray. A second scene in the same movie house has far more sinister consequences. Now, the wartime chronicle depicted in the newsreel has as its offscreen counterpart the handcuffing and arrest of Bruno Lattes on the theater floor.

Because De Sica critiques the garden mentality from without, whereas Bassani does so from within, the film must meet its obligations to history by fully representing the events that Bassani merely adumbrates in the prologue and epilogue. Thus, Alberto's death and funeral are dramatized, as are the signs that foretell disaster: the concentration camp reports at the pensione in Grenoble, Mussolini's declaration of war, the roundup of Lattes, the ceremonial eviction of the Finzi-Continis, and their final wait for deportation.[18] It is in this scene that De Sica announces his definitive departure from the cinematic 'garden' of consolation by literally opening out his film to universal history. He does so by photographing Micòl and her sobbing grandmother against the background of a map of the world in the classroom where they are being held for detention. The grandmother's weeping expresses the family members' collective grief at a paradise forever lost, and their entrance into a global order whose worst iniquities will be visited upon them. The figure of Micòl in this scene is of surpassing importance to an interpretation of De Sica's 'antigarden' strategy in adapting Bassani's text. Her unclothed diva image in the Hütte, where a profusion of soft, blond curls had framed a face of exceeding glamour, has given way to a chastened figure of grief and sobriety in the black-clad, severely coiffed Micòl of successive scenes: those of Alberto's death and funeral and of her farewell to the house on the eve of deportation. It is as if Micòl's disenchantment of Giorgio in the Hütte had occasioned her own imagistic transformation, and now the fetishized siren became the *mater addolorata* who cradles her grandmother, infantilized by old age and grief, in the pietà pose reminiscent of Cesira's in the concluding shots of *Two Women*. So radical a change of feminine iconography cannot help but have metacinematic implications for a film that rejects the 'garden' of conventional visual pleasure for a rigorous confrontation with Holocaust chronicle.

The film's last flashback occurs in this schoolroom setting – it is Micòl's childhood memory of completing and submitting her final exam as a private student and skipping off in the relief of its aftermath. Through this memory of social privilege and academic success, Micòl reexperiences the essence of the garden condition – perfect childhood innocence and bliss preserved intact within the sanctuary of memory – just as she is most violently torn away from its protective confines. In this juxtaposition between garden oblivion and present historical consciousness, between the Finzi-Continis' private Eden and this schoolroom map of the world, lies the difference between what De Sica's film could have been and what it is. In that comparison, the filmmaker was able to revisit and subsume an entire cinematic career, dedicated alternately to crowd-pleasing exercises in entertainment and to uncompromising explorations of social injustice. 'I am happy that I made it,' De Sica told Samuels of *The Garden of the Finzi-Continis*, 'because it brought me back to my old noble intentions' (De Sica, 49 above).

It is in his adaptation of the novel's two seders, or Passover suppers, that De Sica gives powerful voice to his 'old noble intentions.' The narrator's seder is described with direct reference to the genocide that awaits most of the guests at this celebration. 'It was not a happy supper,' the protagonist tells us of his own family's holiday observance.

Though set with great care, indeed, for this very reason, the table in the breakfast room had taken on an appearance quite similar to the one it presented on the evenings of Kippur, when it was prepared only for Them, for the family dead, whose bones lay there, in the cemetery, down at the end of Via Montebello, and yet They were quite present here, in spirit and in effigy. Here, in their places, we were seated, the living. But our number reduced, compared to the past, and no longer happy, laughing, vociferous, but sad and pensive like the dead ... I look at uncles and cousins, most of whom, a few years later, would be swallowed up by German crematory ovens: they didn't imagine, no surely not, that they would end in that way, but all the same, already, that evening, even if they seemed so insignificant to me, their poor faces surmounted by their little bourgeois hats or framed by their bourgeois permanents, even if I knew how dull-witted they were, how incapable of evaluating the real significance of the present or of reading into the future, they seemed to me already surrounded by the same aura of mysterious, statuary fatality that surrounds them now, in my memory.   (Bassani, 124–5)[19]

De Sica's scene begins on a far more festive note, but when this jollity gives way to collective paranoia, the change provides a sinister commentary on the Nazi-Fascist threat. Unlike the sad little breakfast room where the narrator's supper takes place, De Sica's brilliantly lit dining room has a table covered in white, surrounded by guests singing a traditional postseder song. The scene opens with a dolly shot whose movements in either direction around the festive table keep the space as animated as is its company. When the camera finally pivots to reveal Giorgio to the right, a telephone's ring interrupts the song and beckons him to a booth in the adjoining room. Intercut with closeups of Giorgio's frustrated and repeated *prontos* are shots of the guests whose chanting subsides with each increasingly menacing ring. After the second prank call, Giorgio returns to the table to learn that his uncle has also been the victim of such harassments. When the third call comes, the singing stops entirely as father, uncle, and Giorgio all turn their heads in alarm. A cut returns us to the now familiar booth where Giorgio's angry *pronto* modulates into a relieved and delighted 'oooehi, Alberto!' A collective sigh of relief issues from the guests, who enthusiastically return to their song, which happens to be a musical rendition of a counting game used to teach children Old Testament lore through numbers. The juxtaposition of scriptural numerology with the increasing tally of harassing phone calls is not without a bitter appropriateness. As Andrea Gurwitt insightfully observes, the novel's direct confrontation with impending Nazi horror in this scene finds its filmic counterpart in these menacing phone calls, which serve as powerful dramatic devices for introducing the public threat into the privacy of the home (Gurwitt, 56).

The scene of the Finzi-Contini seder is one of far greater formality than that of Giorgio's family, with a burnished wood table stripped of its white cloth, crowned by a crystal chalice. Prophecy, thus visualized, becomes the scene's central dramatic motif. Whereas in Giorgio's house the guests remained anonymous, here the camera plays the part of the gracious host, introducing us to the celebrants individually by slowly panning each one in close-up as he or she greets the new arrival.[20] After a polite interrogation of Giorgio, the company turns its attention to the chalice, whose beauty, luminosity, and centrality to the mise-en-scène suggest important analogies to Micòl herself. Like Micòl, it hails from Venice, and like her (dazzlingly blond and dressed in white), the chalice is the only other radiant element in this shadowy setting. Surrounded by a ring of cards that depend upon it for meaning, the chalice suggests Micòl's own solar centrality to the family system that orbits around her. As Alberto summarizes the chalice's oracular performance for Giorgio, the camera constantly cuts to Micòl, though she remains wordless throughout this segment. When Alberto predicts that the war will end with the total victory of the forces for good, a cut to Micòl's face coincides with the sound track's *concludere* before the camera returns to her brother and then zooms to the chalice.

The scene ends with a visual statement of Giorgio's insubstantial place in the Finzi-Continis' universe as the final shot reveals his face reflected in the polished wood of the table, suspended like a pale moon inside the ring of cards surrounding the goblet. For Giorgio will indeed be spared the ordeal of redemptive sacrifice that awaits the Finzi-Continis. In the play of light and shadows and the imagistic linkage of Micòl with the prophetic theme of the film, De Sica establishes her as the Pascal lamb, the sacrificial victim of World War II history. The darkness is the racist policy whose shadows have already cast themselves in this room in the report of academic discrimination that Micòl suffered in Venice, and in Ermanno's exhortation to Giorgio to hurry and complete his degree before it's too late. From an *ex post facto* perspective, Micòl's radiance in that darkness is both poignant and auspicious – poignant in its transience, auspicious in its anticipation of 'the total victory of the forces of good.' It is this faith in the exemplary power of human suffering to elevate mass consciousness that underlies neorealist filmmaking and attracts De Sica to the novel as a way of returning to his earlier 'noble intentions.' Micòl's sacrifice thus serves a double salvific purpose, redeeming history as the arena for human salvation and enabling De Sica to reclaim his neorealist past.

For Bassani, there is no atonement for the Fall in the historic order. Paradise can only be regained through art, which alone can restore the primal unity left behind in Eden. Where De Sica's film bears witness to the history whose future course can be entrusted to an enlightened and progressive mass public, Bassani's novel can only be a monument, a purely imaginative revocation of lost opportunities and lost lives. It is Micòl's language, with its disparity between meaning and expression, which prompts the protagonist's concluding meditations on the limits of his own commemorative act. 'And as these, I know, were only words, the usual, deceitful and desperate words that only a true kiss would have prevented her from uttering: let them, and only them, seal here what little the heart has been able to remember' (Bassani, 197) (the Italian *ricordare* also means 'to record'). In the contrast between the novel's ending, which focuses self-reflexively on the artistic process of commemoration, and De Sica's final shot of the empty garden, whose lifeless confines conjure up Auschwitz, lies the key to the film's adaptive strategy. This is De Sica's cinematic equivalent of Bassani's composite garden-cemetery image, for the film's farewell montage of the Barchetto del Duca includes a shot of the front gate closed with lock and chain and ends with footage of the unkempt tennis court surrounded by a fence resembling the barbed wire of the *lager*. In the unsubtitled Italian version of the film, phantasmatic images of Micòl and Alberto playing tennis are superimposed on the court in an eery conflation of past and future – a special effect that the English-language distributors chose to delete from their prints. This entire sequence in both versions has as its musical accompaniment the Kaddish, or Jewish lament for the dead, with recognizable references to Micòl, Auschwitz, and Treblinka incorporated into the Hebrew lyrics. Thus Bassani's delicate alignment of funerary and garden imagery is turned into a wrenching historical indictment by use of such specifically cinematic devices as montage and sound-image juxtaposition. It has been De Sica's task to transform Bassani's gorgeous Etruscan monument to Micòl into a plea for moral accountability, and he has done so by removing her epitaph from its literary garden and by rewriting it in a medium whose neorealist past is revitalized by the encounter. Like Giorgio, who rejects the garden in the end, De Sica finally refuses the Eden of cinematic escapism by opening his film out to history and forcing us to accept the consequences.

Notes

1 On the garden's impenetrability, see Guisi Oddo De Stefanis, *Bassani entro il cerchio delle sue mura* (Ravenna: Longo, 1981), 131.

2 For Micòl's status as 'knower,' see Marilyn Schneider, *Vengeance of the Victim: History and Symbol in Giorgio Bassani's Fiction* (Minneapolis: University of Minnesota Press, 1986), 123; and Bon, *Come leggere*, 37.

3 On the novel's dual perspective, see Anna Dolfi, *Le formi del sentimento* (Padua: Liviana, 1981), 44.

4 De Stefanis sees the novel as a 'foscoliano sepolchro.' See *Bassani entro il cerchio*, 95. Schneider argues for the 'urgency of funerary ritual' where 'death – or better, the burial of the dead – preserves the memory of life' throughout Bassani's fiction. See *Vengeance of the Victim*, 3. On the temporal distance, see De Stefanis, *Bassani entro il cerchio*, 95.

5 On the politicized critical reception of Bassani, see Schneider, *Vengeance of the Victim*, 7, and Bon's helpful anthology in *Come leggere*, 85ff.

6 Schneider in *Vengeance of the Victim*, 125ff., argues that Micòl's distance is a pre-condition to the novel's writing. On her function as muse, as Stilnovistic Beatrice or Montalian Dora Marcus, see De Stefanis, *Bassani entro il cerchio*, 98.

7 EDITORS' NOTE: *stilnovist*: from Dante's *dolce stil nuovo* ('sweet new style'), implying a woman who so embodies God's beauty and truth that her lover purifies his earthly desires and achieves saintliness.

8 Gian Carlo Ferretti sees in Bassani the coming together of two contradictory tendencies – that of 'prosa d'arte' and that of anti-Fascist politically committed writing: 'Bassani lives lucidly the conflict to the breaking-point, becoming in this sense the most emblematic writer of his generation.' Quoted in Bon, *Come leggere*, 94.

9 For the ground-breaking study of Edenic prototypes to these Renaissance literary gardens, see A. Bartlett Giamatti, *The Earthly Paradise and the Renaissance Epic* (Princeton: Princeton University Press, 1966), especially his chapters on Tasso and Ariosto.

10 Stanley Kauffmann, for example, complains that the plot is divorced from its political theme. See his review in the *New Republic* 166 (19 January 1972), 33. Colin Westerbeck, JR., on the other hand, cites the parallel between Jewish political disappointments and Giorgio's romantic ones. See 'Deportation from Paradise,' *Commonweal* 95 (3 March 1972), 525.

11 Garbo's precedent is invoked by Arthur Cooper in 'Viva De Sica,' *Newsweek* 79 (10 January 1972), 58: and Pauline Kael in 'The Fall and Rise of Vittorio De Sica,' *Deeper into Movies* (New York: Bantam, 1974), 459.

12 Douglas Radcliff-Umstead notes the importance of this return gaze in *The Exile into Eternity: A Study of the Narrative Writings of Giorgio Basanni* (Cranbury, N.J.: Associated University Presses, 1987), p. 164, n.17.

13 See Laura Mulvey, 'Visual Pleasure and Narrative Cinema,' *Screen* 16 (1975), 6–18.

14 Indeed, Manuel De Sica's music sets the tone for the nostalgia that suffuses the garden scenes, as proved by the fact that the director would listen to his son's score to prime himself for the filming. See Franco Pecori, *Vittorio De Sica* (Florence: La Nuova Italia, 1980), 102.

15 On the temptation to make a film that indulges exclusively in such pathos, see Vito Attolini, *Dal romanzo al set: Cinema italiano dalle origine ad oggi* (Bari: Dedalo, 1988), 225.

16 I argue this extensively in the introduction to *Italian Film in the Light of Neorealism* (Princeton: Princeton University Press, 1986).

17 Bassani's famous refutation of the film, revealingly entitled 'Il giardino tradito,' is reprinted in Bassani, *Di là dal cuore* (Milan: Mondadori, 1984), 311–21. In 1970, he had collaborated with Vittorio Bonicelli in drafting a screenplay that was later submitted to Ugo Pirro for modifications. The resulting script so compromised the integrity of the Bassani-Bonicelli version that the novelist disassociated his name from the production.

18 For an excellent comparative discussion of the narrative structure in novel and film, see Eskin, 'The Garden of the Finzi-Continis,' 171–5.

19 This passage exemplifies the ambivalence that Pasolini sees at the center of Bassani's realism: 'The numerical and mental narrowness of the Jewish bourgeoise of Ferrara' vs. 'The grandeur that is conferred by the "diaspora" and by the tragedy of persecution.' Pasolini, *Descrizioni di descrizioni* (Turin: Einaudi, 1979, 265). Bon notes that in this passage, Bassani abandons his customary ironic detachment and adopts a tone that is 'essential, definitive, hallucinated.' See *Come leggere*, 43.

20 Gurwitt further notes that this seder is photographed with a predominance of close-ups, emphasizing the isolation and individuality of its celebrants, while Giorgio's seder guests were photographed in groups to emphasize their collective identity (Gurwitt, 62).

References

Bassani, Giorgio. *The Garden of the Finzi-Continis*. Translated by William Weaver. New York: Harcourt, Brace, Jovanovich, 1977.

Bon, Adriano. *Come leggere 'Il Giardino dei Finzi-Contini.'* Milan: Mursia, 1979.

De Sica, Vittorio. In Arthur Cooper. 'Viva De Sica.' *Newsweek*, 79 (10 January 1972).

Doane, Mary Ann. 'Film and the Masquerade: Theorizing the Female Spectator.' In *Screen* 23 (September–October 1982).

Eskin, Stanley G. 'The Garden of the Finzi-Continis.' In *Literature/Film Quarterly* 1 (Spring 1973).

Friedman, Lawrence. *'The Garden of the Finzi-Continis.' Magill's Survey of Cinema*. Volume 3. Englewood Cliffs, N.J.: Salem Press, 1980.

Gurwitt, Andrea. *Selective Focus: Film Adaptations of 'The Conformist' and 'The Garden of the Finzi-Continis.'* Honours thesis, Wesleyan University, 1988.

Kael, Pauline. 'The Fall and Rise of Vittorio De Sica.' *New Yorker* 18 December 1971.

Koszarski, Richard. 'A Garden of Diffused Memoirs.' *Village Voice* 23 December 1971.

Parker, Jim. *'Requiem: The Garden of the Finzi-Continis.' Time Magazine* 17 January 1972.

Samuels, Charles Thomas. *Encountering Directors*. New York: Putnam's, 1972.

Walrond-Skinner, Sue. *A Dictionary of Psychotherapy*. New York: Routledge & Kegan Paul, 1986.

The Magic Mountain

COLIN WESTERBECK

Westerbeck's essay on A Brief Vacation *was published in March 1975, shortly after De Sica's death. It points to De Sica's debt to Thomas Mann's famous novel* The Magic Mountain *for the milieu of the more than perfect fairytale sanitarium which is represented in both stories. Both novel and film represent the sanitarium as something of a Shakespearean magic forest in which characters by their very removal from the real world gain a clearer understanding of it. Both novel and film also depict cross-sections of western civilization and identify crises central to our culture. At the same time, Westerbeck's reading of the film gives us a clearer understanding of the thematic links between De Sica's neorealist masterpieces and this last flowering of his social conscience. His ideological sensibility led him, as Westerbeck suggests, to examine the role of gender structuring within a culture in which males hold most of the power. Clara's choices in life are largely choices made by men to whom one renders subservience. The issue of patriarchy is particularly visible in De Sica's late films.*

When Vittorio De Sica died a few months ago, he had just released a last film which is remarkable because it could easily have been his first film.[1] It has been a quarter of a century since De Sica did his classic work – *Sciuscià / Shoeshine* (1946), *Ladri di biciclette / The Bicycle Thief* (1948), *Umberto D.* (1952) – as part of the neorealist movement in Italy. Yet this final film, *Una breve vacanza / A Brief Vacation* (1974), again renews and extends the vision that those neorealist films established as De Sica's own. Whereas most of De Sica's earlier films deal with periods of

Colin Westerbeck, 'The Magic Mountain,' *Commonweal* 102 (28 March 1975), 19–20 extreme adversity in their characters' lives, this film is about a period of relative happiness. But this doesn't represent any basic change in De Sica's sentiments. His films have always suggested a sort of two-sidedness to human experience. Often in the earlier films, the only thing that mitigates for us the characters' suffering is the implication that life at its best is not really much different from what it is at its worst. *A Brief Vacation* may show us the other side of the picture, but it is the same picture De Sica had been painting since he began as a director.

The happiness that is experienced by Clara (Florinda Bolkan) in *A Brief Vacation* is a result of her being sent to a sanitarium to recuperate from TB. From the satanic mill where she works wielding, literally, a hose of fire, she is transported to the cool, snowbound world of the northern mountains. At home she is buried alive by the demands her invalid husband, in-laws and children make upon her. But at the sanitarium she finds herself in the company of well-to-do women who befriend her. At home everything is dirty, nothing works, and the weather is always overcast. It is a world almost without light. But in the mountains the light is dazzling, everything is white, and everything works as it should.

As distinct a contrast as the world of the sanitarium presents, however, from the time Clara arrives there life at the sanitarium begins to coincide in odd ways with her life back home. [On] her last day at her job, for instance, she became so exhausted that she fell asleep over her lunch in the factory commissary and missed getting anything to eat. [On] her first day in the commissary at the sanitarium, she walks into a scene where a girl at her table is also missing her meal. This time it [the abstinence] is done voluntarily and as a romantic gesture – the girl is staging a hunger strike because a doctor she was having an affair with has been transferred – but the very frivolousness of the girl's gesture only makes us more aware of how it compares with Clara's missed meal earlier. Like other things that happen at the sanitarium, this incident seems almost to mock the grim routine of Clara's life back home.

Back home, before she could bring herself to go to the doctor's for her examination, she had to buy some new underwear and [take] a bath at a public spa. But at the sanitarium, when one of her friends, a model, departs, she leaves behind a whole table of cosmetics and clothes for Clara. Having had to pay for necessities before, Clara is now given luxuries; yet again, by reminding us of her life back home, the gift at the sanitarium becomes more an omen of her return to that life than a diversion from it. The culmination of her new life at the sanitarium is an affair she has with another patient. He is everything her grasping, exploitative husband isn't, but he too is nonetheless an echo of her life back home. She met him the day she went to the doctor's, when she allowed him to buy her coffee until her brother-in-law happened to see them together. And when she rediscovers this man up at the sanitarium, her brother-in-law again becomes an interloper by unexpectedly driving the family up for a visit just as Clara is on her way to meet her lover.

Like her family, the people at the sanitarium ultimately seem to make demands on Clara in ways that also use and even abuse her. When one of her girlfriends tries to kill herself because she can't face her disease, Clara is elected to go see her in the hospital and is drawn into a bitter fight the woman is having with the nuns and doctors. Clara only just returns from that ordeal when the model pleads with her to come along while she sees her boyfriend. The model says she needs moral support to resist the fellow's overtures to leave, but after Clara submits to the embarrassment of this confrontation, her friend at once gives in to the man as if that's what she wanted to do all the time. In the end a doctor who has flirted with Clara and been rejected sees that she is having an affair with someone else, and he immediately declares her cured so that she is banished back to the squalor of her home.

The parallel construction that De Sica put on Clara's story binds her present happiness to her past unhappiness. It makes us see the two as inseparable. The one condition can never escape its association with the other. The parallel construction is also typical of the way De Sica always expressed this sense he had of life. In *Umberto D.* there is a moment when Umberto looks out the window of the lodgings from which he is being evicted and contemplates suicide. The camera assumes a point-of-view shot, showing us the street as Umberto sees it, and then suddenly zooms down on the cobblestones below as if Umberto were jumping. But he hasn't jumped, and the next morning when he leaves, as he looks up at his room one last time from the street, the camera again assumes a point-of-view shot. Now the shot inverts what Umberto saw the night before and controverts the finality of what he felt. That matched pair of shots, like all the matched episodes in Clara's story, sustains a kind of momentum in life, a capacity for simple endurance, which seems for De Sica to transcend all other emotions.

All De Sica's great films have been stories of how people either exercise or acquire this capacity to endure, and the reason all his characters have needed such a capacity is that they have all been exiles in life, outsiders who had no choice except to endure hardship. Umberto turned out of his rooms, Antonio turned out of his job in *The Bicycle Thief*, the Finzi-Continis turned out of their garden, Clara turned out of the sanitarium: what they all share is the fate of being dispossessed, disenfranchised, cut off, stranded.

Clara is an outsider in both her own family and the sanitarium where she momentarily escapes from that family. At home, her husband, his brother and his mother all suck the life out of her by their loveless dependence. But at the sanitarium she is from the beginning just as much an outsider, for the whole premise of such a place is that one should want to leave it. All her friends want to do so, but she of course would like to stay. Precisely because of the happiness the sanitarium affords her, Clara is really as alienated there as she was at home. The fact is that the only society into which Clara really fits, the only decent company for her to keep, is that of Umberto, Antonio and all the other extraordinary, lonely figures with whom De Sica peopled the screen.

Editors' Note

1 De Sica's last film would be *Il viaggio* / *The Voyage* (1974).

Filmography

1940   *Rose scarlatte / Two Dozen Red Roses*
1941   *Maddelena zero in condotta / Madeline, Zero for Conduct*
        Teresa Venerdì / Mademoiselle Friday / Doctor Beware
1942   *Un garibaldino al convento / A Garibaldian in the Convent*
1943   *I bambini ci guardano / The Children Are Watching Us*
1945   *La porta del cielo / The Gates of Heaven*
1946   *Sciuscià / Shoeshine*
1948   *Ladri di biciclette / Bicycle Thieves / The Bicycle Thief*
1950   *Miracolo a Milano / Miracle in Milan*
1952   *Umberto D.*
1953   *Stazione Termini / Indiscretion of an American Wife*
1954   *L'oro di Napoli / Gold of Naples*
1956   *Il tetto / The Roof*
1960   *La ciociara / Two Women*
1961   *Il giudizio / The Last Judgment*
1962   'La Riffa' / 'The Raffle' (an episode of *Boccaccio '70*)
        I sequestrati di Altona / The Condemned of Altona
1963   *Il boom*
        Ieri, oggi, domani / Yesterday, Today and Tomorrow
1964   *Matrimonio all'italiano / Marriage, Italian Style*
1965   *Un monde nouveau / Un mondo nuovo / A Young World*
1966   *Caccia alla volpe / After the Fox*
        'Una sera come le altre' / 'A Night Like Any Other'
        (an episode of *Le streghe / The Witches*)
1967   *Sept fois femmes / Woman Times Seven*
1968   *Amanti / A Place for Lovers*
1970   *I girasoli / Sunflower*

Il giardino dei Finzi-Contini / The Garden of the Finzi-Continis
'Il leone' (an episode of *Le coppie / Les Couples*)
1972   *Lo chiameremo Andrea*
1973   *Una breve vacanza / A Brief Vacation*
1974   *Il viaggio / The Voyage*